margarita wednesdays

Center Point
Large Print

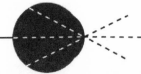

**This Large Print Book carries the
Seal of Approval of N.A.V.H.**

margarita wednesdays

MAKING A NEW LIFE
BY THE MEXICAN SEA

Deborah Rodriguez
with Ellen Kaye

CENTER POINT LARGE PRINT
THORNDIKE, MAINE

This Center Point Large Print edition
is published in the year 2014 by arrangement with
Gallery Books, a division of Simon & Schuster, Inc.

Certain character and place names and identifying
characteristics have been changed and some characters
are amalgams. Some events have been reordered,
combined, and/or compressed.

The text of this Large Print edition is unabridged. In other
aspects, this book may vary from the original edition.
Printed in the United States of America on permanent paper.
Set in 16-point Times New Roman type.

ISBN: 978-1-62899-170-3

Library of Congress Cataloging-in-Publication Data

Rodriguez, Deborah.
Margarita Wednesdays : making a new life by the Mexican Sea /
Deborah Rodriguez. — Center Point large print edition.
pages cm
Originally published: New York : Gallery Books, 2014.
Summary: "Deborah Rodriquez's memoir of her journey of self-
discovery and renewal after she was forced to flee Afghanistan in
2007"—Provided by publisher.
ISBN 978-1-62899-170-3 (library binding : alk. paper)
1. Rodriguez, Deborah. 2. Americans—Mexico—Biography.
    3. Women—Mexico—Social life and customs—21st century.
    4. Beauty operators—United States—Biography.
    5. Beauty shops—Social aspects—Mexico.
    6. Americans—Afghanistan—Biography.
    7. Divorced women—United States—Biography.
    8. Middle-aged women—United States—Biography.
    9. Authors, American—21st century—Biography.
    10. Mental healing.
    I. Title.
F1210.R5849 2014b
972.08′4092—dc23
[B]
                                                          2014015590

This book is dedicated to
my three beautiful grandchildren,
Derek, Italya, and Kai,
all made in Mexico

He upon whose heart the dust of Mexico has lain will find no peace in any other land.

—ANONYMOUS

margarita
wednesdays

THE EXPLOSIONS SEEMED TO HAVE COME OUT of nowhere, their familiar *pop-pop-pop* catapulting me from under the covers and onto my feet in a flash. I instinctively dropped down and covered my head with my arms, the rough knotted wool of the Afghan rug scraping my bare knees as I slid to the floor. The cool air from the open window did little to calm my racing heart. I tried to breathe, but couldn't. I tried to call out, but nothing came from my mouth. My eyes were sealed shut against the flash of light still visible through the lids.

Then, silence. I took one deep breath, then another. The familiar aroma of frying peppers filled my nostrils. My stomach growled. A rooster crowed, echoed by his distant cousin miles away. I cautiously opened one eye, then the other. Three crumpled marigolds from the celebration the night before lay wilting on the terra-cotta tiles by the door. This wasn't Afghanistan, this was Mexico. And I was okay. Hell, I tried to remind myself, I was better than okay.

I stood and drew back the shutters to see the sunlight just beginning to bounce off the B&B's rounded tiles, then pulled on my long cotton sweater and padded across the courtyard to find out what was going on. My host, and friend, Cynthia, was making coffee in the kitchen, a pot of salsa bubbling on the stove by her side.

"Morning, Deb!" She came a little closer. "Are you okay?"

"I'm fine," I assured her, the residue of sweat on my forehead no doubt giving me away.

"Are you sure?" She took my elbow, pulled out a heavy wooden chair from under the table, and gently guided me down into it. "Coffee?"

I nodded. "Um, Cynthia, didn't you hear anything a little while ago?" I was beginning, not for the first time, to doubt my own sanity.

Cynthia let out a little gasp. "Oh my God, Deb. I should have warned you. I'm so sorry!" She handed me a steamy blue cup. "It's just the Catholic church setting off their *cohetes*."

"Co-het-*whats*?"

"Skyrockets."

"Whatever happened to good old-fashioned church bells?" I asked. "Why on God's green earth would they be setting off explosions at the friggin' crack of dawn?"

"It's an old Mexican tradition. The loud noise from the rockets is supposed to scare away demons and evil spirits. They go off in the mornings a lot here in Pátzcuaro. It can get a little loud around holidays and saints' days, but you get used to it."

"I highly doubt that."

Cynthia laughed. "Seriously. Even you, Deb. Do I need to remind you again how far you've come?"

"Please, let's not start on that. At least not until I've finished my coffee." I sighed. But I knew Cynthia was right. I had healed greatly since the day I'd decided to make Mexico my home. And if there was one thing I now understood, without a doubt, it was that there are certain things that just take more time than others to overcome.

THE SUV ZOOMED AWAY FROM THE SERENA Hotel in Kabul as if in the middle of a chase scene. A decoy SUV and a taxi followed close behind as camouflage. We raced past cars, fruit stands, vegetable shops, and pedestrians, leaving a thick trail of dust behind.

In the front sat our Afghan driver and an Australian friend and customer, Jane, who worked for a private security agency. Calamity Jane, I thought, as I watched her chug the vodka she had neatly concealed in a water bottle, and as I saw her repeatedly checking the safety on her semiautomatic gun. This girl was locked and loaded and all business. In the back with me was my twenty-six-year-old son, Noah. We had just returned to Kabul together, two days earlier. My younger son, Zachary, was scheduled to fly in from Northern Cyprus, where he had been studying at Girne American University. It would be the first time we'd all be together in this beautiful country I had called home for five years, a sort of summer family vacation. Fleeing for our lives was not included in the itinerary.

But shit happens. And in those past two days, a lot of shit happened.

It was spring 2007, and I had headed home to Afghanistan from the States on top of the world. A whirlwind tour promoting my book about the Kabul Beauty School had left me giddy with pride, and I was looking forward to getting back to work with my girls at the school. But there were things that had to be dealt with, things that weren't perfect. Even before I left Kabul, rumors had started bubbling up that the beauty school was a brothel, and that the Afghan government was planning on launching an investigation. I was also worried about the government's reaction to my book, which they were *supposedly* rushing to translate into Farsi. My mention that I had first come to Afghanistan in 2002 with a Christian humanitarian organization could very well put me, and those around me, in jeopardy. Over there, you can be arrested and threatened with death if someone reports you for converting to Christianity. Of course, there was nothing religious about the school, nor was there anything illicit. I'm far from a preacher, or a madam for that matter. I wasn't sure how seriously to take these rumors. After all, with all that was going on in Afghanistan at the time, how important could a redheaded hair-dresser be?

And on top of it all, I had, to say the least, a

challenging domestic situation to deal with. Three years earlier, I had married an Afghan man—Samer Mohammad Abdul Khan. The fact that Sam already had a wife and seven daughters living in Saudi Arabia turned out to be the least of his undesirable qualities.

It had all started off fine. For once in my life I felt like I was making a rather practical decision when it came to a man. Sam's help in keeping the school running was invaluable, and he offered the kind of protection any Western woman doing business in a war-torn nation would—literally—die for. My association with Sam would work wonders for my reputation among the Afghan people, a reputation that was already in the toilet simply due to the fact that I was an American. Besides, I liked having a man in my life, and Sam was kind and respectful, and never imposed his religious or cultural values on me. We were introduced by friends, and after we had been furtively sneaking around for a while in a country where, for Afghans, dating a foreigner was strictly forbidden, marriage seemed like a logical option.

But about a year and a half in, Sam began a friendship with "The General," one of the most notorious warlords in Afghanistan. There were warlords in my living room! I quickly learned to phone before entering if I saw an SUV with blacked-out windows and a running motor parked outside the house. The headiness that came from being that close to power had a bizarre effect on Sam. He began calling himself a general (or actually became one, it was never clear to me which), and was soon strutting around Kabul in full regalia like a bantam rooster cruising the henhouse. And he was drinking way too much vodka, not a good thing for a man who had been living in bone-dry Mecca, whose alcohol tolerance level was close to zero, and whose reaction to the slightest provocation was to reach for the nearest gun. Usually my defense became a game of possum—it was easier to pretend not to notice him or to feign sleep than to stir his macho blood. It didn't always work.

It had become clear that Sam didn't love me. I was just a war trophy, an American woman who came with connections, and better yet, cash, or so he mistakenly thought. I began to distance myself from him, learning Dari and throwing myself into the challenges of the beauty school and the coffeehouse I had also opened. But the more I worked and the more successful I became, the more he seemed to resent me. He took my independence as a threat to his manhood, no doubt humiliated by the taunts from his warlord buddies about his inability to control his foreign wife.

It was hard to see through Sam's posturing exactly how much of it was a charade and how much a reality. Was Sam one of the good guys or one of the bad guys? And, I was beginning to wonder, was he really on my side? Sleeping with the enemy would be bad enough, but sleeping with *my* enemy? I realized I had made a huge mistake, and wanted nothing more than to leave Sam. But I had heard way too many stories about women in my situation, and none of them had a happy ending. Bringing shame to an Afghan man can have dire consequences, with women often having acid thrown in their faces, disappearing, or being murdered in retaliation.

Leaving Sam would have meant leaving Afghanistan, and all I had built there, forever, and that was something I could not bear to do. I was changing lives! Me, a hairdresser from Michigan, making a difference in a place few dared to go, at least not by choice. And it wasn't by being a doctor or a diplomat or a philanthropist, but by doing the only thing I knew how to do—hair. I had fought tooth and nail for the school and was unbelievably proud of our success. And I wasn't about to let anybody down. My only option was to come up with an exit plan that might allow me to continue my work and live my life on my own terms. There were still a lot of pieces of that puzzle missing by the time I was headed back from my American book tour.

During a layover in Dubai, Sam called to warn me that my security situation had gotten even worse. He said that two bombers had been intercepted near the beauty school. One claimed that he had been paid five thousand dollars to blow it up. But when I made calls to Afghan friends with connections to the police to verify Sam's account, nobody had heard a word about it. It became hard to know who to trust. I'd seen so many foreigners go rogue from staying in Afghanistan too long that I couldn't even be sure anyone was telling me the truth. Then Sam turned the tables to say my sources were involved in a cover-up. Next he told me that I might be thrown in prison if I returned to Kabul, only to change his tune an hour later in another call. What, I wondered, could have changed in one little hour? Though I wanted to believe him, I was beginning to suspect a setup. Of course, I was nervous. But I was Deb the Hairdresser, and I could deal with anything.

Then came the last straw. Jane, in the course of her workday, had picked up some chatter that made it clear my situation had become a dire emergency. Within forty-eight hours of landing in Kabul I was frantically dialing the embassy. I held the phone to my ear and heard the ring on the other end. It was five minutes after five on a Thursday, the start of the Afghan weekend. I bit my lip nervously. *C'mon, pick up, pick up!*

"Hello, United States Embassy. This is Mary, how can I help you?"

I heaved a sigh of relief. The embassy would help me. How could they not? My girls from the salon and I would go there all the time to provide haircuts, manicures, pedicures, and other treatments for embassy staff. Once I was even asked to powder Dick Cheney's forehead when he was in town. I tried to speak slowly and calmly enough for Mary to understand, but my emotions were running high.

"Hi, this is Debbie Rodriguez from the Kabul Beauty School. I'm in trouble. I was just told that there's a plan to kidnap my son. I need help. I need a safe place. Please, please help me," I pleaded.

"The embassy is closed right now," was the indifferent answer.

"The embassy . . . is closed right now," I repeated in disbelief.

"Feel free to call back during open hours. Thank you for calling."

"Please, Mary, you have no idea! I'm Debbie Rodriguez from the Kabul Beauty School!" I cried, raising my voice a few octaves. "I need help *now!* I could be dead by tomorrow morning! Hello? Hello?"

She hung up. Seriously?

WHERE MY GOVERNMENT FAILED TO HELP ME, my friends could. That's the lucky thing about being a hairdresser—you know everyone. Jane quickly sprang into action.

"You and your son have ten minutes to get

outta there," she said in a flat, clipped tone. "And that's it. I'll pick you up at the German restaurant down the road. Be ready."

"Pack up your things! Now!" I yelled to Noah as I tore up the stairs to my bedroom.

"What?"

"We have to go!"

"Go where?" He stood in my doorway, bewildered, as I grabbed my two biggest suitcases and began to fling the rumpled, dirty clothes I had just unpacked from my trip to the States back inside.

"Just pack!" There was no time to think. I don't think it really occurred to me that I'd never be back. In went my jewelry, still in its travel case. I instinctively tossed in two beautiful pairs of boots I had bought in Turkey. Shoes went flying through the air one by one without the thought of making a match.

My suitcases thumped down the stairs behind me, keeping time with my pounding heart. I paused at the sound of laughter drifting from the salon, fighting back my urge to run in and hug my girls good-bye, to tell them everything would be all right, that I'd be back soon. But it was too risky. Any explanation would have to wait until my return, after things blew over. After one last quick glance around my living room, I ran out the gate with a confused Noah trailing behind, the two of us dragging our suitcases through the mud as I frantically led him to Deutscher Hof Kabul.

"Lock the gate behind us!" I screamed to Abdul, the gatekeeper, "and don't let anybody in!" Ingrid, the restaurant manager, quickly cleared the room of perplexed diners, and made me sit. My shaking hands struggled to keep the water she handed me from sloshing over the edge of the glass. Where would we go? How would we go? I had no money on me, no plane tickets, no nothing. But Jane had it handled. She would get us to Dubai, and from there we'd be on our own.

Noah and I were whisked to Kabul's Serena Hotel, at that time the most secure place in the country, where we were to hide out while the escape plans were being hatched by Jane and her all-volunteer extraction team. In the hotel, the doors were triple-locked behind us. I was allowed one call. "Make it fast," barked Calamity Jane as she handed me my phone. "Don't give away your location, and don't give away your situation."

I didn't have to think twice about who to call. As I started to dial the number I had dialed so many times before, but never for this reason, I thought back on the evening five years earlier, when Karen and I had made "our plan."

THE BARTENDER SLAPPED DOWN TWO WHITE bar napkins in front of us. "So, what are we celebrating tonight, ladies?"

It was Wednesday, and for my best friend and me, it was our one night of the week to catch up, have a margarita or two, and share a good laugh. But on this particular Wednesday night, our conversation was rather sober. It was my last call before leaving Holland, Michigan, for my first trip to Kabul.

Karen was the type of mom who always made sure her children were decked out in the right safety gear, for fear they would suffer a broken bone, or a hangnail. Her kids called her Safety Mom. "Will you be with the group the whole time? Do they provide security?" she asked in between sips, with barely a pause to swallow.

"I don't really know about the security," I said, trying to sound reassuring, "but I'm sure we'll have it."

"Still, we have to have a plan in case . . . you know . . . ," she said. We looked down uncomfortably at our drinks. I was going into a country we had just bombed the hell out of and that was in massive need of rebuilding. I motioned to the bartender for another drink and lit a cigarette.

"At our last meeting they told us to bring a substantial piece of gold."

"Define substantial," Karen said, peering over her glass.

"In case . . . I guess . . . if we have to pay our way out of a situation." I took a long, nervous puff at my cigarette, then looked away. I didn't want to freak her out. I didn't want to freak myself out. The unfortunate reality was that Kabul still wasn't a very safe place.

Karen sat up and smoothed out her shirt. I could see a plan brewing in her head. "Okay, so here's what we'll do," she said, using the tone I'd often heard her use with her kids. "We need a word or phrase that will tell me you're in trouble and that I need to call somebody."

Knowing Karen, and knowing who she knew, I had no doubt that she would be able to get me out of any situation safely. Though I didn't even want to *think* about why I'd need her, I went ahead and humored her. "You're right! We need a code word."

We spent the rest of the night channeling our inner 007s, kicking around different words and phrases—*bun in the oven, the goose is cooked, the armadillo can't cross the road.*

"When was the last time you actually said the goose is cooked?" I teased. "And really, an armadillo?"

"Okay, then, who on earth would believe that you or I have a bun in the oven?" She laughed back.

We finally settled on *the turkey is in the oven.* I'm not sure why we chose that one. It wasn't even November. I blame it on the margaritas. But I was glad to have a plan.

NOW, AFTER THE FIASCO CALL TO THE U.S. Embassy, I wasn't so hopeful. One ring, two rings. What time was it there, anyway? *Please don't go to the machine,* I prayed. Karen's deep voice came through on the other end.

"Hello?" I said, not sure whether I was talking to a person or a machine.

"Debbie?" was the reply. She sounded peeved. I admit that I may have, on more than one occasion, called her in the middle of the night. But there was no time for apologies, so I went straight to the point.

"The turkey is in the oven." I couldn't believe what I was hearing myself say, but I was seasoned enough by now to know that phone lines in Kabul were hardly secure. My words were met with silence. In the meantime, Jane the Australian mercenary was motioning to me to wrap it up.

"What?" replied Karen, groggily.

I tried once more, slower. "The turkey . . . is in . . . the oven." I closed my eyes and prayed she would remember that conversation from years ago. "Wait!" She remembered. *Thank God!* "Are there . . . giblets with the turkey?"

I paused and looked at Jane, now holding her hand out for my phone.

"Are there giblets with the turkey?" Karen persisted.

I scrunched my forehead, trying to remember what she could be referring to. And then I understood.

"Yes," I said, looking at Noah. "The big giblet. Right now, it looks like it will come out okay, but if you don't hear the timer go off within twenty-four hours, it's time for a backup plan."

"Gotcha." I felt a little relief knowing that Karen had my back; if push came to shove she would do whatever she could to summon help. Of course, what she didn't know was that I had already struck out with our own embassy.

"Thanks, Safety Mom." I hung up and placed the phone in Jane's firm hand. She popped open the back, removed my SIM card, and gave it back to me. It was go time.

With the convoy ride behind us, we bustled through check-in and then immigration, draped, tied, wrapped, and veiled beyond recognition, thanks to the Afghan disguise Calamity Jane had insisted upon. I didn't say much as we sat waiting for the plane to leave Kabul airport. I kept glancing nervously out the window to make sure that my husband, Sam, or one of his thugs wasn't coming after us on the tarmac. I knew it was dangerous for a wife to leave an Afghan husband without permission, and that house arrest, imprisonment, or even an honor killing was often the fate of an errant woman.

When we finally did lift off, I hid my face behind my headscarf and allowed the tears to stream endlessly down my cheeks. My sweet son held my hand tightly, not knowing quite what to say. For two and a half hours and a thousand miles my mind raced with questions. What just happened? Where did I go wrong? How do I keep Noah safe? How do I keep myself safe? Where the hell should I go? Where the hell can I go?

The first thing I did once we landed in Dubai was to call Karen to let her know we were okay. Safety Mom had sat by the phone for twenty-four hours straight, at the ready to pull some strings to persuade Holland's mayor, our congressman, and the governor to come to my rescue, if need be. That was my girl. The next step was to connect Noah with his brother in Northern Cyprus. He would be safe there. But me? I had no clue. With just two suitcases to my name, the options were few. I had lost my life, my work, my home, everything I had thought was mine to keep forever, all within just a couple of days. For the first time in my life, I was truly scared. I felt guilty, worried about the girls I had been forced to leave behind. And I was alone.

Karen graciously offered me a place to stay, my hometown being the obvious solution—but not to me. Holland, Michigan, is one of those towns you don't get out of. You grow up there, you go to school there, you marry a Hollander, you die there. You just don't leave. But I had. And going back did not seem like an option. My sons were no longer living there, my father had passed away, and my mother was involved with a new man, unfortunately a man who didn't seem to think there was room for us both in her life.

There didn't appear to be anything left for me there.

The truth is, I had become a sort of mini-celebrity in Holland, due to my book. And now everything had gone up in smoke. If I did move back, I'd have to tell my story over and over and over, answer the same questions again and again, at the grocery store, at the bank, over margaritas with my girlfriends. I just couldn't see it. I wasn't even sure what that story was. My life had just crashed and was burning around me, and I was trying to figure out where the fire was and who started the fire and how to put the fire out and salvage my life, and I knew I couldn't do it in Michigan. I would have rather lived alone on a mountain. And that's exactly what I did, sort of.

IT WAS A CALIFORNIA GUY WHO CAME TO THE rescue. Mike and I had met years before, and he was well versed in my Afghanistan adventure. So when he heard I needed help, he kindly offered the lifeline of his home on top of Bell Mountain Road in the Napa Valley. My decision was a quick one. I desperately needed somewhere to go where nobody knew me, where I could lick my wounds in private and try to pull myself back together. And Napa? The land of Cabernet? One of the top ten vacation spots in the world? I pictured massages and mud baths, gourmet dining and hot-air balloons, right?

Wrong. I found myself in the woods. On top of a mountain in the woods. In a community of hard-working, teetotaling vegetarians who pretty much kept to themselves. Not that that was a bad thing, because all of a sudden I found myself among some very caring, nurturing people who seemed to thrive on helping those in need. And, at the time, I certainly was one of those. But they were also extremely conservative, and my bling-toting, chain-smoking, foul-mouthed, tequila-loving, bacon-craving self was still very much intact, despite my recent upheaval.

My first few weeks in Mike's ranch-style house were spent frantically trying to reach anyone I could in Afghanistan. Desperate to find out what was happening, I'd stay up all night to be on Kabul time, trying to connect on Skype, staring at my laptop screen, waiting anxiously for e-mails to come in. I needed to figure out the truth about what was going on. *What can I do? Who can I call?* I'd finally drift off into a fitful sleep, only to wake in a panic once I remembered what had happened. When I was able to connect with the salon, Sam would inevitably be there. I later found out that he had been spreading lies about my departure, saying that I had gotten tired of living in Afghanistan, had made my money, and was now off somewhere living the good life. The girls also later let me know that Sam had forced them to hand over a portion of the money I had sent them via Western Union. In the meantime, getting back to Afghanistan was all I could think about. I realize now that I was in shock, like someone who had just been involved in a horrible car crash or witnessed a devastating earthquake.

But deep down inside I knew it was too risky to go back, and when a sense of reality began to sink in, I froze. Mike's blue futon became my home base, where I'd watch TV—endless episodes of

Army Wives and *Boston Legal*—for hours on end. The Kardashian sisters became my life. Weird things had begun to happen to me when I tried to leave the house, like the day I burst into tears when I couldn't find the car in the Safeway parking lot. In fact, I was crying a lot, mostly inside the car, panicked that I'd lose my way among the twisty mountain roads and crisscrossing highways of the valley. I began to mistrust the GPS lady and her constant "recalculating," and the fear became so overwhelming that I stopped going out.

And that scared me even more. Who the hell was this person? I had traveled all over the world and never once had been nervous about finding my way. Ethiopia, Pakistan, Syria, India, Morocco, Malaysia . . . no problem! But something inside me had drastically changed. And now I was a self-imposed prisoner in a little house on top of a mountain in the middle of nowhere—and spending way, way too much time alone.

One day, not long after I had arrived, Mike suggested a road trip. He and his friend Shelly had planned a weekend of camping in Yosemite National Park.

"Camping?" I asked, pressing the pause button on the remote.

"It'll do you good, Deb." Mike ran his ruddy hands through his cropped hair.

"Yeah, but are you talking *camping*-camping, as in sleeping bags and dirt and stuff?"

31

Mike laughed. "Of course it's camping-camping. It'll be fun. Just tents, flashlights, a Coleman stove. Really roughing it. You can sleep in the back of the truck if you want."

I thought, wow. I had gone without electricity, but at this point in my life I'd never *choose* to go without electricity. I've slept on the floor because I *had* to sleep on the floor. But this is a first-world country. After all I'd seen in Afghanistan, I had to wonder why on earth anybody would want to have this kind of make-believe adventure. I saw no point in it whatsoever.

"And we might even get to see a bear!" Mike added, his voice rising half an octave with enthusiasm.

A bizarre image of Yogi Bear and Boo-Boo with black Taliban turbans wrapped around their little fuzzy ears popped into my head, but out of gratitude toward Mike, and to escape the loneliness and boredom that had become all too familiar, I agreed to go.

The first night wasn't great. My back had gone out, and the rock-hard truck bed felt like a slab of cement. I lay there as still as a fallen statue, and even with my eyes open the entire night I couldn't make out a single shape. It was that dark. And the noises! Hoots and howls and crackling and rustling. I had no idea what was out there. At least in Kabul I knew that a long high whistle meant a missile, and I could tell the difference between an incoming and outgoing rocket just by its sound. But in Yosemite I was terrified. The covered pickup felt like a coffin. Too scared (and achy) to even get up to pee, I sweated and hyperventilated for seven hours straight.

By the time morning came I was a wreck. My back was throbbing, so when Mike and Shelly said they wanted to make a pit stop before we started touring around, I told them I'd wait in the truck. As they crossed the parking lot toward the restrooms, I leaned back into the headrest and tried my damnedest to relax a little, breathing deeply to ease the pain and calm my brain. Who was that person last night? I asked myself. I had been truly scared, and I'm not scared of anything! Please. Where was the Deb who, not that long ago, was fighting mercenaries on the streets of Afghanistan?

KABUL WAS ON HIGH ALERT. RIOTS HAD BEEN triggered by a military convoy losing control of one of its Hummers. Many foreign businesses had not reopened. I was just finishing up morning classes at the beauty school when a sudden, overwhelming craving for a coffee and a quesada from the coffeehouse just five blocks away hit me.

"Debbie, you really must wait for Actar to drive you," Akmed Zia pleaded, standing between me and the door.

"I'll be *fine*," I insisted, grabbing my purse from

the counter. Really, how much trouble could I get into in five little blocks?

I had made it just two blocks down Wild West Street when I saw the men. Hundreds of them coming right toward me. Shit, another riot, I thought as I frantically searched among the walled compounds lining the street for somewhere, anywhere, to duck into. The mob was on me in a flash—I flattened myself against a wall, lowered my head, and tried my best to blend in, my heart racing as I realized I had been idiotic enough to leave without my headscarf. Just jeans, a big T-shirt, and my flaming red hair. But they weren't running, I realized. They were walking, slowly. Maybe it's some sort of a nonviolent protest, I thought, but I knew how those went. Peace and love for the first part, and all-out slaughtering for the second. I had no desire to be the uncovered infidel who set things off.

As the crowd began to pass, I sucked in my breath, daring to look up for just one brief moment to see a body. A corpse enveloped in a white sheet, held aloft above their heads. The funeral procession passed silently by, the mourners too grief-stricken to even give me the time of day.

I'd never been so happy to see a dead guy in my life. But feeling slightly less cocky by this point, I decided to stop at a friend's compound to borrow one of their guards for the last three blocks of my walk. The request felt a bit ridiculous, but having an Afghan man at my side was a safer way to go, me being a foreigner, a woman, and an uncovered woman at that.

Reza and I were just about to cross the narrow, pitted street when a speeding Hummer came barreling toward us. Children, bicyclists, donkeys, dogs were all flying to get out of the way. Then there was a sudden, loud crack, and the Hummer's giant tire began to bounce down the street, missing us by inches, landing smack on top of a taxi.

The taxi driver leapt out to assess the damage. A crowd began to gather, which made me nervous, considering that this was exactly how the riots had started not that long ago. I sent Reza to the taxi to calm the driver down, and turned my attention to the folks still sitting in the disabled Hummer. It was hard to tell if they were U.S. military or private security, but I was sure that no matter who they were, they wouldn't want another riot to start on their watch, and that they'd quickly right their wrong and offer to pay for the damage.

I started across the gravel to see what I could do to help. My five years in Kabul had taught me that giving a little money and getting the foreigner off the street as quickly as possible could go a long way in keeping a situation from escalating. But by now the taxi driver was yelling, and people were pouring out of their shops to see the big foreign Hummer that had destroyed the little Afghan taxi.

Reza ran over to me, frantically waving his arms in the air. "Debbie, we have to act fast. We must do something!"

"Go find out how much he needs," I said, turning back to the tan Hummer, when the doors flew open and out jumped a ponytailed blond woman and a stocky young man, both in black flak jackets, dark glasses covering their eyes and automatic rifles pointed at the crowd.

"Don't!" I yelled, running over to push the rifle noses down. "Are you guys okay? Anybody hurt?" They shook their heads. By now it was obvious that they weren't military. I led them behind the Hummer, out of view from the crowd that just seemed to be getting bigger and bigger. "We need to handle this fast, and you guys need to get out of here."

"How much?" I mouthed across the street to Reza.

"One hundred," he mouthed back.

"One hundred dollars, and it will be over," I reported to the mercenaries. "Everyone will be happy."

"Uh, that's just not doable. Our orders in this type of circumstance are to A, provide a business card, and B, remove ourselves from the situation." The young man turned to his partner for confirmation.

"C'mon, guys! If you do that all hell will break loose. You have no idea how sensitive this situation is." I couldn't help but think what would happen to my business if anything went down here. For sure a security alert would go out, and the beauty school, salon, and coffeehouse would all be off-limits to half the people in town. And the other half would be too afraid to come anywhere near us.

The blonde was on her phone, dialing for backup. Reza was staring at me anxiously, waiting for an answer. I rushed across the street.

"Don't worry," I assured the taxi driver in loud, slow Dari. "The foreigners will make good. Don't worry." Reza echoed my words at the top of his lungs, his voice bouncing off the shabby store-fronts.

Just as I finished, a trio of black Hummers screeched to a halt beside us, spitting out six huge men with weapons drawn and ready for a fight.

"Are you guys stupid or what?" I yelled as I ran back across the street. "Is this your first fucking rodeo? I'm telling you, we will have a riot on our hands if you keep this up." Again I walked from gun to gun, pushing the noses of the rifles down toward the ground. I was sick of our neighborhood being overrun by tanks that would practically demolish a car in a blink. For those of us who lived there, Afghans and foreigners alike, just trying to lead a normal life was getting near to impossible. Too much stupid shit was happening. And now the place was crawling with private security companies who seemed to be making up the rules as they went along. They had their guns, and they'd do whatever they wanted to do to whomever they wanted to do it to. And if there is one thing I can't stand, it's bullies.

By this time the Afghans weren't sure which was more entertaining—the taxi driver ranting over his broken car, or the crazy woman fighting with the mercenaries.

"Back up! Back up!" the mercenaries screamed at me.

"You need to clean up your mess!" I screamed right back.

"We're not cleaning up anything! Back up!"

By now we were nose to nose, or rather nose to noses, me right in the face of this chorus line of idiots, their guns once again poised for action.

"Lady," the biggest one of the group shouted, "this isn't your concern. You need to back up! Now! Let's roll, guys!"

"Roll? You were fucking rolling, man! Your guy was rolling so fucking fast that his tire didn't just fall off, it *flew* off and nearly took off my head! The cabbie just wants a hundred bucks to fix his car. Just do it, man!"

"I said, let's roll!" he shouted again, louder.

As he raised his arm to signal for the rest to follow, I swiftly grabbed his wrist. "You are not going fucking anywhere until this guy gets his money!" I hissed.

By now the crowd had grown silent. You could almost see them placing mental bets on who was going to win this fight.

"Who the fuck *are* you?" he yelled in my face.

"Who the fuck am I? Who the fuck am I? I'm Debbie, the fucking *hairdresser,* asshole, and I am telling you to hand over the money *now!*"

Behind him, the team of mercenaries started rummaging through their pockets. One handed me a twenty, another a ten. Before long I had the hundred dollars and started to head over to the cab. I turned to the mercenary leader. "Now get out, and get out fast."

They loaded up, rogue tire and all, and were gone in a flash. I cautiously scanned the silent crowd as I handed the driver his money, knowing things could still go either way, and fast. All of a sudden I heard a single clap, then another, until the crowd erupted into a cheering, whistling serenade that followed Reza and me as we ran, laughing, all the way to the coffeehouse.

WHERE HAD THAT WOMAN GONE? I DESPER-ately needed her back to talk some sense into the other one who had panicked at the sound of falling leaves the night before. I deepened my breaths and closed my eyes. When I awoke with a start thirty minutes later, I was surprised to find myself still alone in the truck. Ten minutes more passed, and still no Mike, no Shelly. Must be one long line for that toilet, I thought. After ten more minutes I checked my phone for messages. No reception. All of a sudden it felt as though a switch had been flicked on inside my head, and I began to panic. What if something had happened? What if they fell off a cliff? What if they ran into a bear? And the weirdest thing is, all I could think of was how would I ever get myself home. Who would I contact? Was there anyone who would help me? I could have sworn my heart was going to beat its way right out of my chest.

After a few more minutes I was circling the truck, gasping for air, tears streaming down my cheeks. Too scared to wander even twenty feet away, for fear I couldn't find my way back again, I must have looked like an escapee from a mental hospital to the park ranger patrolling the area.

"Is everything okay, ma'am?" he asked as he approached with caution.

"It's . . . I'm . . . my friends . . ." I sobbed, the snot dribbling down my lip.

"Deb! What's going on?" I turned to see Mike coming toward me, with a dripping chocolate ice-cream cone in each hand. "Are you all right?"

And that's when it began to hit home that I really wasn't.

BACK ON TOP OF BELL MOUNTAIN, MY BIZARRO self continued to reign.

On top of that, the passivity that had seeped into

my veins somehow convinced me that allowing myself to become more than just friends with Mike would be okay.

I was already sort of notorious for my questionable choices in men. Though they weren't always to blame for the failures in our relationships, I had by now gone through a boatload of bad matches, including my polygamous wannabe Afghan warlord, to whom I was still married, who could now have me stoned to death for adultery, and who was the reason I couldn't go back home to Kabul in the first place.

But this one, at that time, seemed different. Mike and his mother, who lived next door, were like a big hug and a soothing Band-Aid rolled into one, particularly after what I had been through. It seemed to just be part of their way to take others under their wing—they liked to save and fix people. So I did my best to settle into my new role as the needy person in the group. Who knew? Maybe I just might find my happy ending after all.

Despite my attempts at fitting in, things quickly started to go from bad to worse. I was still often too paralyzed to leave the house, and inside the house I wasn't faring much better. The bare white walls seemed to be closing in on me. Of course, there was no way I was going to make new friends if I didn't get my ass off that futon, so I had nobody to talk to. And for once in my life, I had nothing to say. The only thing I felt like talking about was Afghanistan, and the only people I really wanted to be with were people who had been through the same sort of things I had. I didn't figure there were many of those in the Napa Valley.

To complicate things even further, a mini media backlash to the success of *Kabul Beauty School* arrived at my door with an unexpected slap in the face. I felt I had been doing everything in my long-distance power to make sure my girls in Kabul would be okay. I was hardly prepared to deal with the accusations to the contrary that were being made, accusations that I now suspect might have been instigated by a certain someone over there who, how shall I say, did not have my best interest at heart. *She went there only to make money,* some said. *She endangered those girls,* claimed others. But regardless of how the stone throwing began, it hurt me deeply.

I was an emotional basket case. Opening a can of beans, taking out the trash, or even getting dressed in the morning would suddenly make me burst into tears. I would be fine one minute, then depressed and lifeless the next.

One morning, after a particularly rough night, I decided to swallow my pride and go for some advice. And for that, who better than a fellow hairdresser?

Mike had introduced me to Deena shortly after I arrived in Napa. I figured she already knew a bit about my situation, so I summoned my courage and slowly made my way down Bell Mountain Road to her salon and plopped myself down for a shampoo, diving right into how depressed I had been. "It's devastating, you know, not being able to go back. I miss my girls, and I worry about them." She nodded as she wrapped my head in a towel and motioned toward the chair. I continued to blather on and on. In the mirror, I could see her eyes glazing over. "My whole life was there. Do you know how it feels to leave everything, and I mean *everything,* behind? My clothes, my photos . . . I feel like I even left my soul in Kabul."

Deena deftly twisted a hunk of my hair up into a clip. "I don't get it, Debbie. Why can't you go back to Cabo?"

"Cabo? I said *Kabul.* As in Afghanistan?" So much for my hairdresser theory. Apparently this girl didn't know Baja from Bagram. So, quickly and efficiently switching gears, I filled her in on my night in Yosemite. As I was paying, she wrote something down on the back of one of her cards and handed it to me. *Steve Logan, Therapist.*

I called right away for an appointment, only to learn that Steve Logan, Therapist, was going to cost me $130 an hour.

"An *hour?*" I was barely able to conceal my shock. "That's over two dollars a minute!" I gasped, quickly doing the math in my head.

"Uh-huh," the uninterested receptionist replied.

"That's the fee with the discount for the uninsured. Cash only. You want it or not?" Clearly she was not trained to recognize a woman on the edge.

"That's a discount?" I must have been completely out of touch with prices in the States because to me, that sounded like a lot of money. Most families in Afghanistan don't make that much in a month. For days I kept doing the math, calculating how many people I could have fed back in Kabul, how much rice I could have bought. The hefty price tag didn't even come with a money-back guarantee if I didn't manage to salvage my sanity.

I called my friend Karen back in Michigan, who assured me that I wasn't being self-indulgent and ordered me to stop being so stupid. "Debbie, you're not in Afghanistan anymore."

To me that seemed to be my biggest problem: I wasn't in Afghanistan anymore. I didn't want to be in California. I just wanted to go home. And the only place that felt like home, the first place where I'd ever experienced the feeling that I was living where I was meant to live and doing exactly what I was meant to do, was lethally off-limits. Now I wasn't sure where home was, and it was slowly killing me. I sat in the house for the next two days, counting the hours until my appointment.

I EAGERLY PUSHED OPEN THE DOOR TO THE office to a barrage of tinkling bells and twinkling lights. Dozens of wind chimes and tiny mirrors were suspended throughout the reception area. With no magazines in sight, I sat and concentrated on how I was going to tell my story without using up the entire hour. All I was looking for was a little direction and encouragement that, whatever *this* was, *it* was fixable. And I was determined to do it in one session. Who could afford to take more time than that?

"You see," I said once I was seated inside on a leather love seat, "my story is rather long, and a bit complicated. I spent the last five years in Afghanistan."

Steve Logan nodded his sandy-haired, balding head, clearly unimpressed, as if I'd just told him something he'd heard a million times before—like that I felt underappreciated by my spouse, or that I couldn't sleep at night. That's when I decided to amp it up and try to get my money's worth. "I moved to Afghanistan after 9/11, started a beauty school, married an Afghan a few months after we'd met, learned he already had a wife and seven or eight kids living in Saudi Arabia. I wrote a book, opened up a coffee shop, went back to the States for a book tour, and somewhere in the middle of that my husband turned on me. I went back to Kabul, discovered there was a plot to kidnap my son, then fled the country in fear for my life. I've lost everything, miss my girls from Kabul, feel homeless in my new home, and am rapidly starting to lose my mind. Am I crazy? Is there a cure? You guys don't use electric shock anymore, do you?"

Dr. Steve was expressionless, not amused in the slightest by my attempt at levity. The guy should have been a poker player. He started to jot something down. I was sure there was *total nut job* scribbled somewhere in his notes.

I waited for some sort of wisdom to come out of his mouth. Silence. Did he want me to say something else? Should I have added that my Afghan husband worked for a big warlord in Kabul? Perhaps the fifteen-minute abridged version hadn't been the best approach. I wiped a rogue tear from my cheek. Then I remembered how much I was paying him. Why wasn't he saying anything? Would I get credit for the nontalking time? *Talk, damn it!* The hour was going to be done before he stopped with his stupid notes. *Stop writing and just fix me!!!* I screamed in my head.

Finally he looked up and said, without an ounce of inflection in his voice, "You have really gone through a lot."

I couldn't help but roll my eyes. "I have, Doc, and frankly I'm not doing so well. Do you know what's wrong with me? Can you fix it?"

"Well"—he paused, drawing out his words—"it's likely."

It was likely he knew what was wrong, or likely

that he could fix me? I looked down at my watch. Ten minutes to go. He returned to his notes. Clearly he was not in a hurry. Then he looked up and asked, "Do you live in the area?"

"Yes," I replied. *Really? Focus on me, man, not where I live. I need to know what to do. I'm on the edge of a cliff, buddy, and I need you to help me.*

He took out his calendar. "Let's make an appointment for next week."

What, next week? You're kidding me. He's got to be kidding me. I barely made it through the past two days and you want me to wait until next week? Please, please, don't do this to me!

"In the meantime, I have some homework for you that should really help your healing."

I heaved a sigh of relief. Homework, thank God. Maybe some sort of writing or drawing exercises. I had heard about those. I rummaged in my purse for a pen and paper.

"The area you live in has lots of glowworms," he began, clasping his hands. "I want you to go into the fields at night and sit with the glow-worms."

I opened my mouth, but no words came out. I waited for him to start laughing at his own joke. But his expression remained unchanged as he continued: "I also want you to mow the lawn in your bare feet and get in touch with Mother Nature."

And that's when his little timer went off. *Ding!* My hour was up!

I just sat there as he wrote up his bill and motioned me toward the door. I could barely utter a thank you. No meds, no workbook, no "things I need to be grateful for" list. Nothing. It would have felt better to burn my money than to give it to this quack.

I left his office in stunned silence, and $130 lighter. At that point, I had lost all hope. There seemed to be no light at the end of the tunnel, unless, of course, it was just a bunch of glowworms.

IN THE MEANTIME, I WAS BECOMING INCREAS-ingly disturbed over my inability to appreciate the life I had. I may have been living a lot of people's dreams out in sunny California, but it didn't seem to be mine. I was that square peg hopelessly hoping to suddenly fit into that round hole. But it wasn't happening, and I hated myself for that.

It was doubly tough, because despite my reputation as the life of the party, there is a part of me, deep down inside, that's really a homebody. There is nothing I love more than snuggling up in my own space, surrounded by my own stuff. But this wasn't my own space, and this wasn't my own stuff.

I'm a treasure keeper, just like my mom. We both need to have familiar things around us. She kept everything—all my teeth, my drawings, my crummy report cards. She would have kept my fingernail clippings if my dad had let her. Me, I'm more of the souvenir type, filling home after home with memories of the places I've been and the people I've met. So when an electrical fire destroyed her house in Michigan during my stay in Afghanistan, my mother and I were both devastated. Thank goodness she and Noah, who was living with her at the time, got out unharmed. But she had everything in that house—my first rocking chair, my dad's pipe, my old prom dresses, our family photos, my kids' baby books—most of it gone. And my stuff? My home was going to be in Kabul, so being who I was, I had found a way to have a bunch of my things thrown into a shipping container, and nine months later it arrived at my door. Every trip to Michigan involved lugging back at least one extra suitcase crammed with more of my little treasures. I can only guess where all that stuff is now. I'm sure Sam has given away or sold most of it. I did see a photo on Facebook of the wife of one of his friends, a woman in Kabul, wearing my pashmina scarf and the blue dress made from fabric I bought in Turkey. I remember that woman complimenting me on that outfit once. In the photo, I could see she was even wearing the gold filigree earrings Sam had once given me.

Now, after having everything ripped out from under me in Kabul, an obsession with homelessness was beginning to gnaw at me. The nightmare of my mom's fire, memories of not being able to get my hands on the last photos ever taken of my dad, it seemed to be all crashing down on me. But it was clear that it was about more than just losing my possessions; it was about losing control of my life. I was no longer in charge of my own fate. My home had become a symbol of that. And trying too hard to make somebody else's home my own was turning into a disaster.

On top of that, as strange as it sounds, even though I still longed for the craziness of Kabul, here in peaceful, safe Napa my fears just kept getting worse. A beautiful display of fireworks at a family graduation ceremony left me shaking uncontrollably. A trip across the Bay Bridge became a nightmare when I found myself driving the off-ramps in circles, unable to find my way out. So when I was invited to tag along with Mike on a trip to Oregon to pay a visit to a sick relative, I jumped at the chance for a diversion. Maybe a change of scenery after a couple of months on top of that hill would be just what I needed to yank me out of my dark place.

The entire family was aware of my situation and treated me gingerly, doing their best to include me in conversations with the folks coming in and out to share what would probably be their final good-byes with Aunt Joan. But I found myself petrified that someone would talk to me, ask me what I did for a living or about what I had been doing in Afghanistan. And as much as Afghanistan was all I really wanted to talk about, inevitably it would always come around to the question of when I was going back, and having to say the words *I can't go back* was like plunging a knife into my own heart. Every time I said them out loud, the pain would bring me precariously close to the edge. I didn't want to believe it, but in reality I had to face the fact that I would probably *never* be going back. So I just sat in that living room, trying my best to disappear into the plaid sofa.

At some point during the weekend Aunt Joan said she was expecting her nephew and his son to be stopping by on their way back from a fishing trip. As if on cue, two dark, lumbering men came through the door smelling like fish and lugging a large ice chest. The younger one headed to the kitchen as the older one greeted Joan with a hug and a kiss. As I sat there wondering who let the Native Americans into this totally white-bread family, he sat himself down at Joan's side and took her hand gently into his own. His voice flowed softly and sweetly with news of life on the reservation, his fishing trip, his son in the other room. He finally stood to make way for more visitors who had arrived, and made his way to the chair next to me.

"Hi," he said, extending his hand. "I'm Larry." He cocked his head and squinted at me, no doubt wondering right back at me who let the crazy redhead into this group.

"I'm Debbie." We shook hands. "I came with Mike. Really just along for the ride. I've never been to Oregon, so I thought I'd check it out."

"And?" he asked.

"Nice. But wow, so remote!"

"I love it up here, especially when the salmon are running. It's a great excuse to see Aunt Joan." His warm smile drew me in.

"So you don't live around here?" Small talk! I was actually carrying on a normal conversation, something I hadn't managed to do in a long, long time. I listened as he spoke about fish and red-wood trees with the same gentle tone he used with his Aunt Joan. An aura of quiet strength seemed to surround him, and in his peaceful presence I felt a welcome calm wash over me.

"You really live on an Indian reservation? I don't think I've ever met anyone who lived on a reservation." Suddenly I felt like an idiot.

But Larry just smiled. "Yep, but in a house, not a tepee."

Larry made me laugh. He continued with some goofy Indian jokes and some silly stories about his childhood with Aunt Joan, and for the first time since I had arrived in the States I began to feel a little normal. I began to feel a glimmer of hope, all from a little small talk with Indian Larry.

Through the kitchen door we could see Larry's

son trying to lift a huge fish out of the ice chest. He stood and tenderly grabbed my arm. "C'mon. Let's go gut us some fish." I stood and followed like a little girl, hanging on his every word.

Obviously at home in this kitchen, he quickly pulled what he needed from the cupboards and drawers. I sat on a stool and watched as he nimbly slid the knife down the salmon's shiny belly. Away from the prying eyes in the other room, I pulled a bottle of Merlot out of my oversized purse. Larry reached for a coffee cup.

"Join me?" I asked, as I poured.

Larry shook his head. "I don't drink."

"Oh, sorry."

"No need to be sorry. I gave up the stuff ten years ago."

"Wow, good for you."

"Yeah, it took me almost losing everything . . ." Larry glanced over at his son. "Then I finally took control of my life."

"That's impressive," I said, quietly placing my cup on the counter. "So it has worked out for you?"

Larry shrugged. "Pretty much. I felt like it was time to do something important, something that would make a difference in my community. And I couldn't do that being a drunk."

I nodded silently. "And?"

"So, I went back to school. Imagine, a fifty-year-old Indian, back in school. Got my B.A., then went for my master's in psych."

"Really?" This guy was something.

"Uh-huh, did my thesis on post-traumatic stress disorder among the First Nations people."

I pulled my stool closer. "PTSD?"

"Yeah, it's a huge problem on the reservation. A lot of people suffering from PTSD don't even realize they have it."

I sat in silence as he explained how all sorts of things can cause post-traumatic stress disorder—physical or psychological abuse, experiencing a life-threatening event, or even just witnessing any of those things could do it. Emergency workers often get it and, of course, people with occupations that expose them to war as well.

"Hairdressers?" The word came out uncharacteristically softly.

Larry's fillet knife froze in midair. "Excuse me?"

And just like that poor salmon lying motionless on the counter, I began to spill my guts. I told Larry everything: about the beauty school, the threats, the escape with my son, how I now panicked over little things, my irrational fears, night terrors, feeling frozen, dead, not able to enjoy anything or anybody. He nodded his head knowingly.

"It's weird, you know. In Kabul I wasn't really afraid of anything. I knew I wasn't always safe, but I didn't go around feeling unsafe, either. I was living what I thought was a normal life. Now I'm afraid all the time. I can't make any sense out of it. I just want everything to go back to normal. I want my life back."

I was baring my soul to a stranger. I couldn't seem to stop the words, or the tears, from flowing. Larry listened quietly, his almost black eyes hardly blinking.

I didn't know this man, but he seemed to know something, and somehow I felt he might be saving my life.

I heaved a giant sigh as I finished my story. Larry carefully put down the knife, grabbed a towel and wiped off his hands, then walked outside and motioned for me to follow. The air was still. Larry pulled out a pack of cigarettes and offered one to me. I quietly declined and reached into my purse for a tissue. He inhaled slowly and, just as slowly, exhaled.

"You'll be just fine," he assured me, staring off into the cloudless sky. "Sit for a year. Feel. Heal. Cry. Laugh. And get a cat."

HELLO, MY NAME IS DEBORAH RODRIGUEZ. I'm a hairdresser, and I have PTSD.

Having a name for what might be wrong with me didn't make it all that much easier. PTSD. Four letters that when strung together sound strangely like a sexually transmitted disease. Or when turned into words and said out loud—post-traumatic stress disorder—like a car engine malfunction. I have been called many things in my lifetime—eccentric, wacky, larger-than-life—but the one thing I always had a hard time accepting was a label.

Of course, I had considered the possibility that I might be suffering from PTSD even before my conversation with Larry. I had lived in a war zone for five years. Things were popping and dropping around me all the time, rattling the windows and rocking the house, but they usually missed their targets. Sure, it left me a bit unnerved at times, but I resided above the Kabul Beauty School, not on a military base. No one shot at me, nor did I know anyone who'd been shot. I never witnessed

56

combat. I felt safe ninety-nine percent of the time. I do hair—the biggest dangers in my workplace are carpal tunnel syndrome and tripping over an electrical cord. So it was hard for me to reconcile my experience with that of a soldier out in the field. I almost didn't feel worthy of the diagnosis.

But the fact was, I was suffering. And after the glowworm incident I wasn't about to go back to therapy. Steve Logan, Therapist, had ruined that option forever. That, and I still had no insurance. I decided to follow Larry's advice. First I got the cat. Then I sat.

Larry had suggested that I should try not to shake anything up for one year—no major life changes. No marriage, no divorce, no big purchases. Just keep things simple and do my best to feel everything. A year sounded like an eternity, but I decided to give it a try.

I felt everything, all right, but wallowing in all that loss, grief, and loneliness left me exhausted, and even more depressed. I was eating too much, and was spending an inordinate amount of time and money shopping online. How many pairs of black leggings can one girl use? I even ordered bathing suits, and I'd rather poke myself in the eye with a needle than be caught dead in a bathing suit. All I could think about was Afghanistan, and by now those around me were so sick of listening to my blathering that I could see their eyes glaze over whenever I uttered the word *Kabul*. But I wanted so badly to hold on to that life, and I had so much more to say about what I had witnessed over there. So I began to write my stories down. I believe now that disappearing into those stories, which later became the novel *The Little Coffee Shop of Kabul*, is what kept me from totally going over the edge. I gave my story the happy ending I wished had really happened.

I tried to find a job, but even though I had founded a successful nonprofit in Kabul and had helped hundreds of Afghan women learn a trade, the big charitable organizations wouldn't give me the time of day—I had no college degree. I briefly considered going back to school, but after checking out the requirements, the years it would have taken me to finish seemed like a lifetime.

Even my rock-solid fallback profession, hair-dressing, turned its back on me. Knowing I was in no position to start my own business in California, as the costs would have been out of this world, I mapped out a strategy for making the rounds of the local salons. I'd dress up to the nines and hit all the high-end places, offering my expertise as a color specialist. Who could resist a hotshot, internationally renowned (thanks to my book) hairdresser with years of experience to share?

I waltzed through the heavy glass doors of the first salon on my list, all dolled up in my trendiest handmade designer suit and my Turkish leather boots. The place was a mass of chrome and mirrors, with power cords descending from the ceiling, and not even a wisp of discarded hair visible on the glossy black hardwood floor.

"I'm Deb Rodriguez," I said to the twenty-something tattooed, miniskirted girl behind the reception desk, and held out my hand for a shake.

"Do you have an appointment?" she asked without moving a muscle in her face, or anywhere else for that matter.

"Is the owner here? I'm interested in a job."

The girl nodded a little, her eyes dipping down to my feet and back up again. "I can let you speak to the manager if you'd like," she offered in a monotone voice. She lowered her chin and spoke softly into a tiny mouthpiece snaking from beneath her blunt-cut bob.

A pale, skinny, black-clad guy appeared at her side, shears hanging from his right index finger. "How can I help you?" he asked with a patronizing smile.

As I filled in Edward Scissorhands on who I was and what I wanted, rattling off my résumé at rapid speed, even pulling out a copy of my book for good measure, I could sense his growing impatience by the way his eyes began to dart around the room. Behind him, the mirror showed a salon at full throttle, every station occupied and every hairdresser in motion. Then, in the midst of the familiar commotion, I suddenly caught sight of myself—a lime-green striped candy cane among a sea of black cool. My gorgeous raw silk, broad-shouldered, shawl-collared, custom-tailored jacket, the one that had made me so chic in Kabul, was now making me stand out like an alien from another planet. That, and my long, straight redheaded extensions, which the insides of this place had probably not seen in years, if ever. And my makeup! My eyebrows! What was I thinking? They were way, way too Afghanistan for Napa. My heart sank as the blood rushed to my cheeks. I'd been out of the country so long that I had lost all sense of style. The Deb who had always prided herself on being trendy and cool was suddenly and woefully out of touch. I was trendy and cool in Kabul, but now I was a walking victim of the sorely outdated copies of *Vogue* that were the only issues circulating over there. A living, breathing *What Not to Wear.* I had lost my cool. I looked like a freak.

I was told that the only position available to me might be shampoo girl. Minimum wage. But I knew what this guy was thinking. Nobody wants an old hairdresser. At my age, you either come with a huge clientele in your hip pocket, or you don't come at all. And you certainly don't come with a green-striped suit.

My only other option would be the quick-cut places. This time I wore so much black I looked like Elvira. At my first stop, everyone looked like they were fresh out of high school. And I was told that I'd have to do a haircut every fifteen minutes. Are you kidding me? What about that consult? What about the color? I made that first stop my last.

So I continued to sit. The boredom was stifling. I craved the chaos of my old life. I was an unemployed drama queen without a script. What I needed to feel was alive. I probably should have been on meds.

In my relationship with Mike, I was taking the passive-aggressive approach. But mostly passive, to be honest. I knew I was too much of a mess to be in any relationship, but I never seemed to be able to summon the wherewithal to leave. Lucky for him, he was away working most of the time, and when he was around I did my best to put on my happy face and keep it there. I suspect that much of the fulfillment he got out of the relationship came from being my savior, the knight in shining armor. *My little Afghan refugee,* he once called me in front of his boss.

Any attempts I made at independence were pretty pathetic. For instance, I refused to bring my clothes into his house. So instead of packing up and going it on my own, I simply bought a closet and put it in the garage. Moving my clothes into his closet would have meant I was staying, and I knew, in the long run, that I shouldn't, and maybe even couldn't.

"You need the girl next door, and I'm definitely

not her," I'd tell Mike over and over, the guilt of letting this relationship happen eating me up. "If you really knew who I was, I doubt you'd even *like* me." At that time of my life, I didn't much like myself, either.

Needless to say, our relationship was faltering. Only Mike didn't seem to realize it—it was as though we were involved in two different relationships. I think his first warning sign should have been the forty-foot shipping container I set up in the garden. I had been sold on the beauty of shipping containers in Kabul, where there were so many of them constantly arriving, then sitting empty, that people got very creative. Even the American embassy recycled containers as apartments, creating a whole trailer park compound for their employees. In Napa, I wanted a girl cave, a place to escape. With an enthusiasm I hadn't been able to summon since returning to the States, I draped the ceilings of my very own shipping container in velvet and painted the interior in an *Arabian Nights* theme—bright blues, oranges, and reds. Always the hairdresser, I installed a salon chair, a sofa, and a mini fridge. My shipping container was the only place where I could indulge in a glass of wine and a cigarette without fear of offending Mike or his mom.

In a last-ditch, halfhearted attempt at salvaging what little I saw between us, Mike and I boarded a cruise to Mexico. It was a compromise: I had sworn I'd never go on a cruise, and Mike had vowed never to set foot in Mexico. So there we were.

I was curious about Mexico. Hell, I was curious about everywhere on the planet. But in Napa I had sort of befriended some of the Mexicans who worked as landscapers and carpenters around the neighborhood. They made me feel more comfortable and welcome than anyone else around there had. I was clearly more Mexican worker than Napa housewife. One young guy in particular, Carlos, would entertain me with stories of his life near Guadalajara, while he and his uncle laid bricks on Mike's patio. As he spoke, one half of my mind would travel back to the streets of Kabul, while the other half began to soak up the sights and sounds described in his tales. Soon I was peppering him with questions about Mexico. I was intrigued.

"If you love it so much, why are you here?" I asked one afternoon. Of course, I should have realized it was all about the money.

"But you could live like a queen down there," he told me.

"Are you going to take her down to meet your family?" I asked when his new baby was born. He lowered his eyes to the ground. I wanted to crumble into a ball and disappear. Later I heard his landlord turned him in to the immigration authorities. I never saw him again.

• • •

ON THE CRUISE, ANY HOPES MIKE HAD FOR some steamy shipboard sex were dashed by day one. The backward-moving ocean made my head spin, and I spent hours shut up in our cabin wanting to puke my guts out, then suffering panic attacks from feeling so confined. A visit to the dining room would send me rushing back to my cell, nauseated by the sight of buffet plates piled as high as Mount Everest with every fried, breaded, cheesy, greasy, gravied food you can imagine.

One evening, while we were sailing relatively smoothly toward Cabo San Lucas, I tentatively ventured up to the bar, Mike in tow. The accented bartender had looked to me to be by far the most interesting person on board, and I thought that a little cross-cultural conversation might be a good diversion. I had run out of things to say to Mike.

Two stools down, over Mike's shoulder, a man with unnaturally black hair smiled and raised his glass. I returned the gesture and momentarily felt just a little bit better. As I took a sip of my wine, I watched a short, roly-poly woman bounce up to the dark-haired man and plant a big juicy kiss smack on his lips. I envied the joy that seemed to be oozing from this woman as the two of them cuddled and joked. Then she turned and held out her hand. "Hi there. I'm Robin." She jerked her thumb toward her partner. "That's my husband, Chris. Who are you?"

Before long Chris and Mike were deep in conversation, and Robin and I were sharing a bottle of Chardonnay and swapping stories. Hers belied her cheery demeanor.

"We have six kids," she said, holding up that many fingers.

"Seven!" her husband corrected, pausing from his chat with Mike.

Robin giggled. "Oh yeah, that's right."

"And no, we are not Mormon," Chris added. "Catholic."

Robin and Chris had been living a very comfortable life in Tucson, Arizona—five children, a house with plenty of room to spare, good jobs, nice cars—when all of a sudden tragedy struck. Robin's brother was poisoned and stabbed to death by his own wife, the mother of their two young kids. Robin and Chris spent every dime they had in court fighting a brutal custody battle over their niece and nephew. They sold their home, the cars, everything they could to keep the kids away from the murderer's family. Now they were nearly broke, and all nine of them were squished under one tiny roof, but they were together. And Robin was celebrating.

When it came time for me to tell my tale I felt a little embarrassed. My problems seemed almost trivial in light of what she had been through.

Robin reacted to my reluctance by taking my hand in hers. "You have a smile on your face, but sadness in your eyes."

So I began to talk. And I talked, and talked, and talked some more. By the time I had filled in Robin on the highlights and the lowlights of my life, the bar had almost emptied.

"You, I must say, have quite a story," she said when I had finished, raising her glass in a little toast.

"*I* have a story? Well, I do. But *you,* I have no idea how you've gotten through all you have."

"I have my faith," Robin said as she grabbed the pendant around her neck and gave it a kiss. "It's the only way. Whenever I feel hopeless or weak I take my santo and hold it as tight as I can, and I am reminded that there is something much bigger than myself watching over me." Robin hopped off her stool and clasped both my hands in hers. "You need a santo."

"A santo?"

"A saint," she explained.

"But I'm not Catholic," I protested. "I'm somewhat spiritual, but not very religious." I surprised myself a little by saying that out loud, but it was the truth. As a kid, the Pentecostals had taught me to believe in heaven and hell, salvation, divine healing, the laying on of hands, speaking in tongues—but saints just weren't anything special, as far as I knew. But what did I know? By this point in my life I had been exposed to an entire medley of religious beliefs and traditions, and I took pride in my ability to see beauty in all of them. But I had witnessed too much hypocrisy to commit to any one thing. I saw it in my own town, my own church, my own home. In Afghanistan it was the same. In his attempt to have me convert to Islam, Sam had given me an English copy of the Koran. It was full of wonderful wisdom for daily life. But, just like at home, in the wrong hands its messages could be intentionally misinterpreted, conveniently paraphrased, and used to manipulate instead of inspire.

Robin persisted. "It doesn't matter. God doesn't care if you're a Catholic or not. Trust me, it's just what you need. You'll touch it, hold it, and it will remind you of your good life, but will also point you forward to where you are going."

"Where do you get a saint? I've never shopped for one of those before."

Robin laughed, her sandy curls jiggling around her face. "They're everywhere in Mexico. Tomorrow we'll leave the boys to their own devices, and you and I will go saint shopping in Cabo."

"But how will I know which saint to pick?"

"You don't have to worry. The saint will pick you."

THE WARM BREEZE WHISPERED PAST MY EARS as Robin and I wound our way around the dockside shops. I started to feel, for the first time in months, as though I could truly breathe again. My muscles seemed to melt right into my bones, and I even caught myself humming a little Jimmy Buffett while we walked.

Robin stopped in front of a display window crammed with souvenirs—T-shirts, refrigerator magnets, masks, shot glasses, ceramic donkeys dressed in serapes and sombreros. It was hard for me to imagine I was going to find my salvation here. She gently pushed me through the door and pointed down the aisle toward the religious paraphernalia. All the saints looked the same to me. I searched to find one that wasn't too flashy, a saint that would just blend into the rest of my jewelry, and as I stood there staring at the dozens of shiny silver disks on display, all but one began to fade. I placed three hundred pesos on the counter and put it around my neck.

Robin was waiting for me outside. I held out the pendant. "Which one is this?"

She nodded with satisfaction. "It's the saint that you need. It's the Virgin of Guadalupe. You know, there's nothing like the mother to take your worries to her son."

I was definitely one to leave myself open to all possibilities when it came to a higher being, and I soon found myself seeking comfort from the little santo hanging from my neck, and from the thought of a woman who had lost so much, yet had it all.

The rest of the cruise was pleasant enough. In Puerto Vallarta, we all took a cab ride into the old part of town for shopping and dinner. In Mazatlán, we had been told that the port wasn't that attractive, and there didn't seem to be enough time to really explore the rest of the city as much as I would have wanted to. So I opted for their world-class marlin fishing instead. But back on board that evening, as I listened to some of the passengers describe the cliff divers and the museums and the art galleries, and their trek down a charming street called Carnaval, which led straight to the shopping at Plazuela Machado, I regretted my decision. Especially because I didn't catch one fish. But Carnaval Street? A place with a name like that was a place I had to see. I vowed to do some research when I got home.

MY YEAR OF SITTING HAD COME TO AN END. I didn't really feel all that different, although I did notice that I wasn't crying quite as much, at least no longer every day. I continued to constantly get lost, but it didn't mean I had to pull over to the side of the road in a state of panic each time. But inside, the pain and confusion were churning around together in a nasty dance, flinging out doubts that were multiplying like rabbits, each one a reminder of how much of a failure I was. I had failed at relationships and marriages, and somehow, even though I had been forced to leave Kabul, I felt like

I had failed big-time at the one thing I was most proud of—the beauty school. And now I was failing at the slightest attempt at a normal life. I didn't even know who I was anymore. Somewhere between Kabul and California, I had lost my way.

The thing was, life on the mountain with Mike was safe and secure. For the first time in my adult life, I was being taken care of. And for a free-spirited woman heading toward fifty, who hadn't done a lick of planning for her future, that was huge. Plenty of women would have killed for what I had. So why was it so hard for me? Half of me, racked with guilt over not appreciating what I had, still yearned for the ability to adjust to life on the mountain. The other half just wanted to run away.

ABOUT A MONTH AFTER MIKE AND I RETURNED to Napa, I found a little house in Mexico. It seemed to just happen, sort of. The truth was that, as was my habit whenever I traveled anywhere, I had turned every stop on the cruise into a game of "could I live here?" You name it, I've fantasized it. Iceland? Too much fish. Japan? I felt too big. India? Made me crave a Whopper. On this trip, the first two ports of call, Cabo San Lucas and Puerto Vallarta, were immediately crossed off the list, both being a bit too touristy for my taste. But I just couldn't seem to get Mexico out of my head. I wanted to own a house. And once I started looking into the possibility of Mazatlán, I couldn't stop. It seemed to tick all my boxes. Proximity to the ocean? Check. Plenty of English speakers? Check. Culture and history? Check. Sam's Club and Walmart? Check. I booked a flight to return for four days, to see for myself what this town was all about, and within twenty-four hours, I was hooked.

The ride in from the airport was a major disappointment—dry, barren, dirty, and covered in graffiti. At first Mazatlán felt like a huge prank that had been played on me. I began to seriously doubt my instincts, and started to seriously regret spending the money on the flight. But when the taxi turned down into Olas Altas, and deeper into the Centro Histórico, I almost gasped. It was France and Germany and Spain and New Orleans all rolled into one, with a beach!

Roger the Realtor had four houses on his list for the next morning. And guess where the first one, and the best one, was? On Carnaval Street.

In retrospect I can see the natural progression of things, from my garage closet to my backyard shipping container to my tiny bungalow in Mazatlán. I'd always kept an escape hatch, a place to call my own, even if it was just a closet. Having a house had always been important to me. I was just twenty-one when I rescued an old house slated for a tear-down, moved it onto some property my dad gave me, and never looked back. The real estate bug must have been in my genes, as it followed me throughout my life—I always managed to own my own home, even when I was earning the lowest of low salaries. The last house I owned, before I went to Afghanistan, now belonged to one of my exes. I got nine thousand dollars in that divorce, and he got everything else. I would have paid him to get out of that marriage. Wait, I guess I did.

But in California, with the cost of living so high and my job prospects so low, I just hadn't been able to see how to make buying a home work. After sinking money into starting the coffeehouse in Kabul, putting my son Zach through college, and purchasing my car, I only had so much to work with. And, to top it off, I had no credit. Not that I had debt, but being out of the country for so long meant no viable credit history. Purchasing a home in California was out of the question. My little nest egg would have rapidly disappeared, with nothing to show for it. And then what?

The house in Mexico somehow felt like the right thing to do. After all, it would cost me less than most of the cars I saw whizzing around the roads in Napa, not that I was planning on buying one of those, either; I'm just saying. So I scooped up what remained of my book earnings and rationalized it as a good investment, and the perfect getaway place. I would go, or Mike and I would go, for a few months out of the year and vacation on the beach. I realize now that there had been another, stronger force driving my decision.

Mike had heard me talk about my desire to have a little place somewhere, but he never took me seriously. Buying an old Moroccan *riad* in the Sahara was an idea I bounced around for a while. When I overheard him telling the rest of his family to "just pretend you believe her—it's a phase, it will pass" as if I were a two-year-old, I was furious. So when I actually put my money where my mouth was, Mike was speechless.

"It will be fun," I assured him over breakfast one morning. He rolled his eyes. "Seriously, you'll see." It crossed my mind that he was keeping his mouth shut just to keep me happy.

So imagine my surprise when Mike dumped me. Or rather, when his mother dumped me on his behalf. One Tuesday morning I woke to the sound of someone sobbing from our hallway.

"Shirley?" I asked. "Are you okay?" I opened the door to the sight of Mike's mother in her velvet tracksuit, bent over in misery. I reached out to keep her from falling over. "Oh my God! What happened?" I had never seen her so emotional, let alone shed a tear. My immediate thought was that Mike had been in an accident.

"Oh, Debbie!" She heaved. "I'm so sorry . . . You and Mike . . ." Her voice trailed off into another sob.

I was confused. No one was dead? "What about me and Mike?" I asked.

Her swollen red eyes looked into mine and I could see that she probably had been crying for hours. "That you two broke up! I'm so sorry, Debbie . . ." She held me tight. "I'm going to miss you." I was dumbfounded. I have been dumped via e-mail, phone, text, and the old-fashioned Dear John letter, but this was a first. I had just been dumped by my boyfriend's mom.

Then, as if the universe had forgotten the art of subtlety, two days later I sat in a courtroom in front of a judge, tearfully fighting for an annulment from my Afghan husband. Fortunately, after a few grueling hours, it was granted. I was now officially not married, again, at least outside of Afghanistan. But the stress of all that had gone on in the past few days left me completely deflated. I couldn't imagine feeling any worse.

So, finally, I did what I should have done much, much earlier. I gave myself permission to leave. I hadn't been planning on making Mexico my new home, but the little house on the sea seemed to be all I had left. The day after the annulment, I crammed everything I owned into my red Mini Cooper, and Polly the cat and I headed south for Mexico.

THIS SHOULD HAVE BEEN THE SCENE IN MY life movie where I'm tooling down the coast, hair flying in the breeze, belting out a song of girly liberation, pumping my fist out the rolled-down window. If only. The stretch from Napa to Palm Springs, California, is, for the most part, hot, boring, and long. And I was a mess. The car was littered with crumpled tissues, empty soda cans, and sticky candy wrappers. The air was stale with Marlboro Menthols, and the only sounds to be heard were Polly's mews and my own curses at anyone who dared to pass a little too quickly, swerve a little too close, or even just look at me sideways.

All I wanted was to be in my house, and it was all I could do to stay focused on that goal. You'll be fine, I tried to tell myself over and over. Just trust the GPS lady, do what she says, and you'll be fine. You can figure everything else out after you get there. It will be fine. "We'll be fine, right, Pol?"

Riiiiggghhhttt, answered Inner Debbie, my worst

critic, her nasally voice dripping with sarcasm.

"I wasn't talking to you! And who invited you, anyway?" I answered out loud.

What, you thought I wasn't coming along?

Apparently I had expected too much when I hoped to leave my doubts behind, back in Napa. Instead those doubts seem to have multiplied, weighing me down with even more baggage than I had arrived there with.

You've got more baggage than Paris Hilton on a three-week luxury cruise.

I couldn't argue. My life sometimes seemed like a series of one-act plays starring the same character, a gutsy heroine who over and over seems destined to triumph, yet somehow never quite does. Oh, I was great at survival. That skill set kicked in long ago, after my first husband, whom I had met in college, fathered not one but *two* children with women who were not me, including one who was (until then) my best friend. I am not kidding. I was only twenty-five, with two little boys, when things finally fell apart. We were married too young, and our union had already been a rocky one, with both of us to blame. And to complicate things even further, my soon-to-be-ex-husband was working alongside me at my mom's salon, and had built up a clientele bigger than my own, which wasn't hard considering my double duty as a mother. So when, in the heat of the moment, I presented Mom with a "he goes or

I go" ultimatum, and she chose her cheating son-in-law over her own daughter, I had to force myself to bottle up that triple betrayal deep down inside somewhere, put on a smile, and figure out a Plan B. But not before slashing his tires in a fit of rage.

Wow. You go, girl! But what about that Plan B? Did you actually believe that escaping your mom's salon to work in a prison was a wise career choice? What kind of woman thinks that conducting mess hall pat-downs on a bunch of thieves and murderers would be better than doing perms?

Inner Debbie knew way too much about me. But she wasn't telling the whole story. Yes, I did move on to work, briefly, as a prison guard. But when I took that job, I was a single mom who needed to feed her kids, and a steady salary, health insurance, and a 401(k) were luxuries I had never before enjoyed. You do what you have to do. Unfortunately, they stuck me on the second shift, which meant I never, ever got to see my boys, and I was likely facing a sentence of nine more years on that same schedule. What kind of a life was that? No amount of money or security could make that okay. I think I knew it was time to leave when Zachary told his first-grade teacher that Mommy couldn't make it to the parent-teacher conference because she was in jail.

The day I quit, after a year on the job, I had been

working the yard. My long blond hair extensions were gathered up into an *I Dream of Jeannie* ponytail on top of my head, the only practical solution to guard against the brutal wind whipping off Lake Michigan. The captain called me into his office.

"Anything wrong, sir?" I asked, knowing there wasn't. I was doing a good job. Nobody had escaped, and no one had been killed on my watch. I had already complied with the captain's request that I trade in what he called my "disco pants," which were actually quite nice and baggy, for the regulation skintight, black standard-issue ones that elicited catcalls and whistles from the sex-starved inmates. He motioned for me to sit.

"Your hair."

"Excuse me?"

"It's your hair. You can't wear it like that."

I had to laugh. "It's just a ponytail, you know, because of the wind?"

"Just take it down from on top of your head."

"What do you mean?"

"You know, just pull it down an inch, so it looks more normal."

"I can't. You see, this part . . ." I held out my extensions for him to take a look. "This part isn't mine. And when I pull on it too much, it gives me a headache. I can't work with a headache, can I? And anyway, what exactly does 'more normal' mean?"

I could see by the way he shifted his weight from foot to foot that he was losing patience with me. "Just move the damn thing down an inch. Nobody is going to take you seriously with hair like that."

"Well, nobody is going to take *you* seriously with those three measly twelve-inch-long strands combed over your bald head. Who do you think you're kidding?"

I swear I could see the steam coming out of his ears. "An inch! That's all I'm asking."

I knew I was right, and I wasn't about to back down. I easily got more respect from the inmates than I got out of the men who worked in this prison. Within the system, there had been way too many dropped hints about the exchange of "favors" for a promotion. And I was sick of it.

"You know, if you want my ponytail moved, move it yourself. On second thought, no." I unhooked the wad of keys from my belt and flung them on his desk. "I'm outta here."

After the prison stint I tried to go back to my old standby, hairdressing, but at that point, with no customer base and no insurance and almost no money, it all seemed so hopeless. An opportunity (and yes, a man) dropped into my lap, one that just seemed too good to pass up. Bobbie was a Bahamian who lived in Chicago. There was a lot of money to be made down in the Bahamas, he told me, diving for lobsters and crayfish. We were moving to the islands, where we would build a house on the water. I was truly intrigued by the idea of showing my kids the world beyond Holland, Michigan. It would be an adventure!

So I sold my house, bought a pop-up tent, packed up the boys, and moved to Mangrove Cay. My vision of living on an island, spending long, sun-kissed days combing the sand with my sons, sounded way better than raising a couple of latchkey kids I never saw. Nothing was worth missing the opportunity of seeing them grow up. And I did make it work, for a while. We began construction on the house. Earning a living from diving was proving to be difficult, so for extra money I'd fly to Nassau once a month and buy Twinkies, Juicy Juice, and Doritos in bulk, then sell them out of the back of my battered old car to hungry schoolkids on lunch break and families at sports events and festivals. In our temporary home, we had no water, we had no electricity, but for the first time in my kids' lives I was there to greet them at home every day after school, even if it was just from the flap of a tent. It was the packs of flesh-eating sand fleas that, after six months, drove me away from the Bahamas, back to Michigan, and into my next marriage.

Who did you think you were, Elizabeth Taylor or something?

It was clear that the loudmouth inside wasn't about to let up on me. On the contrary, I was no

Elizabeth Taylor. One thing I never understood about myself was the fact that although there were always plenty of prettier and thinner and smarter women around, I never seemed to be able to date a man for long before he'd ask me to marry him. And though I knew that "no" was an option, and at times may have been the wiser choice, I just couldn't seem to get myself to say it out loud.

With Mr. Right, I at least forced myself to try. I told him maybe. We met at the mall, where, with my last five hundred dollars plus a two-thousand-dollar loan, I had set up a holiday kiosk to sell plaster gargoyles. I had come across them during a trip to Chicago and couldn't get over how cool they were. So I found the factory that made them and was soon in possession of a boatload of gargoyles—two-inch gargoyles, six-hundred-pound gargoyles, and everything in between. My dad had always told me I could sell ice to an Eskimo, but here I was, trying to persuade conservative midwestern Dutchmen that a scary cement sculpture was something they just couldn't live without.

One day Mr. Right came by to check out my gargoyles, with three kids just as adorable as he was in tow. Soon he was dropping by every day, bringing me coffee or cocoa or tea. We talked about our families, his amateur acting career, my love of travel. I learned he even went to the same church that I had recently visited a few times. I was smitten. I left the mall seven weeks later with enough money for a down payment on a home, and a new boyfriend.

Then he asked me to marry him. Though things had been going extremely well, I was determined not to make another mistake. So I suggested we date for a year and then revisit the question.

Our dates always involved seven people—with his two sons and daughter, and my two boys—all of them between the ages of eight and thirteen. We traveled around with our own little Brady Bunch, which to me seemed like a good way to keep things from moving too fast. Mr. Right, who sang at church and played Jesus in the Easter pageant, encouraged me to play my trumpet at every service. It was so much fun to pick up the instrument again after nine years. I loved the powerful feeling that came from blasting out those sweet notes all the way to the back pews. And after a nearly perfect year, one that felt almost too good to be real, I said yes.

It was a fairy-tale wedding. All the kids stood up for us, and each and every member of the new family added a ring to the third finger of his or her left hand. After a romantic Italian honeymoon (for two), we all settled into a farmhouse big enough for the whole gang. And though we worked different shifts, Mr. Right managed to keep the weekday passion alive through hidden notes and frequent phone calls.

It was only six weeks after the marriage that I sensed a change. He had begun to distance himself from me. No more phone calls, no more notes. And when we were together, he seemed to have no patience for me. I suspected depression. He claimed the depression was mine. Then one day it simply stopped. He suddenly seemed to hate everything about me—my body, my hair, my smile, my kids. It was as though just the smell of me when I entered a room would make him sick. I had no idea what I had done.

By now he was making sure we were never alone. His weekends were spent being Super Dad, a role I still admired him for. Then one Sunday, on a weekend when my kids were at their dad's, I headed out to the car with my trumpet, anxious to get to church early to warm up before the crowd arrived. There, in the driveway, was Mr. Right hurrying all his kids into the van.

"Why so early?" I asked. He didn't answer. I never saw Mr. Right and his kids again. Soon we were divorced. I later heard he had moved to Florida and come out as gay.

For once Inner Debbie didn't seem to have much to say. And I really didn't need her to remind me about the next disastrous relationship, the one that sent me packing to Afghanistan. I had married a preacher—a jealous, hot-blooded, hot-headed Latin preacher. At least something good came out of that union, even if it did come from a place of dark desperation. But honestly, when you leave during a screaming match with your husband, swearing that you'd rather die in Afghanistan than live one more day in Michigan with him, you know it's time to go.

The truth was, I had already started making an attempt to head down a different path well before that confrontation with my preacher husband. I'd always yearned to be more than just a hairdresser. To me, hairdressing was what those girls did who got pregnant in high school, or who weren't smart enough or rich enough to go to college. I didn't look at my trade as something to be proud of. It was just something I had settled for. What I really wanted to do was help people, and to the younger me that meant either cop, firefighter, or military. But back then, at least where I lived, girls just didn't do that. I considered becoming a missionary, but the thought of cramming religion down people's throats just didn't fly with me. That, and I hated the outfits.

But times had changed, and now that my kids were nearly grown, I was determined to turn my energy toward something that mattered. By that time I was too old to be accepted by the police academy or the military, and I wasn't even close to being in good enough shape to battle a raging inferno. So when I came across a Christian organization in Chicago that was offering disaster relief training, I jumped at the chance.

Two weeks without my husband was like a spa vacation, that is, if your spa focuses on teaching CPR and the basics of decontamination. Then, two weeks after my training was complete, the terrorist attacks of 9/11 hit. I was on a plane to New York within hours of a call to come help. Day after day, I'd massage weary firefighters' callused, pungent feet and listen to the horror stories of what they'd been through, happy to be able to give them even a few brief moments of comfort and calm, while at the same time trying my best to ignore the cell phone constantly buzzing in my pocket. My controlling husband and my sorry life seemed far, far away. Even in the midst of all that chaos and despair, or perhaps because of it, it became abundantly clear to me that it was time for my life to change, big-time, and that I was capable of being the one to make that happen. So when I heard that the organi-zation I was working with was putting together a team to be sent to Afghanistan, I immediately began to campaign for a spot. I would spend a month, I thought, putting my training to work helping those who had suffered from the Taliban's brutal regime. It would be the start of my new future.

Speaking of Afghanistan . . .

"C'mon, do we really need to go there? I did a lot of good things in Kabul."

Sure, the reproachful Debbie inside reminded me, *but let's not forget that you ended up run-ning away from there, too.*

That one really hurt. On my best days, I understood that I didn't run away from Kabul at all. I hung in there until it became impossible to do anything *but* leave. In fact, it was a voice inside, much like the one now bumming a ride to the border, that convinced me to stay as long as I did. *You can't leave, you'll let everybody down,* it would say, over and over. *You have no choice.* And honestly, if it had been just me on the line, I probably would have stayed. I had become used to putting myself out there, and had become weirdly inured to the danger. But when my son was threatened, the mother lioness came roaring out of me and whacked me back into reality. Staying would have, no doubt, ended in something I'd rather not even imagine. No, it did not end the way I wanted. Of course, I was still struggling with the pain and guilt of leaving everything, and everyone, behind. And no matter what my situation might have been at home, I went to Afghanistan in the first place thinking I might, for once in my life, actually be able to do something good, perhaps make a difference. When the opportunity came to use what I knew best in a way that could help other women gain their own independence, to share the tricks of a trade that had, more than once, saved my own life, it seemed like it was all meant to be.

And where did that leave you? Running away again?

"I am *not* running away."

You always run away.

"I do not!"

Do so.

"Cut it out!" I answered out loud. "Can't you see I'm trying to drive? And that, I might add, is a big deal for me these days."

Big deal? Driving? Who are you kidding, Rodriguez? You're nothing but a . . .

Whoosh! My heart jumped into my throat as the gust from a barreling eighteen-wheeler thrust my little Mini off onto the gravelly shoulder of the road. I slowed to a stop, shut off the ignition, and turned around to check on Polly, who was frozen in a crouch, her green eyes wide with fright.

"It's okay, baby," I lied, lighting a cigarette, the one I swore would be my last, with a shaking hand. An oven blast of sweet, dry air flooded the car as I slowly lowered the windows. In the distance I could see a range of snow-covered peaks jutting out from the flat desert floor. On either side of me, a strange vineyard of giant white fans turned lazily in a synchronized waltz, in rows and rows stretching out for miles against the cloudless blue sky.

Personally, I had to admit that it was hard to believe I was actually doing this. Mike (or rather Mike's mother) breaking up with me might have been just the kick in the ass I needed to get me on the road to a new phase in my life, but I was far from feeling sure about it. If only I could simply reach across, open the passenger door, and boot that belittling voice inside out into the scrubby sand. I still had more than a thousand miles to go before I reached Mazatlán, and she was starting to really, really piss me off. Instead I pulled back onto the highway and turned up the radio to try to drown her out.

Was I running away? How can you run away from something you never really had in the first place? Napa was not my life. It was more like my rebound life, the one your girlfriends warn you against and the one you jump into because it's easier than facing up to the reality and pain of what just hit you. In Napa I had been on hold for two years, trying to make something work that probably never should have happened at all.

THE SKY HAD TURNED INTO A MELTED NEON Creamsicle swirl by the time I pulled up to the Days Inn on Palm Canyon Drive. I barely had enough energy to pour a bowl of Friskies for Polly before flopping down on the bed, the stiff polyester bedspread practically cracking beneath my weight. If I hadn't been too exhausted to pray, I would have. But what would I have asked for? I would have had to come up with an actionable scenario, a clear-cut vision for what I wanted my new life to be. But, as usual, I didn't really know what I was getting into, so instead I just held on to the little santo around my neck and hoped that this time things would turn out differently.

5

"MAYBE I COULD DRIVE A TAXI DOWN THERE. I'm getting a lot of experience, right? What do you think, Pol? Or maybe I could, if worse comes to worst, sell time-shares? We both know I'm a good talker. How does that sound?"

Polly didn't answer. We were on our way to Tucson, and my poor cat was moping in her carrier, miserably wedged in the backseat between mountains of vacuum-sealed space-saver bags that, for some reason, seemed to be expanding by the minute. I was trying hard to keep Debbie Downer from entering the conversation. But I couldn't deny that my lack of a plan was more than a little scary. My future was staring me down like a pissed-off pit bull. It was hard to look away, but more frightening not to. Even the cactuses standing tall by the edge of the road, waving at me like funny, giant green men, couldn't distract me from my anxiety.

One thing was for certain. I was not going to be a hairdresser in Mexico. Though I knew I was damn good at it, my dismal attempts at getting a salon job in California had done a real number on me. Realizing that I was being looked at as an old hairdresser was like getting a kick in the teeth. The whole experience only served as a reminder of the negatives of the profession. When I really think about it, I can't really say I ever actually wanted to become a hairdresser. Though it had been kind of fun playing hairdresser in my mom's salon when I was little, folding the towels and taking the rollers out of the old ladies' hair while they sat under the dryers, I was all too aware of what it actually meant to be a real one. I can, to this day, picture my mom on the couch at night, heating pad stuffed under her spine and swollen feet propped up on a cushion, her smile slowly thawing from having to remain cheerful whether she felt cheery or not. Back then I wanted to be a princess. That, or a famous opera singer. My doting mother never failed to indulge me in my fantasies. Nevertheless, when I turned fifteen, she sent me to beauty school. "It's a great skill to fall back on," my overworked and underpaid mother insisted.

So for a year after earning both my high school and beauty school diplomas, I worked in my mom's salon. It was expected. It was easy. But I wanted more. Though I had struggled in school, I longed to be an educated, sophisticated world traveler, a woman of importance. So I told my mom that I wanted to go to college. "Oh, honey child," she crooned in her sweet southern drawl, "you know you're not college material." After one year at John Brown University in Siloam Springs, Arkansas, I proved her right.

I fell back on hairdressing, of course. And when, a few years later, with a husband, two kids, two cars, and a house, I called my mom sobbing, she was perplexed.

"Are the kids okay?" she asked as she rushed through my front door, scanning the room for any signs of an accident or mishap. I nodded.

"Are you okay?" She took my chin in her hand, my tears cascading over her fingers and onto the floor.

"Yes. I mean, no. Oh, Mom, I just don't know what's wrong with me. I'm miserable, and I have no right to be." She went into the kitchen and put the kettle on the stove. I followed. "I mean, I should be happy, right? I have so much." Mom nodded. I plopped down on the kitchen chair. "I just don't get it. Why doesn't this work for me? I still keep feeling there has to be more."

Mom poured the hot water over a tea bag and handed me the cup. "I'm not sure, baby girl," she answered as she stroked my hair. "But I do know one thing. You can do anything you set your mind to. What do you want?"

"That's the problem," I said, sobbing. "I just don't know."

She pulled a tissue from under her sweater

sleeve. "Well, that just doesn't make any sense. You're a dreamer. Always have been. Come on, what does your heart tell you?"

"I'm a hairdresser. I'm already a mom. What else *can* I be?" I whined.

"Listen to you. You don't have to be just one thing, or even two. You can do anything you want. And that, child, is not a reason to cry."

"I know, Mom." I sighed. "I just wish I could figure it out."

My mother sat down across the table. "You know, you always did want to be a princess. It's not too late . . ."

I snorted a laugh in response.

"Well, that's not very princesslike of you," she admonished, producing yet another tissue.

"Thank you, Queen Mother."

"Debbie, I think you can be a mother, *and* a hairdresser, *and* a princess."

And as she reached across the table to take my hand in hers, I wondered if this woman, whose own mom had died when she was just a baby, who married at sixteen to escape a household of fourteen kids, living a dirt-poor existence in the Arkansas cotton fields, who remained trapped in a disappointing relationship until death did them part, had once wished for someone to tell her she could be a princess, too.

I carried my mom's words with me wherever I went. They were there as I patrolled the prisoners' bunks for shanks and battled the misogynistic prison staff, they were there while I was swatting away the killer insects on the Bahamian beach, and they were there when I boarded that first plane to Afghanistan. I heard them every single time I stepped out of the supposed comfort zone, which, for me, was never particularly comfortable in the first place.

It wasn't until Kabul that I finally embraced the hairdresser in me. I saw that I was doing as much, or maybe even more with my scissors and dyes than a lot of people with fancy degrees and big titles achieve in a lifetime. Over there, I realized that it was about so much more than simply doing hair. For the first time in my life, I respected my job, and myself. I wasn't "just" a hairdresser any-more! I was living proof that anyone could make a difference. You just needed a lot of determina-tion, a good amount of energy, the willingness to take a few risks, and a good sense of humor.

But a few risks too many, and you might find yourself like I did—lost, confused, and starting all over again. By the time I got to Napa, I could no longer hear my mom's voice. I couldn't even call her for a reminder. By that time she was starting to forget things, and wasn't really capable of helping me much. I was pretty sure she wouldn't have it in her to tell me that I could be a princess anymore.

So now, with hairdressing and reigning over a

kingdom of adoring subjects out of the picture, what was left? What would I do in Mexico? I didn't have a clue. Part of me pictured myself spending the rest of my life sitting quietly on the beach, sipping a margarita. I was tired. Tired of men, tired of moving, tired of being scared, tired of being confused. But who was I kidding? I'm not one to sit quietly, anywhere. All I was hoping was that being in Mexico would give me the chance to figure things out.

I tried to focus on the one thing I knew was waiting for me down there—my little house on Carnaval Street. I could not wait to settle into my own place. After all that time in California squatting in someone else's home, I was more than ready to plant some roots.

Mexico I could afford, at least for a while. The way I figured it, my savings would last for maybe a couple of years, if I was careful. So in a way, I realized, I should consider my house in Mexico to be an investment in my future. It was my house that would allow me the time to figure things out, to fix myself. That's a lot of pressure for one little house, I thought. I hoped it could take it.

THIS WAS TO BE MY LAST DAY IN THE U.S.A. The skyline of Tucson faded in the rearview mirror as Polly and I headed south down Interstate 19 toward Nogales, Mexico. We were off to an early start. Who knew what I'd find at the border? I began to picture humorless guys in sunglasses with machine guns, narcos and federales in blood battle, trigger-happy Border Patrol agents chasing down fleeing immigrants. In another life, those kinds of guys might have been a piece of cake. Now I just wished them gone, gone from my imagination and anywhere else they might be lurking.

Driving through that flat, barren landscape on a road that seemed to go on forever in a hypnotic straight line, my thoughts turned to my mother. How I wished she could see my new home. Hell, she might have even enjoyed this road trip, if things were different.

I had been able to convince my mom to visit me once in Afghanistan. She had never been out of Michigan, and by this time I was beginning to see signs of a slipping mind and slowing body, so I knew the time was short for her to enjoy an adventure. I really wanted her to see where I lived, meet my friends, and maybe do some hair in the beauty school. I was anxious for her to under-stand why I had chosen to make my life half a world away, and desperately wanted to hear her tell me that I had done well.

We arrived in Afghanistan together after a shopping spree in Dubai. She saw a lot during that first week in Kabul, but we both were yearning for a road trip. Of course, I doubt she understood what a road trip in that part of the world really meant, but I decided it was time for us to do something we'd both remember forever.

So one morning a bunch of us packed into a van and headed twelve hours north through the Hindu Kush mountains, into the open country-side leading to Mazar-i-Sharif. The next day we decided to have a picnic in the countryside near the Afghan-Uzbek border. It was really beautiful up there, with the fields in bloom. Mom kept insisting that Sam pull over so she could pick some flowers. I didn't have the heart to tell her they were opium poppies. We eventually did pull over for lunch. Sam was excited about a new gun he had bought, so as we feasted on roasted lamb, naan, and pomegranates, we began to take turns at target practice, aiming at an abandoned old tank in the field. Seriously, that's just the kind of thing you do for entertainment over there. We were all hooting and hollering and having a fine time when all of a sudden the turret on that tank began to turn toward us with a grinding whir.

"Run!" Sam yelled.

"Run, run!" I yelled at my mom.

"Why? Why?" she yelled back.

I grabbed her hand and dragged her toward the van, her headscarf slipping down over her eyes, and stuffed her in back while the others franti-cally gathered up the food. As the car doors slammed shut I started to laugh, uncontrollably. So did Mom.

Mom told me she'd never go on a picnic with me again. But she sure got her adventure. Oh, and when she returned to the United States, one of her customers asked her what her favorite part of Afghanistan was. Mom smiled and said, "Dubai."

But now, all alone in another desert, I wasn't sure I was equipped to handle that kind of drama anymore. Vultures circled overhead as the road began to bend and turn, taunting me with every twist. *Go north, go back. Move ahead. Drive south. No, wait, turn around. C'mon, just go.* Around me, the scorched brown hills stretched out for miles, broken only by the chain-link border fence that even I could have climbed over had I wanted to. This measly barrier couldn't even keep the cows in, or out. I could see them squeezing under, heading north in herds in search of that elusive greener grass.

My pulse quickened as the first green border crossing sign loomed into view. As my last glimpse of American soil disappeared into the distance, the reality of settling in another foreign country began to seep in. I wasn't going to know my way around, and the little Spanish I knew was laughable. Second nature would be a thing of the past, at least for a while, until I figured out how things worked. The simplest daily tasks, like getting gas, asking for directions, or telling a doctor where it hurt, would become huge chores. Everything that made life easy in the States, gone.

And, on top of it all, I knew nobody, and nobody knew me. I could be dead in my house for days, weeks even, and no one would notice. Well, I thought, being really dead in Mexico is still better than feeling dead in California.

"Here goes nothing, Pol," I said, the inside of my mouth so dry that I could barely part my lips.

It was as if I had entered another dimension. The crossing into Nogales was nothing, just a green light and a guy waving me through, but once on the other side, it was as though someone had changed the channel. Gone were the rows of neat, clean, cookie-cutter houses. Here it seemed more like Afghanistan, with little cement buildings crumbling down into the road. The rise in decibel level was instantaneous. Music blared from rolled-down car windows and open shop doors, mariachi and *banda* and pop all banging up against each other in one big shouting match. Horns blasted. Street vendors shouted out their offerings. *Naranjas*! *Tacos*! *Cacahuates*! Skinny dogs ran down the muddy streets, narrowly avoiding the buses and trucks and carts selling tacos and hot dogs and corn and flowers and newspapers with photos of dead bodies splashed across their front pages. And apparently there were no driving rules in Mexico, only one giant free-for-all, with lanes disappearing into thin air and everyone just rolling wherever they pleased.

The chaos felt almost suffocating, but then again, it also felt strangely liberating.

I was in Mexico, for good this time. And was I going to panic? Of course I was. But first I had to get my visa.

WITH MY SATCHEL CRAMMED WITH A MILLION papers hanging on one shoulder and Polly in the pink carrier slung over the other, I approached the daunting white building.

"Bienvenido, welcome!" A chubby man in a crisp, short-sleeved shirt motioned me over to a counter, his warm smile taking me by surprise.

"Hi. Hola." I plunked down a pile with everything I had; papers for me, papers for Polly, papers for my car.

He began to leaf through the well-worn pages of my passport. I could see the stamps for Syria, Pakistan, Afghanistan, India flipping by.

"CIA?" he asked, with only half a smile. "Military?"

I shook my head. "I'm a hairdresser."

A flash of serious doubt crossed his face. I'd been down this road before, so out of my bag came a copy of *Kabul Beauty School*, the Spanish version, always useful evidence in proving I wasn't a terrorist or a spy.

"Una celebridad!" He began to pass the book around to his coworkers. Everyone seemed amused, except for the long line of impatient travelers growing behind me. Then he handed me a pen as he opened the front cover. "Your signature, please?"

Autograph in hand, he turned back to business. "So, you are vacationing in Mexico?"

I opened my mouth, and for a second, the words caught in my throat. I felt like I was perched on a mile-high bungee platform, summoning the courage to take the plunge. I took a deep breath and shook my head. "No, I live here. I'm coming to live in Mexico."

His smile grew wider as he began to pound his metal stamp down on page after page of my papers—*thump, thump, thump*—each thump feeling like a whack at stamping out my past.

"Perfecto. Now you are a Mexican." He handed me my papers.

"Mucho gusto," I mumbled, stuffing the papers back into my bag. "Mucho gusto!" I repeated, a little louder this time, searching for any leftover courage that might still be lurking in my soul. So there I was. Starting over. This was no south-of-the-border vacation, this was for real. I had my cat, my car, my stuff. My brain felt pulled in a million directions, from relief at having arrived, to scared sick of all the uncertainty, to a nagging self-loathing about not being able to make things work in the States. But in my heart I felt a twinge of excitement. And I felt something else bubbling up from inside—a sense of control that I hadn't been able to summon for two years. It was as if I had just found the corner pieces of the jigsaw puzzle that was my life. All I needed to do was figure out how to fill in the middle. Unfortunately, I never was very good at puzzles.

"Now what do I do?" I said out loud to myself with a sigh. The official took me literally, and pointed down the road to another building, where, after much confusion, a lot of bad attempts at Spanish, some feeble stabs at sign language, and a moment or two when I seriously considered, once again, turning around, as there was no way I was going to make it in a country where I couldn't even figure out how to get in, I finally got my car registration.

I HADN'T GONE FIVE MILES OVER THE BUMPY road that led away from the immigration office when two blue-vested, blue-hatted guys flagged me down. One leaned over, peered through the passenger window, and smiled. The other was saying something to me, but I couldn't recognize even one word. Then they began to compare notes with each other over the roof of my little car. I dug deep into my bag, hoping I had remembered to pack enough pesos for a quick bribe.

"My friend thinks you are very handsome," came a voice through my window.

I stuffed the bills back into my purse and laughed. "Why, thank you. And he is very handsome, too." They waved me on, and I continued through the now-green rolling hills, past little churches and shrines and clusters of flower-strewn crosses to commemorate those who had died on the roads. The landscape grew cluttered with pampas grass and little pink flowers. Men with shiny machetes hacked at the thick grass dividing the two sides of the narrow highway.

That afternoon I drove only until I could see the sun beginning its slow descent toward the horizon. I was worried by all the warnings I'd heard about driving in Mexico at night. If the narcos or kidnappers don't get you, the animals leaping randomly back and forth across the roads surely will. That, or one of the potholes the size of Texas that could swallow up a Mini in a nanosecond. But I was ready to call it a day. My only stop after Nogales had been a gas station, and my only human encounter, outside of toll takers, was the gas station attendant who stuffed my cash into a coffee can and hoisted it up on a pulley to an upstairs window, where his buddy took the payment and lowered the can back down, change and receipt inside. They were kept company by a weather-beaten old woman who stood guard outside the restrooms with a wad of toilet paper and a bucket of water that could be mine for five pesos. I made a note never to travel without tissues, hand sanitizer, and Wet Ones again.

Solé Grand Motel, read an oval sign atop a

tall pole next to the highway. *Toda La Semana $220 X 12 horas, excepto los sabados.* Two hundred and twenty dollars, and for just half a day? I thought Mexico was supposed to be cheap! Then I remembered that it was pesos, did some quick math, and realized that the rate *was* cheap, only about sixteen dollars. Wow. I could learn to really love this place, I thought. I pulled off the road and followed the signs until I came upon a window-less stone façade with the hotel's maroon logo splashed across the front. A soulless rock garden bordered the driveway that led to an electronic gate.

"Bienvenido," came a faceless voice from a box outside the car.

I lowered my window. "I need a room?" I felt like I should be ordering fries and a shake.

"Cuántas horas?"

"Excuse me?"

"Cuántas? Dos? Seis? Doce?"

"One night!" I yelled back into the little box. "Just one night."

"Te gustería un hombre? Una mujer? Un masaje?"

I had no idea what he wanted from me. "A room! One night!"

"Doscientos veinte. Two hundred twenty." I grabbed some bills and stuffed them into the metal drawer, which pulled back with a bang.

"Veintitrés," the voice answered as the gate swung slowly open.

I obediently pulled into a tiny open garage marked twenty-three, and was about to grab my purse and Polly to head out and stretch my legs a bit when the door behind me clanged down shut. A cold sweat sprouted from my forehead as I waited for my eyes to adjust to the dark. As soon as I could make out the outline of another door to my left, I had no choice but to enter. Anything had to be better than getting locked inside this hot box.

And much to my surprise and delight, on the other side of that door was one of the nicest hotel rooms I'd seen in a long time. Marble floors, a king-sized bed, a sitting and dining area, big-screen TV, fluffy towels embroidered with the motel's logo, the works. I reached for a chair to put down Polly's carrier. It didn't budge. Nor did the one next to it. I tried the ashtray on the table. Glued down. What kind of clientele did they get at this place, anyway? When I turned and saw the packaged condom next to the mints on the pillow, I finally got it.

But the room was so clean and spacious, and my carful of stuff was sure to be safe in the garage, and I was dead tired of driving, so I settled in to what I learned later was one of Mexico's many no-tell motels. When I thought about it, it was kind of a civilized setup. In Afghanistan, of course, there was no such thing. One of my girls over there had told me a heartbreaking story about her sister, who had a husband who would lock her in her room with the kids, taking the key so he could bring women to the house. She would watch them come and go each night through the keyhole. Other men over there would bring young boys and prostitutes to parties, or frequent the Chinese restaurants that were, in reality, fronts for brothels.

I filled Polly's litter box and poured her a meal, and realized that I hadn't eaten all day. The room service menu offered all sorts of tempting snacks and drinks, so I went all out. Twenty minutes later a bell rang at my door, but in the seconds it took for me to answer, whoever had delivered my tray had already disappeared.

I kind of liked this place, where things were so anonymous that I almost felt invisible to myself, which, I have to admit, was sort of a relief. Maybe the old Deb could simply disappear into the Sonoran Desert—only just not literally. In my mind that was way too much of a frightening possibility. But what if Mexico really could grant me a clean slate? What would that new Deb look like? Between bites, I began a list:

1. New Deb thinks ahead. She does not make rash decisions. She does not live her life as though it's her own personal extreme-sporting event. She will no longer be known as "Crazy Deb."
2. New Deb does not need a man. She might *want* a man, but if and when the opportunity

arises she will be very, very selective. No more college sweethearts (too late for that), no more beach bums, no more closeted gays, no more abusers, no more wannabe warlords, and no more Mr. Nice Guys to make her feel like shit for not being able to be so nice herself. If there is another man, he will be the last man standing. Oh, and by the way? Marriage is not a mandatory thing.

3. New Deb does not wallow in her past. She will learn from her mistakes, not obsess over them to the point that she becomes a basket case who is constantly second-guessing herself and sobbing all over the place, eating too much, and making everyone around her crazy, and . . .

4. New Deb will be skinny! Well, maybe not skinny, but at least healthy and fit. She will cut out the junk food, she will ride a bike, she will not fall prey to the margaritas. She will, for once in her life, learn to feel good in her own skin. New Deb promises to love New Deb no matter what size she is.

(Here, I have to admit, I paused to finish my tacos and drain my beer.)

5. New Deb will never pick up a cigarette again. Ever.

6. New Deb is not afraid. She is as strong as she once thought she was.
7. New Deb will be her own best friend, not her own worst enemy. She will keep herself from taking two steps back every time she takes one forward.
8. New Deb will never pack her life in boxes again. In Mexico, she will find a way to make her head content and her heart full. And that's that.

After a long, steamy shower I snuggled into bed, eager for the diversion of old reruns and cable news, courtesy of the remote that was bolted to the bedside table next to me. But as I surfed, it appeared as though the only things with even slightly visible reception were four porn channels and a soccer match, none of which was enough to keep my eyes open at that point. So I just drifted off all by myself, dreaming about the New Deb in my dark, quiet, safe, sex motel.

THE NEXT MORNING DIDN'T START OFF SO great. I found myself on the road way too early, thanks to the plaguing doubts about my move that had boomeranged back into my head at 4 A.M., and which were still running through my brain like hamsters on a wheel. Would I be able to make a living down here? Would I make friends? Was Carnaval Street a wise investment, or the biggest mistake I'd made in my life? Maybe things would seem clearer by daylight. It was still dark. Really, really dark. And I seemed to be the only person out at that ungodly hour.

Suddenly the darkness was broken by three arcing beams of light about a hundred yards up the road. As I approached, I could make out a trio of dark-clothed figures waving me over. My instincts kicked in as I stepped on the gas, not sure whether to congratulate myself for avoiding a setup or berate myself for being stupid enough to try to outrun the police. To this day, I still have no idea who those guys were. Regardless, I pulled over at the next gas station and parked under a very bright light, and waited for the sun to come up.

But even the light of day didn't do much to soothe my nerves. The two-lane road was that in concept only. You could be going eighty miles per hour in the right lane only to come up against a huge bus at a dead stop right in front of your bumper. No place for you (or him) to pull over even if you had time to, just a drop-off that would turn a Mini into a pancake in one quick second. And the left lane? An overturned semi in the median was proof enough to me that it wasn't a much safer option.

Then there was the humidity. I could almost hear my hair frizzing up as I rolled down the window to pay yet another toll. The hot, thick air shoved its way in like a pushy commuter boarding the 5:10 to the suburbs. At least it was a sign that I was getting closer to the sea.

Just fifteen minutes into the state of Sinaloa, a couple of guys in military uniform stopped my car. A shiny round face appeared at my window. "Qué está en el carro? What's in the car?"

What wasn't in the car? I asked myself, my mind scrambling to remember the Spanish word for cat, panicking at the thought of me being kidnapped and Polly left abandoned in the desert, or of poor Polly being catnapped and the Mini being carjacked and me left to die by the side of the road. The officer motioned for me to open the door and step out. My legs felt like rubber, and I could feel that morning's hastily downed coffee making its way back up.

"Cat. I have a cat in there," I pleaded in a voice that sounded nothing like mine.

He bent down to peer under the Mini's roof. I felt faint.

"Fruta?" the guy holding the gun asked.

"What?"

"Fruta?" He called his partner over, and pointed inside. "Gato!" I finally remembered. "Gato!" But they weren't paying attention. They were too busy laughing. I followed their gaze toward the backseat. The only things visible were Polly's whiskers poking out from the carrier, stuffed between the space-saver bags that had by now, apparently due to the heat, expanded to the max,

109

filling the car's interior like a giant marshmallow man.

No sooner had I recovered from that episode than I came to the road sign for Culiacán—the headquarters of the dreaded Sinaloa Cartel, allegedly the most powerful drug-trafficking organization in the Western Hemisphere. A narco city that boasts of more homicides than any other city in Mexico. I had been warned, and had planned not to slow down, not to get gas, not to do anything but hold my breath and get through this town as fast as I could. I was beginning to feel like a character in a video game, leaping and hopping and ducking to avoid disaster at every turn.

By now the jungle-green roadside had turned into farmland—flat, flat, flat—with nothing but cows that I, in an attempt to remain alert, actually started to count as they whizzed past my window. Yes, I was counting cows. I was up to forty-seven when I saw it. Right beyond the road sign for Mazatlán, a dark sapphire stripe glittered under the blaze of the overhead sun. The Pacific! Palm trees swayed in the ocean breeze. It was like entering paradise. I rolled down the window and let the briny air fill my nostrils with each deep breath I took. I was almost home, as scary as it sounded to call this strange place home. I may not have had a clue about anything that was to come, but I did know how much I was looking forward to seeing my house. My tiny bungalow that had gone practically overnight from seaside getaway to my lifeline.

I'm still not sure how to interpret what happened next, though in retrospect I'm sure it had to be some sort of omen. At first I could have sworn it was snowing. Airy flecks of white started blowing past my window, rapidly multiplying into a swarm as I continued down the road. They drifted up against the windshield one by one, then three by three, and then before I knew it in a flurry so thick I could barely see two feet in front of me. Butterflies. Billions of them. Everywhere I turned, there were butterflies. Butterflies as far as the eye could see. I could feel the unfamiliar stretch of my lips against my teeth as a grin began to spread across my face. "We're home, Polly. We are finally home."

6

YOU KNOW HOW SOMETIMES YOU HOLD ON TO an incredibly vivid memory of a place in your head, only to end up gobsmacked by reality upon your next visit? Maybe it was the remote little inn where you stayed for your honeymoon, whose carpet stains and peeling wallpaper were invisible to you at the time. Or that childhood home you revisited. You could have sworn the house was a lot bigger when you lived there.

I am happy to report that, despite my worries, that did not happen to me when I returned this time to Mazatlán. I really can't say it was love at first sight when Roger the Realtor had first led me to the house on Carnaval Street, on my last visit. But it was Carnaval Street! I could not believe there was a house for sale there. It must be meant to be, I thought. But the façade of the crumbling little box we stopped at looked like the aftermath of a bubble gum factory explosion. It was pink. Pink, bumpy cement. Pink all over, with a flat roof, one tiny window with blue and red and green and yellow opaque panes covered by a handwritten "Se Vende" sign, and a house on either side, with not even a hair of space between them. But something happened when I went inside. Though it was clear that you'd have to wedge your way through the narrow shower to get to the bathroom sink and toilet, and I couldn't tell if that frosted glass in what I realized was the house's one and only window was there to hide the street from view or vice versa, the high ceilings and century-old tiles made the tiny house feel strong and solid and wise. It took fifty-two steps to circle the entire space, which I did three times before I sat myself down on the cool green floor, where the colored light streaming through the window splashed down like a bright, blurry Christmas tree. I wanted this house on Carnaval Street. How could you live on a place called Carnaval Street and not be happy?

Now, months later, I was back. And after the basic renovations I had overseen long-distance, including sanding and smoothing and the three coats of paint it took to turn that bubble-gum pink into a respectable ochre with forest green trim, my house was even better than I had imagined. Perhaps it was due to the fact that it was all mine, but I felt something being inside this house that I hadn't felt in a long time. I felt safe. Maybe it was just the lack of windows.

I did hole up a lot at first. Though *shy* has never been a word used to describe me, it was clear that what had happened to me in Afghanistan and festered during my time in California limbo had snuck across the border with me. Trust, specifically when it came to trusting myself, had become an unreliable partner, and confidence—*real* confidence, not the crazy kind that compels one to, say, take off and drive halfway across Mexico—seemed as elusive to me as a marriage proposal from George Clooney. Even in my own home I was still a Debbie I had a hard time recognizing, and a Debbie who, frankly, was not much fun to be around. Especially in a hot little house with limited air-conditioning.

Had I been more calculating or, to put it more honestly, had I been more in control of my life, I probably would not have chosen summer as the time to move south of the border. This wasn't like Kabul heat, where at six thousand feet you could almost see the sun's rays sucking the moisture from your skin. Here you were constantly drenched in a sticky sweat, as if you'd allowed an ice-cream bar to melt down your arms, onto your body, and in between your toes. If you had to wrap a scarf around your head you'd suffocate. At first I survived by jumping, soaking wet, from the shower to a spot in front of the fan and back again, or by sitting amid bags of frozen broccoli on my couch. I read a lot, and waited every day, all day, for the cable guy to arrive. In Mexico, waiting for the cable guy is sort of the same as waiting for the cable guy anywhere, but instead of saying they'll be there on a specific day within a specific range of hours, they'll only commit to a general time frame. As in "he will be there between now and when Jesus comes." *Mañana*, *mañana*, they say when you call to check. For weeks I waited. No TV, no Internet, no landline. No communication with anyone but myself. Oh, I did have a cell phone, but without even one person in Mexico to add to my new "Five Friends Free" plan, it sat idle.

In the meantime, when evening would start to fall, my daily prayers for the cable guy appearing to remain unanswered, I began to notice my neighbors across the street gathering on their front steps. Music and friendly shouts and quiet laughter would echo off the low-slung cement buildings. Since it felt no hotter outside than in, I forced myself out to explore. I was determined not to start out in Mexico the way I had ended up in California, as a housebound hostage held prisoner by my own demons.

At first I'd just venture down a few buildings toward Abarrotes Josi, the local grocery. Carnaval Street comes to life in the evening—women in plastic chairs gossip around a game of bingo, babies get passed from lap to lap, and the older kids join each other for a game of soccer or tag or jump rope in the middle of the street. The street seemed to be the women's domain. I figured the men must have favored cantina life. "Carro! Cuidado!" A synchronized warning would echo off the houses whenever a car approached, sending all the kids running for safety. Not a lick of English could be heard on Carnaval Street, which suited me just fine. I always found a sense of comfort being surrounded by words I couldn't understand, conversations that couldn't distract me, arguments that didn't involve me. I had enough noise inside my own head for all of us.

It wasn't long before I found myself continuing down Carnaval Street a little farther than usual, down to the Plazuela Machado. It was twilight, and under a fading pink sky the lights around the square were starting to twinkle like fairy dust through the palm trees. Gleaming white-covered dining tables spilled out from under the spotlit arched façades of the restaurants lining the streets. I was hungry, and those tables looked so inviting. But being one who always hated eating alone, it took me three slow loops through the stalls in the center of the plaza, and one hundred fifty pesos plunked down for a pair of handmade earrings and a little woven purse, before I got up the courage to sit.

A cute waiter approached with a smile. "Buenas noches."

"Buenas noches," I said back with a smile.

"Qué va a tomar?"

"Vino tinto, por favor," I responded, proud of

my mastery of the language, at least when it came to ordering a glass of red wine.

As I sipped under the darkening sky, the tables around me started to fill with young couples, groups of older men, mothers and daughters and children and friends, some greeting others with kisses as they made their way to their own tables, others waving a polite hello across the street. I was tempted to wave to an imaginary acquaintance myself, just so I wouldn't seem so alone.

"Can I get you something to eat?" The waiter's perfect English jolted me out of my pity.

"Wow! You speak really good English," I said, a bit too eagerly.

Again he smiled that beautiful smile. "Thank you. I have worked hard at it."

"Are you from around here?"

He nodded. "I was born in Mexico."

"I'm from here, too! I mean, I live here now, too. I just moved here."

"Well, welcome to Mazatlán." He extended his hand. "My name is Sergio."

"Debbie. Pleased to meet you." My voice sounded rusty from neglect. "Join me?" I asked, forgetting for a moment that he had a job to do.

Sergio laughed. "I wish I could. Let me bring you some chips and salsa, and you can just relax and enjoy all this."

Indeed, a spectacle was unfolding around me. Fire dancers spun their flames to the beat of drums, pausing occasionally to let the hip-hop kids strut their stuff. To my left, a long-haired blues singer raised her sultry voice in competition with the painfully off-key Beatles imitators on the opposite corner of the square. Across from me, a sad clown with a painted smile knotted balloons into swords and dachshunds and Mickey Mouse ears. I could barely hear myself think, which, I thought, was not a bad thing. And I was no longer alone—the relentless parade of street vendors winding their way from table to table were there to make sure of that. One, a beautiful girl selling flowers almost as tall as she was, seemed to be raking it in. I scanned the plaza for a mother or father or big sister trailing behind, but saw no one.

I told Sergio to bring whatever he recommended from the menu, and he returned shortly after with a plate of crusty, golden shrimp circling a shallow dish of pale red glaze. "Camarón. In Mazatlán, we have shrimp coming out of our ears. Maybe sometimes you can't find money at the bank machines, or your packages at the post office, but you can always find camarón. Enjoy."

And I did. That first bite of shrimp fried in coconut batter tasted like paradise. And washed down with the mango margarita Sergio had slipped onto my table? A fiesta in my mouth. It sure beat Kabul, where the sheep you'd see grazing in the garbage pile outside the hospital by day could very well end up being the mutton kabob on your plate that night.

The battle of the bands intensified as more performers joined in, eager to fill their tip jars with pesos before the night's end. The tables around me remained packed, the diners slowly nursing the remnants of their drinks, still chatting away as if they had just sat down together minutes before, instead of hours. Families continued to stream into the square, little boys running, girls perched on their fathers' shoulders, babies in strollers. I wondered if there was something happening I didn't know about.

"What's going on here?" I asked Sergio when he came to take my plate.

He laughed. "It's Saturday night."

"And?"

"And it's summer."

This was nothing like my summer Saturday nights, where my entertainment consisted of sitting on the front porch watching my kids catch fireflies.

"Some of these people live here, and some are here on vacation. Summer is when the gringos leave and the Mexicans come."

Leave it to me to be the one bucking that trend. "But why are all these kids up so late?"

Sergio looked at me as if I were an alien. "It's Saturday night," he repeated.

In an instant a loneliness bubbled up inside of me

like a warm shaken soda. It had been two years since I'd seen my kids. Yes, they were grown, Noah trying to make a go of it in Chicago and Zach, now married, selling insurance in Washington, D.C. But they were still my boys and here we were again, in different countries, in different time zones, in different worlds. But at least this time I knew I could be there in a flash if they, or my mom, needed me.

Sergio brought the check. "Can I get you a taxi?"

"That's okay, I can walk." I was suddenly anxious to get back to my house.

"Where do you live?"

"Carnaval Street."

Sergio checked his watch. "But you must not walk home by yourself at this time of night. A woman alone in any country should not be wandering around after ten o'clock." He walked me to the corner, where a line of little white golf carts were waiting. "Calle Carnaval. Cuánto?" After some negotiation with the driver, Sergio picked through the coins in my palm to make sure I had the correct change. "And not a peso more," he warned me, helping me into the backseat.

And as I bounced home over the potholes, I heard Sergio's words. *A woman alone.* That I was. In a totally foreign place. What if something happened to me? How long would it take for anybody to know I was languishing in a hospital ward, or notice that I'd been kidnapped, or find me dead in the shower? Or that I'd slipped into a downward, penniless spiral, to the point of no return. Like my thoughts, the taxi seemed to be going in circles, winding around the one-way streets and hitting dead ends on a trip that should have been a clear, straight shot. I had no idea where we were. The town seemed to take on a completely different look at night. At one point I thought I recognized the hot dog cart that was usually at the end of my street, but I could have sworn they had been selling oysters from that very same cart just a few hours earlier. Finally, a U-turn brought us upon the unmistakable purple house six down from mine, and the familiar faces of my neighbors, still on the street where I had left them.

I FILLED MY DAYS AS BEST I COULD, ADORNING my house with enough color to cheer a pregnant nun. Up went the wall hanging I had carried from India and the painting I bought in Morocco, both placed weirdly low on the wall, thanks to a too-short ladder and a too-high ceiling. Polly kept busy standing guard over the cockroaches, some as big as Chihuahuas, that regularly wandered in under the door, our house being just one of the many stops on their daily patrol through the neighborhood. They strutted down the street as if they owned the place, which by all rights they did, seeing as cockroaches have been around longer than any of us. Polly would swat them, along with any of the little iguanas that dared to enter, back into the street with a quick whack of the paw. Sometimes I'd catch her playing footsies with a pair of little white paws inching in from under the gate. Sure, it was easy for *her* to make new friends. *Meow* was *meow* in any language.

By now I was leaving the front door open with the gate still locked, just as I had seen my Mexican neighbors do. One day I noticed Josi the grocer stop and bend down in front of my gate, picking up the white-pawed cat I now recognized as hers.

"Gato!" I said through the gate, pointing at my own chest. "I have a gato, too."

Josi nodded. "Dónde?"

I didn't know the words to explain how Polly was still sometimes a little shy in this new country, still a little too wary to socialize with people. Or wait, was that myself I was thinking about?

"Gata negra," I added, hoping Josi wouldn't rush away. By now five or six other neighbor women had stopped at the gate, eager to see Polly. So I had no choice but to pry my poor cat from her safe place under the sofa and show her off. As I held the petrified Polly up proudly, I could feel her muscles stiffen and watched as her long black hair stood up on end. The women oohed and clucked, and shuffled away. At the time it never occurred to me that Polly was the first long-haired black cat they'd ever seen. They couldn't decide, I later learned, if I was an Egyptian, based on my looks (!) and love of cats, or a witch, based on Polly's looks and fear of humans. The truth was that the only cat I liked was my own, and the only human she cared for was me.

Of course, with the front door now permanently open, the music from the street let itself in without an invitation: opera, bongos, ballads, top-forty hits, oldies, and once an entire *banda* group blaring its tubas, trombones, and accordion at 5 A.M. Seriously. A full-blown collision of polka and mariachi, complete with microphones and speakers, right outside my door. There were people dancing in the street, waving beer bottles in the air, and using my windowsill as a bar top. I couldn't tell if the party was starting early or ending late.

The music in Mexico never seemed to stop. Better yet were the sounds of vendors making their rounds, shouting or singing out whatever they had to offer that day. Shoe shines, shrimp, doughnuts, knife sharpeners, each one had its own unique calling card. A steam whistle announced the guy selling hot plantains and sweet potatoes as if he were a train arriving at the station. You knew the gas truck was approaching whenever you heard the theme from *The Good, the Bad, and the Ugly*. Even the mailman sounded like a New Year's Eve reveler as he passed on his green bicycle. And the honey man? We quickly fell into our own little routine. *Honey for my honey? No honey today, honey.*

One day I saw a nurse in a white uniform going house to house.

"Influenza?" she called out when she reached my gate, pulling a needle from her bag.

"Um, no thanks, I think I'll pass," I answered, shaking my head.

Another time a gaggle of three young boys, who couldn't have been more than twelve or thirteen years old, were offering to take blood-pressure readings for five pesos.

During the day, I wouldn't dare venture farther than down the block to Josi's grocery, for fear I'd miss the cable guy. Every day the sweet car-wash man sitting on the corner with his bucket and rags would be sure to smile and say "Buenos días," engaging me in a conversation I barely understood half of. Every day I'd step over Michael Jackson and Roy, Josi's two little dogs, who spent their days flattened like pancakes on the cool sidewalk under the store's ancient Coca-Cola sign. Every day I'd buy bottled water or little candies, or a pepper, an onion, and just two eggs, and two Tums for later. When I once asked for Tylenol, Josi handed me one measly tablet. But I loved having an excuse to drop by often, for a little broken chitchat with her before I had to go home to wait some more.

As the shadows grew long, and it would become clear that yet another day had passed without me getting my connection to the world beyond Carnaval Street, I'd make my way down to the plaza to chat with Sergio and the other English-speaking waiters who had become my only friends. And each night I'd see the same girl selling her flowers, all by herself. She'd hug and smile for pictures with strangers, posing too close for my comfort with men she didn't know. Somebody had obviously taught her some skills. But whoever that somebody was was nowhere to be seen. I worried about what she'd have to sell once she became too old for flowers.

ONE TUESDAY I WAS LOCKING THE GATE behind me when I finally spied the cable guy. It was the eve of one of the millions of Mexican holidays, so I knew I had to make this man mine before everything shut down for days of partying. I jumped in front of his truck and pointed frantically at the tiled numbers over my door, waving my work order in his face, desperate to bring some noise besides my own thoughts into my silent house, and aching for a connection to the world beyond Carnaval Street. I didn't care if I got a full lineup of telenovelas; I just needed to not feel so alone. He shook his head and started the engine. "No, no está en mi lista."

"Listen, please. Please!" I clasped my hands in prayer, not budging from the street. I must have looked like a lunatic.

He paused for a moment. "I can only give you the básico cable. For the television."

"No, I need Internet!"

He shook his head and began to back up.

"One hundred pesos!" I shouted.

"One hundred pesos?" He stopped and shook his head again.

"Five hundred pesos!" I stuck my head in through the passenger-side window. "You give me a full connection in the next thirty minutes and I'll give you five hundred pesos. Cash."

The truck zipped away from the curb. "I'll be right back."

I have no idea where that man went, but I do know that he came back with everything. As the sun went down that night, and the rest of the neighborhood took to the street, I gleefully settled onto my couch with *You've Got Mail* (in English!). The light from the TV seemed to draw passersby like moths—my neighbors had no qualms about peering through my gate whenever the inside was bright enough to make out the details of the renovations. They were curious to see what I had done to the house, and even more curious about me. After the part where Meg Ryan tells Tom

Hanks, "You're nothing but a suit!" I got up to make myself a sandwich. I was just cutting the bread when suddenly I heard someone moaning. *Oh baby, that's it, do it to me, do it now.* Odd. I didn't remember *that* happening in the movie, and I seriously doubted it could be coming from my ancient neighbor's room on the other side of the wall. I rushed back into the living room, where full-blown, full-volume porn was pouring from my TV, in full view and earshot of all those passing by. I frantically dived for the remote, and in my nervous fumbling pressed the volume instead of the channel button, the raunchy sound track now blaring out onto the sidewalk. Before I could reach the door, I spied a group of kids beginning to gather, so I dived onto the floor and yanked out the plug. That cable guy had obviously been hell-bent on coming through with more than I asked for, as soon became apparent by his frequent drive-bys just to see if I "needed any-thing." I even twice caught him climbing the pole outside my door. When I told Karen back in Michigan the story, she instantly dubbed him my Porn Fairy.

NOW THAT MY DAYS WERE FINALLY FREE, I quickly fell into a routine that forced me farther away from Carnaval Street, down the narrow streets out into the rest of Centro Histórico. First I'd head to the Plazuela República, where the cool vaulted interior of the cathedral offered a welcome respite from the heat outside and the thoughts within. I'd sit in an empty pew under the crystal chandeliers, intent on conjuring up a Deb who would be fun to spend the day with, a Deb who was strong and secure and perfectly happy to be on her own. On more than one occasion I'd succeed, only to burst out into the blinding sun in the beautiful old square to be confronted by a sea of love, where couples of all ages, lacking either time or money for a no-tell motel and with, no doubt, a mother standing guard at home, would sit glued together in a marathon lip lock. It might have been funny, if it didn't make me feel so alone.

Sometimes, when I first started exploring, I'd catch myself navigating the brick sidewalks head down, as I had learned to do in Kabul, where eye-to-eye contact from a woman is a dead giveaway for a foreigner, even one wearing a veil. Here, even with my head up, I'd still feel like a guest on the streets, and would politely step aside to let the locals pass, as though I didn't really belong.

From the square I'd cross over into the Centro Mercado, where I'd stare in wonder at the severed pig heads and chicken feet and giant prickly cactus leaves, and try to imagine what the hell I'd do with those in a kitchen. Coming from a family whose big treat was gas station chicken (yes, literally fried chicken you'd buy at the gas station), my culinary skills were a little limited. My favorite part of the bustling old market was the far corner in the back, where they sold vitamins and dietary supplements and *brujería*— black magic. There were potions for everything. Soaps that promised prosperity, rattlesnake sperm incense to bring rapid good luck, pheromone powders to improve your sex life, salts for a better business, oils to ward off the evil eye, water to make you a better student, double reversible lotion potions to protect you from hexes (and send them right back to the hexer). And if you needed a little extra help? A full array of business cards advertising local professional *bruja*s (witches!) was displayed under glass on the counter near the cash register.

If I wasn't too scared to mess with that stuff, I might have been tempted to try a spell or two, maybe even a love potion to find myself a partner for one of those park benches. But then again, that would probably not have been a great idea. With my history, I'd no doubt be better off finding a spell to keep men away.

The shopping area of El Centro never failed to cheer me up. The crowded sidewalks, honking horns, the smell of street food and car exhaust blending together in a stinky urban perfume, all made me feel alive. The stores chock-full of tacky T-shirts, plastic hair clips, clingy tube tops, and cheap jewelry called to me like a dinner bell to an empty stomach. And the shoes! It killed me that I was cursed with size-nine feet, apparently a size nobody in Mexico ever had a need for. But my favorite discovery was the place that sold princess dresses. Seriously. Rows and rows of big, poufy, shiny, sparkly dresses in every color imaginable —hot pink, lime green, bright orange, and against the wall, virginal white. There were tiaras and crowns and wands. This was a store for me, if only I were about two feet shorter and ninety pounds lighter.

I could feel myself becoming a little more comfortable every day. Yes, I still got lost every time I left my house, but the flashing beacons atop the jumble of radio and TV towers littering Icebox Hill, above Carnaval Street, were always there to remind me that I wasn't far from home. Having the ocean nearby didn't hurt, either. I'd simply look at the little compass I kept on my key chain, find west, and off I went. If I hit the water, I'd know how to make my way home, where I could always start off again in another direction. After taking a quick shower and downing a gallon of water, I often did.

BY DAY, THE PLAZUELA MACHADO TOOK ON A whole different aura. Honking cars inched their way through the streets where I dined by night, and ballet students scrambled to class at the Teatro Angela Peralta, where a never-ending melody tumbled from the windows as aspiring opera singers from around the world practiced their arias, over and over and over. I had become oddly drawn to the theater, fascinated by the tragic story of the woman for whom it was named—a poor, not-so-attractive girl from Mexico City who grew up to become known around the world as the "Mexican Nightingale." Apparently she was a feisty young thing who, after a sad, brief marriage, started both an opera company and an affair with her manager, Don Julian. Her Mexico City patrons, scandalized, did everything they could to ruin her career, even going so far as hiring hecklers to interrupt her performances. She vowed never to sing in Mexico City again. In 1883, at the age of thirty-eight, she began her final tour. One of the first stops was Mazatlán. Her Mazatleco fans greeted her boat at the dock and escorted her to the Plazuela Machado, where they were rewarded by a spontaneous balcony performance of "La Paloma," a famous Spanish song that's all about the triumph of love over death. Little did they know that this was to be her last performance. Yellow fever had hit the ship's crew and quickly spread throughout the entire company, including Angela Peralta. One of the few who didn't contract the disease was Don Julian, who quickly arranged for a deathbed marriage ceremony. As his bride-to-be supposedly had plenty of money and no heirs, his motives remain a matter of debate. Witnesses reported that by the time it came time for the "I do's," Peralta was completely unconscious, and maybe even already dead. One account says that another surviving member of the company supported her limp body by its shoulders, literally manipulating her head up and down in answer to the proposal. Another says that it was a woman hiding under the bed who uttered the assent. Well, at least she didn't die alone.

ON SOME DAYS I'D FIND MYSELF DRIFTING along the waterfront down the Malecón, which to me felt like a boardwalk without the boards. I'd cut back and forth across the palm-lined median, dodging the buses and cars and motorbikes as I alternated between the salty mist splashing up from the seawall on one side and the smells of coffee and shrimp coming from the hotels and restaurants on the other. The old Hotel Belmar held a particular fascination for me, with its crumbling blue balconies, tiered Spanish fountain, and cool fifties-style logo. I'd read a bit about its history, from its debut as the elegant lady playing host to society balls and elaborate weddings in the 1920s, to its heyday in the 1950s as a favorite hangout for John Wayne, who would arrive on his yacht for a vacation of marlin fishing and card playing. Rumor has it he used to get a kick out of taking a turn behind the registration desk, surprising visitors as they came to check in. His fifth-floor room is still there, available for rent like any other in the hotel. But now the Belmar is more decrepit spinster than faded beauty, half of it inhabited by budget-driven tourists and expats, the other half full of empty rooms crammed with discarded beds and shattered toilets and, supposedly, ghosts of guests past.

Often, my wandering would end before sunset at Mamita's, an open-air spot near the ocean, where Analisa the bartender would greet me with a dazzling smile and a glass of red wine. Analisa made me laugh, as she proudly paraded her big fake boobs back and forth behind the bar, with visions of big tips dancing in her head.

"You like my chichis?" she asked me once. "My last boyfriend, he pay for them. Only good thing to come from that relationship."

I loved Analisa and her chichis. I also loved her accent, and the way her sunglasses always matched the color of her nail polish. I envied the fact that even in this miserably hot Mexican summer, she never seemed to sweat.

When the bar wasn't too busy, Analisa and I would chat. Before long, I knew all about the string of bad boyfriends that made my own history look like a Disney movie: the cowardly Mexican one who left her pregnant after his mother deemed her too low-class for marriage, the violent gringo one who had turned on her one too

133

many times, yet another jealous gringo with pockets deeper than hers, the one who footed the bill for her boobs, later complained about their watermelon-like size, and was apparently the only man in the Western Hemisphere to feel that way. But I also quickly learned that Analisa was devoted to her teenage son and, as an unmarried Mexican woman, was culturally chained to her mother's household. No matter how old, in Mexico single women don't move out. It just isn't done. And for Analisa, that meant living in a household that included not only her elderly mother and her own son, but also a brother, a nephew, and a sister with Down syndrome. It was clear why she needed those big tips so badly, and needed them now. Those hot-mama looks weren't going to last forever.

As the sky would start turning from orange to pink, Analisa would turn her attention to the English-speaking regulars who'd fill the place up with their booming voices and enviable familiarity. I'd remain at my seat at the bar with my book and my phone, raising my eyes to watch when I thought nobody was looking. More than once I caught a man getting kicked by his wife under the table, another casualty of Analisa's excellent chichis.

One evening I spotted a familiar face, a guy I had been introduced to at Roger the Realtor's office when I first came down to Mazatlán.

"Bodie," he reminded me with an extended hand. "Bodie Kellogg."

I slipped my book back into my bag. "As in cornflakes?"

He laughed. "Yep, great-grandson of W.K. And this is Snickers." A sweet-looking pup was glued to his side.

"Nice to see you again." My memories of elementary school field trips to the Battle Creek factory made this guy an instant celebrity in my mind. Over the next few months I'd learn Bodie's story. How this scion of one of America's richest families had drifted down to Mexico in a pickup truck a few years ago, looking for a place to live. How, as a self-proclaimed refugee of the sixties, he got involved with ecotourism in the jungle, jaguar-calling in a remote village at the base of the Sierra Madre, anthropological digs in places where kids would giggle at the first gringo they'd ever laid eyes on, tours for the adventuresome traveler into the secluded mountain countryside, where one wouldn't dare go alone. Bodie got by doing all that, with a little construction, photography, and writing thrown in on the side. We weren't talking Richie Rich here—Great-grandpa's millions went directly to the Kellogg Foundation, save for an educational fund for his heirs, which Bodie milked for over ten years, five campuses, and no degrees, which explained why he seemed to know everything.

But that evening what was most apparent to me was that Bodie seemed to know everyone. And as the sun disappeared, I somehow found myself agreeing to join Bodie and some of his pals on a Sunday excursion to a place called Stone Island.

HALF OF ME WAS EXCITED TO MEET NEW people. I was flattered that Bodie thought I'd fit in, since fitting in was something that had eluded me over the past couple of years in Napa. But the other half of me was a nervous wreck. Sunday morning came quickly and started early with a phone call from Bodie.

"Hey, Deb. You're still in for the beach, right?"

I closed my eyes and took a deep breath. "I'm in."

"Great! Meet at Macaws at noon, and we'll take the panga over to the island."

I didn't want to sound stupid, but I had no idea what a panga was. More crucial was the fact that I also didn't know where Macaws was. Bodie rattled off a ten-minute set of directions. As in *turn west at (something that sounded like Generalmente Chichomicholambariña Street) and go east at (another unintelligible street name), follow the street ninety degrees around the traffic circle until the (iglesia something) is at two o'clock, and head straight for the (what sounded to me like bathroom in Spanish).* I was just grateful I lived on a street I could pronounce and spell.

"Bodie, would you mind giving me the same directions again, only this time in girl talk?"

He laughed and switched to a strained falsetto. "Walk to the big white house, turn left at that adorable pink building with the blue door, and then right again where all those hunky car-wash guys are. When you see the ocean, take your first left, look to your right, and voilà. Macaws."

"Bodie, just one more thing, do I turn left or right when I walk out my front door?" I could just hear him wondering how a woman who had been all over the world could be so helpless when it came to getting around.

I packed up my beach bag with a dozen strengths of sun block—I seriously doubted they called this the Tropic of Cancer for nothing—tied up my hair in braids under a big floppy hat, and checked myself out in the mirror. Then the terror set in. I swear I stopped breathing for a minute or two. Being introduced to a group of strangers in a dark, smoky room, fully clothed, is one thing, but at a beach, in unforgiving sunlight, half naked? What had I been thinking? I ran to the phone to politely decline Bodie's invitation, then hung up, dialed, and hung up again, and finally sucked it up and headed to the closet.

Do I wear the big cover-up or the small one? In Afghanistan I had personally embraced the tradition of covering one's entire body. Those big baggy clothes could hide a multitude of sins. I began to rethink my move to a tropical destination. Maybe Iceland would have been a better choice. My mind was racing. *Are these skinny people or fat people? Are they old or young? Shit, this is not the way I want to meet new friends.* Have I mentioned I am a fan of the burqini? It's a wonderful invention. Sort of like a full-length wet suit with a hood, only way looser. Anyway, that day I settled for my most modest bathing suit and my largest cover-up, and off I went feeling naked and exposed, vulnerable in a way that brought back way too many feelings I'd rather not feel.

Bodie was nowhere to be found under the churning ceiling fans in Macaws' open patio. I turned around, anxious to leave before anyone saw me.

"Debbie? Is that you?"

An ethereal blonde in a flowy blue dress stood and went behind the bar, uncapped a bottle of tequila, and started to pour. She held out her hand.

"I'm Sharon. I've heard so much about you!"

I must have looked as mortified as I felt. She smiled a radiant smile and said, "Girlfriend, we all need tequila to go to the beach." I appreciated the empathy but wasn't so sure I should be going down that slippery slope so early in the day, especially in a crowd of new faces.

"Better make mine a double," boomed a hearty Texas twang from the sidewalk. I turned to see a very tanned woman wrapped tightly in a bright blue cover-up. "Bonnie. Pleased to meet you." She helped herself to a glass from Sharon's hand. "Cheers, y'all."

All I will say is that over the next five hours I came to realize why God invented tequila.

THERE'S SOMETHING ABOUT BEING AN EXPAT that sets a person apart from the rest of society. And I don't mean geographically apart from their forsaken home, nor do I mean culturally apart from their new neighbors. I saw it when I lived in Afghanistan. They're just a different breed. Are they born that way? Or does living as a stranger in a strange land make them that way? I think it's a chicken-and-egg thing. Sure, I know all too well that life circumstances are often behind the metamorphosis from pat to expat, and that quite often those circumstances involve money, or lack thereof. In Afghanistan it was all about making a buck; here it was all about stretching one. But still, it takes a different kind of person to not just sit still and let life happen to them. I'm not sure how to define it, but all I know is that they just aren't normal. And in my book, there's absolutely nothing wrong with that.

But there was a major disconnect between what I had experienced among the expat community in Kabul and what I was finding here. Unlike over there, where personal history and credentials are an expat's calling card, to these folks yesterday was yesterday, and today is today.

Let me explain.

That Sunday on Stone Island, as I sat at Lety's surfside restaurant around a long plastic table under a palm frond roof with a dozen mismatched people of all shapes and sizes knocking back buckets of beer, margaritas, rum pulled out of someone's beach bag, and of course, straight tequila, I learned a lot. Here's how the conversation went:

Me: *How long have you lived down here, Barb?*

Barb: *Oh, I don't know. Hey Art,* she brayed across the table to her octogenarian husband, *how long have we been here?* Art just shrugged. Barb turned her attention to a vendor selling baskets table to table. I turned my attention to Art.

Me: *Where are you guys from?*

Art (taking a sip of his drink): *Syracuse. Had a restaurant. I was known there for my dooble entenders.*

Me: *What?*

Art: *You know, double meanings. I'm writing a book. Funny stories. I'm a pretty funny guy, right, Bonnie?*

Bonnie laughed and helped herself to some chips.

Me: *So what's your story, Bonnie? What are you doing down here?*

Bonnie: *Me? You don't want to hear our story.*

Me: *No, really, I do.*

Bonnie: *Nah. Not that interesting. Hey, Nancy!* She turned to a youngish woman at the end of the table, who could have been the third of a trio of Russian nesting dolls made up of Barb, Bonnie, and herself. *You dealing tonight?*

Me: *Deal? What does she deal?*

Bonnie: *Poker. She's a pro. We have a regular game Sunday nights. You play?*

Me: *She earns a living doing that?*

Bonnie: *That, and she ties fishing flies. Has quite a business.* She turned to the guy on her right. *Hey, Eyelashes, you playing tonight?*

The Guy (who did indeed possess impossibly long, dark eyelashes, shrugged his shoulders): *Not sure, depends on if Fernanda is home to watch Reyna.* His British accent was as thick as London fog. An adorable six-year-old was digging trenches in the sand by his side.

Me: *Who is he?*

Bodie: *That's Simon.*

Me: *And?*

Bodie: *And what?*

Me: *What's his story?*

141

Bodie: *Story? Married. To a Mexican. She's a psychologist.*

Me: *But how did he end up here?*

Bodie: *I'm not sure. Do you know, Lisa?*

Lisa: *I think he might have had some big job in New York or somewhere. Quit and moved to Mazatlán.*

Me (giving up on Lisa and Bodie): *Why did you and Sharon come to Mazatlán, Glen?*

Glen (shrugging his shoulders): *It just sort of happened. All I know is we'd never move back, right, Shar?*

Pete: *I agree wholeheartedly. And* (kissing my hand) *please allow me to be the first to officially welcome you to our little paradise.*

Me (pointing to a perky little blonde at the far end of the table): *Who's that?*

Cheryl: *That's Sonja. As in Sonja and Barry.*

Me: *When did they come down here?*

Nobody responded.

Me (to Donna and Rob): *What about you guys?*

At this point Art's chair toppled slowly backward into the sand, bringing the table, the glasses, the guacamole, and Art down with it. I jumped up to help. Everyone else kept drinking.

"Happens all the time," Barb said as she stood and hiked her strapless elastic top up over her boobs and under her armpits. "Gave up bras when I moved to Mazatlán," she said with a laugh so loud it momentarily drowned out the clamor of the *banda* musicians moving up the beach. "Swim, anyone?"

I had never intended to bare my body that day, so I can't explain what came over me when I decided to fling off my cover-up and join the group bouncing around in that salty blue sea. It wasn't just the heat, which was turning our cold drinks into sweaty puddles of water seeping across the plastic table. And it wasn't the booze. It was just that these people seemed so comfortable with themselves, so willing to do whatever they felt like doing regardless of how it might look to anyone else, and so nonjudgmental that you had to wonder if they really concerned themselves with anyone else at all.

Don't get me wrong. These people could gossip along with the best of them. It was the same in Kabul—for expats even a big city becomes a small town where everyone knows everyone else's business. But here the gossip was never mean-spirited, and it usually concerned some-thing the gossipee had put out there herself. Nevertheless, as Glen advised at one point that day with a wink, "It would be wise to never miss a meeting."

And by no means am I saying that these people were unfriendly. Far from it. By the end of that afternoon I had invitations to the poker game (which I declined), to join Barb at her Friday morning painting class (which I accepted), and to Margarita Wednesdays with Glen and Sharon at Macaws (which made me think of Karen in Michigan, and made me love this place even more). But what I realized was that for all of them, dwelling on or even talking about their pasts was considered a waste of time. It just wasn't something that was brought up. In fact, they hardly asked me, the new kid on the block, anything about my own life prior to coming to Mazatlán. How great was that? I could be anybody! Not that I wasn't proud of things in my past, at least some of them, but for once in my life I didn't feel like I had to explain myself, which at that time I wasn't sure I even could. I could be anybody—for one sweet afternoon, I felt like I could just be me.

I may not have learned much about my new friends that day, but I did get back on the panga (which, by the way, is the ricketiest, most crowded little deathtrap of a boat you've ever seen) knowing this: no matter how different we all seemed to be, it was becoming clear to me that we had one huge, undeniable, and indefinable thing in common—that peculiar something inside that had drawn us to life in this odd little city by the sea.

I LOVE THE FEELING OF FALLING IN LOVE. I could feel myself falling hard for this new country, yet I was afraid. My heart was saying yes, but my head was telling me to take it slow, to protect myself from getting in too deep. Afghanistan had taught me the consequences of that. Yet as we all know, the problem with love is that you just can't control the who and the when of it. But for now it remained fairly easy to keep my distance from the soul of Mexico, buffered by the English-speaking posse that was graciously starting to usher me into a world of their own making.

Unfortunately, as is inevitable whenever I start a new relationship, I was gaining weight. The taco-tequila-tostada diet was taking its toll, and I was running out of creative solutions for camouflaging the rolls that seemed to multiply overnight and the cellulite that was puckering up my skin in places I didn't even know could pucker. Why, oh why, couldn't I wear my weight with the pride of a Mexican woman? They'd squeeze themselves into those same skinny jeans they wore twenty pounds ago without a blink of the eye. How they managed to do that in ninety-degree heat and one hundred percent humidity was a mystery to me. By mid-morning I'd be sweating so much that anything I wore would become plastered to my skin like a globby layer of papier-mâché.

Weight issues had plagued me my entire life. To my stick-thin mother, the fact that I took after my father's side of the family was like a knife in her heart. Her acquired southern belle sensibility was, by the time I was old enough to notice, clearly offended by the mere presence of the large, loud, lumbering man she had married for his promise of a better future. I worshipped my mom but saw plain as day that she did not worship my dad. So I did everything possible to become just like her.

Mom had me on diets from the time I was ten years old, and she even joined Weight Watchers herself more than once when I was a kid, casually inviting me to "have some fun and come with" in her desperate attempts to get me to slim down. It had taken her eleven years to conceive, as she often reminded me, and before I was born she was *so* looking forward to having a little doll to play dress-up with. After she gave up on me she turned to real dolls, amassing an impressive collection of Madame Alexanders, dozens of perfect little angels with bee-stung lips and poofy skirts and corkscrew curls crowding the shelves of her bedroom, the same bedroom that ended up in ruins after that house fire. Poor dolls.

I tried everything I could to become thin, including a yearlong bout with anorexia. At seventeen years old, five feet five, and eighty-five pounds, I thought I looked great. My mom was so proud of my "dieting" success. She wasn't aware of my daily doses of Ex-Lax or my self-induced vomiting, and when I stopped getting my period she insisted on a pregnancy test, despite my honest avowal of my virginal status. The doctor told me to gain weight, but I wasn't about to give up this newfound feeling of control over my life, or the satisfaction of being, for once, smaller than my mom. Even she couldn't fit into my size-three pants! So I put rocks in my pockets before my next appointment. It wasn't until my big, beefy boyfriend broke up with me (*you're just too skinny!*) that I came to my senses.

The following year I left for a few months in Japan with a Christian organization. It was my first time out of the country and, determined to follow the instructions we had been given during our training sessions, I never once refused even the tiniest grain of rice from my host family. I couldn't insult them, could I? I ate everything in sight. I will never forget the look on my mom's face when I got off that plane. The pattern continued in college with my freshman thirty—I couldn't just stop at fifteen, like everyone else—and into my on-again, off-again marital history. And it obviously still hadn't been broken.

But now I was turning to the Mexican women for inspiration. Of course, I still wanted to look good, but I was determined not to let skinny be the be-all-end-all anymore. It was time to start feeling good, and time to start feeling good about myself. It was time to join a gym.

So what did I do? I went shopping. I couldn't set foot in a gym without the proper outfit, could I? *Why can't shopping be an acceptable form of exercise?* I whined to myself, adrenaline pumping the way it always did when I'd find myself surrounded by shelves and shelves of bargains. I could stick with this routine, cruising the mall. Why, I'd do it every day! I hated going to the gym, it was so much work. I wandered the aisles until I spotted an adorable pair of purple and black spandex pants, and for one quick second this whole workout thing didn't seem like such a bad idea. Then I remembered what my friend Karen in Michigan always said: *Spandex is a privilege, not a right.* I bought a pair of sweats and went back home.

But when the time came to actually get serious about this whole exercise idea, it soon became clear that the real challenge wasn't going to be finding the right outfit; it was finding a gym that I wasn't going to suffocate in. Mexicans aren't too keen on air-conditioning, because not only is it expensive, but they believe that sweating is actually healthy, unless, of course, you are sweating in air-conditioning, in which case you'll get sick. Go figure. My other two requirements for a gym were that it be female-friendly and close to my house.

Gimnasio Roberto's, a quick bike ride away from Carnaval Street, fit the bill close enough. As I passed under a dubious likeness of Arnold Schwarzenegger hanging over the doorway and climbed the long, narrow stairway up from the street, I could feel the wetness spreading from every nook and cranny of my body. I hadn't even lifted a finger yet and I was drenched, droplets of my sweat leaving dark, round spots on the threadbare gray carpet under my feet.

Let's get physical . . . physical, Olivia Newton-John screamed from the giant speakers hanging on the wall, the bass turned up so high the floors shook. Back down another set of stairs, one flight below, the dark, cavernous gym was lined with more mirrors than a carnival funhouse, and was teeming with a sea of incredibly beautiful people. The women were all Jennifer Lopez—toned, tanned, huge breasts, awesome booties. Everything matched. Tight pink pants were paired with low-cut pink midriff tops, pink sweatbands for the head, pink wristbands, and a pink towel to wipe the machines down.

The men? Enrique Iglesias clones, from their sweaty six-packs up to their perfectly gelled hair. They were all impossibly beautiful.

I snuck into a corner space and eyed the dumpy chick in the T-shirt and sweats staring back at me from the mirror. The makeup I'd never leave the house without was already streaming down my cheeks. I looked like Gene Simmons after a particularly rowdy KISS concert. From every angle, all I could see were those beautiful people, and I knew that if I was seeing them, they were seeing me. I closed my eyes and started to lift, curling up and down and up and down, willing the flesh that was sagging off the back of my arms to magically turn into muscle bulging from the front. Soon the weights were becoming impossibly heavy, and I was struggling to lower them without letting them crash to the floor. I must have let out some sort of uncontrollable bellow or other cry of distress because, to my mortification, when I raised my eyes everyone had turned to look. And that's when I saw her. My angel in a push-up sports bra and the tiniest pair of shorts you've ever seen, shorts that were barely covering an ass that topped a pair of legs as long as I was tall. She was a Bo Derek ten to my Ugly Betty zero. She effortlessly grabbed my weights and lowered them to the ground, her two-inch-long crystal-studded nails reflecting off the mirrors surrounding us. I opened my mouth to thank her but whatever came out sounded nothing like Spanish.

"Debbie," I added quickly, while extending my hand. "Rodriguez."

She looked puzzled. Mexicans are always curious about how I could be a Rodriguez yet speak Spanish so poorly, and with such an atrocious accent. I tell them that I kept the name and got rid of the husband. That always brings a smile and keeps me from having to go into my marital history. And my Spanish *was* terrible. In high school, I could not understand one word in any language that my French-born Spanish teacher spoke, and the Rosetta Stone courses I was now trying to follow only succeeded in putting me to sleep.

The woman introduced herself as Angelica. Then she pointed to the different women in the gym and shouted out their names above the din of the blaring disco music.

Angelica and I both arrived at the gym at around noon every day. We shared weights and traded equipment. She showed me how to use the butt-shaping machines and I made her laugh, mostly through goofy faces and pantomime. She persuaded me to ditch the little backpack I toted from machine to machine, and to follow her lead—water bottle in hand, towel around neck, cell phone tucked into one bra cup, change purse with house keys in the other, and a tube of lip gloss handily stowed in the cleavage. Genius.

Although I thought I could feel myself firming up little by little with each visit, I was embarrassed by the fact that I wasn't able to have a normal conversation with Angelica or the other women in the gym. Here was a chance to make friends with some local women, and I couldn't even talk to them. It felt a lot like Kabul in the beginning, when I had to use an interpreter to communicate even the basics to my girls at the school. Note to self, I thought: find a Spanish teacher ASAP.

"Cuál es tu trabajo?" Angelica asked one day. What do you do for work?

Nothing, I thought. It felt strange to think that, but so far Mexico had proven to be as affordable as I had hoped it would be, and I was managing to stretch my savings as tight as the skin on a pregnant woman's belly. In answer to Angelica, all I could do was scribble with an imaginary pen in one hand, and mimic a pair of snipping scissors with the other.

The next day I handed Angelica the Spanish-language version of *Kabul Beauty School*, pointing out my picture on the back cover. She rattled off something to the other women in the gym, and they all gathered around to take a look.

When I returned the following week, the girl at the front desk was reading my book. It seemed they had been passing it around. She held up the cover for me to see, and smiled as I walked past. I smiled back. I'd finally been invited to the cool kids' table! But as much as they now knew about me, I still hadn't figured out what these girls were all about.

One day I arrived at the gym to find myself face-to-face with a stringy-haired man in sandals and socks and a muscle shirt that revealed everything but muscles, who followed my boobs with his bloodshot eyes as I headed to the machines. I thought I recognized him from Mamita's, but we had never spoken. I averted my eyes as I passed, pretending not to hear whatever it was he was saying to me. Angelica appeared from behind and quickly pulled me away.

"Pinche pendejo," she muttered, which I later learned roughly translates to "fucking asshole." I could now see him on the other side of the room leering at us. "Tu amigo?" Angelica asked.

"No, no, nada, no friend!" I answered, in a panic.

She turned to the other girls in the room, rattled off something really fast, and suddenly the room was abuzz. Angelica then said something else, lowered her fabulous fake lashes at me, and said very seriously, "Cuidada. Eso hombre es malo. Careful."

That evening I popped into Mamita's right before sunset. Analisa instinctively reached for the red wine. "Just water for me," I told her, not without some difficulty. Her perfectly groomed eyebrows lifted toward the ceiling in a question mark. I squeezed my belly in response.

"Ah, good for you," said my friend with zero body fat, as she climbed onto the bar to take a bottle from the top shelf. As usual, the room went silent at the sight of Analisa's perfect ass suspended in midair.

"Sucks," I responded, sipping my water as I waited for her to climb down, a feat that always seemed to take her a little longer than necessary. "And I just joined a gym, but they won't turn on their air. It's killing me." Analisa just nodded. This was not the tree to be barking up for sympathy. "I guess I'm just not as tough as you are, Analisa. Can I have a glass of red wine?"

Analisa placed her hands on her hips and paused, weighing my request.

"Please?" I put down my water. "Oh shit!"

"Okay, Deb. I will get you your wine . . . relax!"

"It's not that!" Out of the corner of my eye, I had spotted the guy from the gym. "It's that drunk over there." I rolled my eyes toward his table and tried to duck out of his line of sight as he downed a shot of tequila.

"Oh, that cochino." Analisa wrinkled her nose. "Yesterday he throw five hundred pesos at me and he say, 'What can I get for that?' "

"Ugh. What did you tell him?"

Analisa laughed and grabbed her boobs. "I told him he cannot afford this. Then I walk away. What else can I do?" She paused and sighed. "You know, Debbie? Sometime I hate this job."

"You should get out of here. Find something else."

"It is not easy, you know." She turned to pour a beer from the tap.

"Hey, Red!" came a yell from across the room. Everyone stopped to look but me. I hated being called Red. I hated being called anything by this creep. "I see you've been hanging out with Angelica! Now that's one chica I'd like to tap!" he yelled as he thrust his hips.

Analisa looked at him, and then at me. "What is he saying?"

"He's such an asshole," I said, without looking up. I lowered my voice. "He stalks the girls at the gym."

"What gym did you join, Debbie?" Analisa asked.

"The one near my house," I said. "You know, on Reforma Street."

Again Analisa just shook her head.

Now the guy stood up and began to rub his crotch against a cement pole in the middle of the room. "Has she taught you to use the pole yet? You can show us what you've got later tonight at Velvets! Hey, guys!" he called out to the room. "Red's working at Velvets tonight!"

I could feel the heat rising from my chest to my hairline as I pushed myself up from the stool and cleared my throat. But before I could make a move, Analisa grabbed me by the arm and sat me back down. "Tranquilo, Debbie."

"What is his problem? Jeez. I *really* don't know how you stand working here." I pointed to the wine bottle on the bar.

Analisa poured. "I need the money, Debbie. Nobody takes care of me. I am the one who takes care of me and my son."

"Well," I said, sipping my wine, "I still think there must be better places to work. Places where you don't have to wiggle your butt in people's faces to earn a living."

Analisa pretended not to hear. "Why you go to that gym with those dirty girls? This is not good, Debbie. People will think you are like them."

"What do you mean, like them?"

"You know those girls at that gym are all dancers, don't you?"

"What do you mean, dancers?"

"You know, what is the word? Naked dancers."

"Strippers? No way!"

"Most of them work at Velvets, or the other clubs. And a man, he can get anything he wants at those places. What time you go to the gym? Not early like me, right?"

I knew that regardless of how late Analisa worked, or how hard she partied, she had a 6 A.M. date with the gym, every single day. I shook my head. "No, I go late."

"Right. And why do you think those girls all look like that?"

"I think they look good!" I protested. "And they're so nice! Are they from Mazatlán?"

"Lots of girls come here to work, some by choice, some no. You know prostitution is legal here, right?"

I had no idea. "But this is a beach town! I never see working girls hanging around."

"That's because you go to bed at eight," Analisa said, laughing. "Anyway, they don't hang around." I just shook my head.

"It's a job. Money." She grabbed a tip off the bar and stuffed it into her tight pocket. "There are not a lot of ways for a woman with not much education to make money here, Debbie."

I should have understood better. Though the women here certainly had more freedom than those I had met in Afghanistan, for those without resources the options still seemed to be few. I'd see them working the hotels, the bars, cleaning houses, selling shoes, at the receptionist desk at the dental office or at the phone company, but that seemed to be about as far as most careers went. Higher education was a luxury many could not afford. And besides, most of them seemed to have babies before they were even old enough to know what sex was.

Even the jobs that were available to women were hard to come by. Hell, work for everyone down here was becoming harder and harder to find, with news reports of kidnappings and shoot-outs and bodies left hanging from bridges, scaring boatloads of tourists away from the country. Yes, things happened, but as I knew all too well, things happened everywhere. Mexico seemed pretty peaceful to me, so far.

I HAD HIRED BODIE TO OVERSEE SOME renovation on the house. Now I was woken up every morning by his crew of four tiptoeing past my door on their way to the roof, the only option for some much-needed expansion to accommodate friends and family I hoped would someday visit. But as soon as the guys would make their way up my killer spiral staircase (which, if my ass got any bigger, I'd never be able to negotiate), all bets were off. On went the radio, full blast, and in came the music straight through the two-by-two-foot open cube between my bedroom and my roof, which was the house's very traditional, very old, and semifunctional "air movement" system (that is, at least when the air was moving, which in the summer was, like, never). And boy did these guys love their music. It was as though they were auditioning for *American Idol*, their voices crowing through the still morning air, reminding me of the muezzins' call to prayer that was my predawn alarm clock in Afghanistan. After the suffocating silence of all those mornings on top of that hill in California, I was delighted to wake once again to the sweet sound of life around me.

Coffee with Bodie became a morning ritual. I think we could have solved most of the world's problems over all that coffee. As the others toiled away on his roof—his one-eyed plumber, his tattooed fresh-out-of-prison gangbanger from Los Angeles, his paper boy/electrician who would show up covered with sweat after his morning deliveries, and my sweet waiter Sergio, who apparently moonlit by day as Bodie's translator and carpenter—Bodie would entertain me with tales of Mazatlán. Spanish conquistadors and pirates, galleons teeming with gold, and silver, starry-eyed prospectors flocking across the land on their way to promised riches during the 1849 gold rush, revolutionaries who escaped through the limestone tunnels snaking out from Devil's Cave, practically right around the corner from Carnaval Street. I learned about the Chinese workers who came down through California and started families with local women. Later, reacting to a Depression-era backlash, a whole slew of them abandoned their homes and businesses and returned to China. Then World War II broke out, and the Mexican government sent ships to rescue the Mexican women and their children, leaving the men behind. Today you can see a trace of what's left of their Chinese husbands in a trail of offspring who provide Mazatlán with much of its legal and medical expertise. You've got to love a doctor named Pablo Wong or an insurance agent named Juan Chong. That, and the food. Like my favorites—the side-by-side Mandarin restaurants, Jade and *Original* Jade, owned by two ancient feuding sisters who split their deceased father's establishment right down the middle, and who to this day refuse to give in to each other.

The French, the British, the Germans—it seems as though everyone wanted a piece of Mazatlán at one time or another. I finally understood the eclectic architecture in Centro, as well as the startling green eyes on some of those kids I'd seen along the Malecón. It had never occurred to me that it was the Germans who had started the famous Pacífico brewery in town, or that they were the ones to blame for all that earsplitting *banda* music everywhere you turn.

With Bodie's encouragement, I began to drop in at Macaws, which I would do when I knew he'd likely be around. But no matter who was there, I would always be invited to join in. Being among this lively group, with their never-ending conversation and bottomless pit of stories, made the afternoons feel like one giant slumber party, without the pillow fights. As the summer rainstorms would come barreling through we'd pull our chairs in tighter, stranded happily together in the haven that was Macaws. The streets around us would become rushing rivers in an instant.

Now I understood why all the curbs were so high that a girl in a tight skirt never stood a chance. Sometimes, along with the flash floods, a horrible, reeking stew of sewage would bubble up from below. It was disgusting. There was shit in the street!

And then, one Saturday morning, there was shit in my closet.

From the day I started to have work done on the house, the question of putting in my own sewer came up constantly. I didn't get it. I had no idea how it all worked, but everything seemed to work just fine, and besides, putting in a new sewer would mean ripping up my beautiful old tile floors, and that was going to happen over my dead body. I should have taken the signs I saw in every public restroom in Centro, that outline of a toilet paper roll with a big X through it, as a warning. That, and the fly-covered buckets that people actually used instead as the alternative for waste disposal. But no, I thought I just must be one of the lucky ones. Until one morning when I flushed and heard the gurgling coming from my shower.

That can't be good, I thought, reaching for the plunger. Job done, I put a load of laundry in the washer and settled in on the couch with a book. Thirty pages later, I was interrupted by a strange odor creeping into the living room. That really can't be good, I thought, reluctantly getting up to investigate. To my horror, back in the bathroom a cloudy brown sludge was flowing over the shower lip and spreading across the floor. Shit everywhere. I frantically dialed Bodie's number, and within fifteen minutes he was at my door with Sergio, plungers and Drano in hand. We poured bottles and bottles of Drano down the toilet and into the shower drain. By now the shit was coming out of every orifice in my house, and the odor was seeping out through the gate into the street. So we ran to Josi's for more plungers, thinking that if we could block off the air, we might be able to literally force this crap out. The three of us plunged and plunged and plunged until our fingers blistered and our arms ached. After more than an hour, when we finally seemed to have everything but the odor under control, I thanked the guys and off they went, smelling like shit. Exhausted, I headed to the bedroom to flop down on the bed. But no. Because there, seeping out from under the tiles in my closet and into the room, was more shit.

I again called Bodie, who quickly found Sergio, who called the one-eyed plumber, who needed to confer with the original contractor who had helped fix up the house, who called sewer truck guys to blow the lines out, who warned me (via sign language) that blowing the lines out could result in shit all over my walls. Not an option. Now what?

By now the entire neighborhood had gathered

around, curious to watch as the gringa got the shit sucked out of her house, only to be disappointed to hear, along with me, that the sewer line, which was tied into the one next door, had somehow, by someone, been completely cemented up. Closed. No access. No outlet. Nowhere for the shit to go. The solution? Drill a hole through the bathroom wall that I apparently shared with my neighbor.

Off we went, Bodie, Sergio, the one-eyed plumber, the contractor, the sewer truck guys, and me, to knock on my neighbor's door. Or rather, as they do here, yell through his gate.

"Hello! Anybody home?" My voice bounced right through the spotless living room and back out into the street. "Hello?" We waited. And waited. Finally, a very, very old man in a sleeveless white undershirt and pants jacked up to his armpits shuffled toward us, his little white poodle scampering behind. "Debbie. Your neighbor," I said, extending one arm and pointing toward my house with the other.

He held up one finger and shuffled away.

"El viejo. Adónde va?" The one-eyed plumber was getting restless, and wanted to know where the old guy was going.

"Hello?" I tried again.

Back he came, all buttoned up now in a crisp white shirt. "Pepe," he said, opening the gate and taking my hand with a little bow. "Bienvenido." He invited us in with a sweep of the arm.

The plumber and contractor began to explain the problem. Pepe just smiled and nodded his head, then reached down to retrieve a glass dish off a side table. "Dulces?" One by one, my entourage followed my lead in accepting his offer, obediently popping the sickly sweet candies into our mouths, while images of a tsunami of shit rushing down Carnaval Street played in my mind.

Suddenly a huge grin spread across Pepe's face. A woman had arrived at the gate, apparently the owner of the house, who had been alerted to the commotion by Josi the storekeeper, and who, after first denying that she had done anything to the wall in the bathroom, agreed to the hole in the wall, only after our promise to her that we'd leave her bathroom in better shape than we found it, much better shape. Pepe walked us to the door to see us out, pressing a little wrapped cookie into each of our hands as we shook good-bye.

With the problem solved, at least for now, Bodie offered to help with the cleanup. Let's just say it wasn't pretty, but we did manage to bundle up every stinking rag and towel, along with the sweaters and jeans and blankets I had neatly folded and stored on the closet floor, and handed them to the laundryman Bodie had phoned, the one who promised to have everything back within a day, but didn't, because somewhere in between, the laundryman got shot.

"Welcome to Mexico," said the gang upon my next visit to Macaws. The violence had now arrived at our front door. Some in Centro had even heard the shots that rang out from the passing red motorcycle, killing the laundryman for who knew what reason, and now any red motorcycle cruising the streets became a source of high anxiety for all of us.

But of course, life went on. And indeed, I felt as though a phase of my initiation period had passed. Little by little, I was starting to belong.

When Bodie wasn't around, sometimes I'd sit and have coffee with Sharon and Glen, who owned Macaws and Casa de Leyendas, the restored colonial mansion turned B&B that housed it. Glen impressed me as the laid-back drummer type he told me he had been before getting sucked too deep into the corporate world. Mazatlán had given him back his sense of humor, and had made him open to anyone and anything. Sharon, on the other hand, seemed a little more aloof. But there was a certain vulnerability about her that I thought I recognized.

One afternoon I noticed a gorgeous photo of a sexy blonde inside the B&B's spacious foyer and seized the opportunity for an icebreaker. "That's a great shot of you, Sharon. How old were you there?"

Sharon rolled her eyes. "That's not me. That's my mother."

"Wow. She was beautiful!"

"She died last year."

"Oh, I'm so sorry."

Sharon shrugged her shoulders.

"But really, I mean it. So gorgeous."

"She would have been thrilled to hear that. She lived to be admired for her beauty."

"Was she a model?"

Sharon snorted a little. "Not exactly."

"Well, she sure looks like one."

"Actually, Debbie, she was a Playboy Bunny."

"Right. And my mom was Cleopatra." There was no way a woman like Sharon, so natural and unaffected, with her hair swept back in a simple ponytail, lips shining with a pale gloss, and a baggy dress that hid what others would have flaunted with pride, could have been brought up by a Playboy Bunny.

"Seriously, Deb. She worked in the club in St. Louis. Serving drinks."

"Hmm," I answered in a lame attempt to sound matter-of-fact. "So she was a cocktail waitress."

"Yeah," Sharon said with a laugh. "A cocktail waitress with two ears and a tail."

"It's a living."

"I guess. She never did hold down a normal job. Bartending, masseuse, those were more her type of thing. She'd do anything to not be dependent on a man." Sharon went into the kitchen and returned with a bottle and two glasses. I checked my watch. Sharon poured. "It's okay, Deb. Late enough. Here's to my mom."

"To your mom. May she rest in peace." We clinked glasses and dragged a couple of chairs into the shade next to the pool.

"I'm not so sure resting is what she's doing, if she has anything to say about it." Sharon kicked off her flip-flops. "We lived like Gypsies, moving all the time. One day, she packed up the car with my two little brothers and me and took off for California. I have no idea what she thought she'd find, but the four of us ended up living in a Hollywood dump with a prostitute as a room-mate. Wild, huh?"

"She sounds like a piece of work."

"Yeah, she was pretty unorthodox, as far as moms go."

"Not that there's anything wrong with that, right?" I wondered what Sharon would have thought of my parenting style.

"To a point." Sharon sipped her wine. "Seriously. Once she told me she slept with some of the Rat Pack back in the day. What kind of a mother brags about that?"

"Seriously," I echoed, not really sure how to react.

"And here's one for you. Once she claimed to have been abducted by aliens."

I tried hard not to laugh, though Sharon herself was smiling.

"Really."

"Yeah, really."

"Well? At least you got her looks."

Sharon laughed. "There is that. But she was relentless with me, always trying to groom me to be a model, just like she always wanted to be. I know I was a huge disappointment to her. But that was her dream, not mine. I'm definitely not the model type."

Wow. The daughter of a Bunny, I thought, looking at Sharon with newfound awe. In a way, though our mothers were polar opposites, I felt like I could relate to Sharon's story. I could still picture the look on my graceful, delicate mother's face when the Sears saleslady would direct her and her big, bulky, bellowing daughter to the Chubby department. "Yeah." I sighed. "I was always envious of my mom's looks, wished I was as beautiful as she was."

Sharon laughed. "I wasn't envious, Deb! I was embarrassed. I never thought she was that pretty. I never thought *I* was pretty. Everyone used to say that I looked just like her. I hated that. I always claimed to have my dad's eyes, and his eyebrows, too."

From my perspective, Sharon must have been one tough little girl. Me? My reaction to the all-too-obvious differences between my mother and myself was my absolute certainty that I was adopted. All that bragging she did about never showing when she was pregnant? Obviously a cover for the mysterious lack of pregnancy photos. Year after year, I'd use my birthday as an opportunity to invite my mom and dad to come clean about my parentage. I knew it was just a matter of time before they'd agree I was old enough to handle the truth. It wasn't until I was fourteen, and suddenly began to see a little bit of my mom's face in the mirror, that I gave up on that idea. I envied Sharon's candor. I was liking this woman who could talk so freely about such a drama-laden life, one who could come through all that mess to end up creating the unbelievably warm, welcoming environment she had built at Casa de Leyendas. The B&B was stunning, perfectly decorated and accessorized down to the last detail. How did Sharon become Martha Stewart growing up with Anna Nicole Smith? I felt honored that she had shared this part of her past with me, that she had opened the door just a little bit wider to welcome me into the group, and into her life. I was getting a sense already that Sharon and I were destined to become good friends.

THE NIGHT I GOT THE CALL FROM BARB WAS when I knew I was really starting to belong. It was ninety-four degrees outside, and not much cooler inside. When my cell rang I barely had the energy to answer.

"Deb, it's Barb," she said very calmly. "Bob is dead."

I shot straight up on the couch. "Oh my God, I'm so sorry. That's terrible! What can I do?" I blathered into the phone, picturing her sweet, elderly husband that day at the beach.

"I can't find Bodie's phone number. I need someone to get rid of the body."

My mind flashed for a second on a Barb I'd never imagined, one holding a bloody knife or a brain-splattered hammer over the kitchen sink. "Um, Barb? Don't you think you should call the coroner? They have those here, right? Or the hospital? Or perhaps the police?"

"I don't think—"

"How did he die, Barb? Where is your husband's body?"

"He died on the living room couch just a little while ago and . . . husband? Who said anything about Art? Bob is our dog, Debbie."

I tried to cover up the sound of my sigh with a little cough. "Of course, that's what I meant. Let me make a few calls and I'll get back to you."

I quickly dialed Bodie's number, anxious to get him started tapping into his network of fellow animal lovers. No answer. With no phone book to be found at my place, I rushed down to Macaws, where Glen and Sharon and Cesar the bartender were just closing up, and we got to work searching for help. In the middle of it all, Bodie called back. Though I swear I made it clear that a dog had died, I learned later that all Bodie heard was "Bob died, and we need to get rid of the body."

Silence.

"We've called a few twenty-four-hour numbers listed for cremation services, but none of them answered," I explained.

Still, silence at the end of the line.

"We thought about double-bagging him and putting him in the parking garage but I think he would begin to stink in this heat. I've asked Glen and Sharon if they have an empty freezer just to keep him cold through the weekend, but all their freezers are full."

More silence.

"Bodie, are you there? We just need a number for someone to take Bob away."

"Maybe you should call the American embassy."

The embassy? *Seriously,* I'm thinking, *you report dead dogs to the American embassy here?* I wasn't about to go down that road. After all, when I had tried to report that my son had received a kidnapping threat and that my life was in serious danger, I got jack shit out of the American embassy. I highly doubted the American embassy was going to be the answer now. It was time to call for reinforcements.

I alerted the rest of the troops, and soon the phone lines were on fire. One vet was too drunk and said he'd come by on Monday. Two others claimed they didn't have a freezer big enough to store the mutt, and that we'd have to wait until after the weekend. The rest of the round-the-clock services didn't even answer. A nice funeral was obviously out of the question. Now it was simply a matter of removing the body from the living room. Bonnie headed to Barb's house to help deal with the dog on the couch. She had an idea, remembering that Roger the Realtor lived nearby in a big house with a lawn. Perhaps Bob could be buried there.

But Roger's big lawn had been recently cemented over, in his gringo attempt at the preferred local style. Roger pointed out the empty lot across the street. We were jazzed, and relieved. "Who has a shovel?" someone asked. Glen said that he thought he might know someone who knew someone who had a shovel, but as we stomped on the hard ground we realized what we really needed was a pick and an ax.

We then considered a burial at sea, but feared the waves would just wash him back up to shore. Mafia-style was floated as an option, as in a bag and some rocks, but we had no boat, and it was late. Maybe a Hindu pyre on the beach? With no wood, and an overeager police force, we knew we'd never get away with it. And in the middle of all this, the reality of losing their beloved Bob was just beginning to sink in for Art and Barb.

Finally, Bonnie, who spoke more Spanish than

all of us combined, got hold of a vet and, though she swore he sounded drunk, successfully persuaded him to come get Bob. We still don't know what became of Bob. All I do know is this: in Mexico, it's not a good idea to die on the weekend. I'd have to remember to be extra careful on Saturdays and Sundays.

WE TRAVELED AROUND LIKE A REVOLVING herd of goats that summer, stopping to graze at the nearest taquerías and quenching our thirst at a variety of watering holes. Now there was always something to do and someone to do it with, no matter what day of the week or what time of day. We'd gather for roof parties at sunset, or wander down to the water to watch the cliff divers floating through the sky.

One Thursday evening a few of us headed to Zaragoza Park, where older Mazatleco couples would tango and two-step long into the night. I had heard that it was a pickup scene for the Mexican geriatric crowd, the place where a widowed grandma or a spinster aunt could go with her head held high, all dolled up with silk flowers in her hair that matched the folding fan in her hands. The men, with their perfect posture and pointy white shoes, led the women gently across the plaza with an air of elegance that seemed to have come from another era. That night a couple of mustachioed men asked me to dance. "No, gracias," I said with a little smile. I couldn't imagine dancing in that heat. It was hard enough to survive just sitting there watching from a plastic chair. Besides, I didn't dance in any weather, at least not in public. Never did, and doubted I ever would. I envied these women as they spun and twirled proudly and gracefully across the plaza.

Sunday nights, we'd meet down by the water to watch the clowns. Me, I got more of a kick out of watching the spectators splayed out in a giant circle on the plaza's hard ground, mothers and fathers and children totally and equally engaged in the silly slapstick, as if it were the original Broadway production of *The Lion King*. They really love their clowns down there. Whole families of clowns have been prancing around in their giant shoes and fright wigs entertaining generation after generation of Mazatlecos for years. And boy, do those clowns rake it in. I've heard they even earn more than doctors. Even so, I'm glad my mom was a hairdresser and not a clown, because then I'd have to be one, too, and I wouldn't be caught dead in those mismatched outfits and that gaudy makeup.

AS THE SEASON CHANGED, SO DID MAZATLÁN. Of course, weather-wise it only dropped a few blessed degrees, but in terms of the vibe, it was as though the volume had been turned up about a hundred decibels. The snowbirds were flocking back from Seattle and Vancouver and Winnipeg and Minneapolis, and along with these fair-weather residents came the charity fund-raisers, the wine tastings, the gallery openings, and more parties than ever. There was a buzz of anticipation along the Malecón, with people shouting and waving to each other, hugging, kissing, showing off new hairdos and clothes as if it were the first day back at school. To me, it felt like those of us who had endured the marathon that was summer were being trampled by a bunch of sprinters with a bit too much enthusiasm. Where were all those guys while we were holding down the fort with our heat rash, wilted hair, and bubbling sewage? Personally, I was proud to carry the badge of honor that comes with being a full-timer, and felt lucky that I had gotten the chance to know the hearty group I met over the summer. I had learned a lot from them, so now I simply followed their lead, embraced the new energy, and dived right in.

It was way too easy to get lost in all that chaos. I was always good in chaos. It didn't leave me much time to think about myself and, for the most part, that seemed to suit me just fine. This perpetual fiesta sure beat that interminable sitting around that the Indian had prescribed up in Napa. I started to think that maybe this was all I needed in the first place. But when I took the rare quiet moment to have an honest conversation with myself, I also feared that, though I was certainly having more fun than I ever did in California, I had allowed myself to become distracted. Mazatlán was one giant distraction. It was easy to live a life without a responsibility in the world, a life disconnected from everything, including myself. And I knew that, in the long run, that would get me nowhere fast. I'd lived a lifetime searching for that someone or somewhere I thought might bring me happiness. And though I was certainly hopeful about my new life in Mexico, deep down I knew that the only one who could make me happy was me, and that the only place I'd find happiness was a place deep inside myself, a place that was becoming increasingly difficult to locate amid all the noise.

I had come down to Mexico determined to do things right this time, and I wasn't about to give up on that. So even if I wasn't yet sure how to work on the inside, in the meantime at least I could keep working on the outside. The hairdresser in me was a huge believer in the look-good, feel-good philosophy.

The gym thing had sort of fizzled when Roberto, the owner, got shot. As happens down here, nobody really talked about how or why. They just padlocked the doors and went on with life. And so did I.

It was a visit to my mother that pushed me to pursue another avenue of self-improvement. Not an actual visit to my mother, but rather it was the *thought* of a visit that prompted me to apply for my FM3 visa, the one that would allow me to leave the country without my car, should I have to do so in the case of an emergency. I wanted to be able to just hop on a plane in the event that my aging mother needed me. So, apparently, in order for me to be granted the rights that this visa offered, the Mexican government needed to see, and photograph, a naked face. That meant a face devoid of all hair, including, for example, hair strategically parted to mask a broad forehead, bangs cut at exactly the right length to cover a droopy eyelid, a curl placed just so to distract from a sinking jawline. Not one stray hair. And they wanted to see your ears, which apparently can only be made truly identifiable when standing face forward at attention with cotton balls shoved behind them until they stick out like a cartoon mouse. "Sin sonrisa. No smile!" The shutter clicked.

"I'm hideous," I cried to Sharon when I showed her my card. "How can I even see anything with those big old sacks hanging down over my eyeballs? And what the hell is that under my chin? Tell me I don't really look like this." Sharon just laughed. "What do you think?" I asked, stretching my cheeks back as far as the skin would allow.

"You look like Bruce Lee," she answered.

"Don't you think I'd look a lot better with just a little work?"

Sharon shrugged her shoulders. "I think you look just fine."

"C'mon. A little lift?" I raised my brows to the ceiling. "A little tuck?" I flattened my chin with the back of my hand.

"It's a big deal, Deb. It's major surgery."

"Ooh, I know what you need, Debbie," piped in Analisa from behind the counter, where, to the joy of both of us, she was now working the day shift. It was adios Mamita's for her. "Cirugía estética vampiro," she said. "I have a girlfriend, she got this."

"Cirugía estética vampiro? What is that?"

"You know, it's like a . . ." She pushed her front teeth out over her bottom lip.

"Why would I want buck teeth, Ana?"

"No, not that. You know." Now she raised her collar, grabbed Glen by the front of his T-shirt, and pretended to bite his neck. "They take the blood."

"Mosquito?" Glen giggled, clearly enjoying himself.

"Vampire! You mean a vampire?" Sharon shouted out.

"Yes! That is what it is. A vampire facelift."

I was picturing a procedure that would leave me with a whiter than white face and long, pointy fangs, not exactly what I had in mind.

"It's where they take your own blood and put it back into your face," Analisa explained. "With shots. It will make you look *joung*. I've seen the pictures."

Sharon shuddered. "There's no way anybody's getting me to do any shots, unless they're shots of tequila." It did sound pretty disgusting, and I had my doubts, but to me needles sounded way better than knives.

Mexico has its own take when it comes to health care. Like at the pharmacy, where there always seems to be some sort of party going on. I've seen a guy there dressed up like a giant Pillsbury Doughboy—although I guess he's supposed to look like a doctor—dancing around outside trying to entice people to go in. There's also often a "nurse" hanging around out front, handing out promotional flyers for all sorts of miracle cures. This is a country where you walk in off the street and the pharmacist offers up Viagra and Lunesta as if they were Tic Tacs or Lifesavers. Where you can get storefront X-rays and blood work done on a whim, any day, any time. But as quirky as it seemed, I hadn't heard anybody complaining about the medical service down here. My only personal experience until now had been the one time I went to the clinic inside the pharmacy with my ears plugged up. A nice doctor irrigated them swiftly and efficiently. Then he triumphantly held up my big glob of earwax for all the world to see. "Mira! Frijoles en sus oidos!" I had beans in my ears.

I persuaded Sharon to accompany me to the

doctor on Juárez Street, the one Analisa had heard good things about. The neighborhood left me thinking twice about leaving my car unattended, but inside, the office was a sparkly white.

"The Vampire?" The graying doctor took my chin in his thick hand and slowly turned my head back and forth. Then he shook his own head slowly back and forth. "Not for you."

"Why not?" I whined, enviously eyeing the posters of Salma Hayek, Cameron Diaz, Penelope Cruz, and the like plastered on the walls of his office.

"Too late. The Vampire can only do so much for a woman like you."

A woman like me? What the hell did he mean by that? Before I could yank my chin from his hand and head to the door, he continued, tapping each part of my face with his pen as he talked. "Perhaps with a brow lift, some work on the eyes, a little lipo under the chin, cheek implants, and then we straighten out that nose, yes. You might look beautiful." He flashed a perfect smile and swept his arm toward the posters on the wall, as if he had personally performed surgery on them all. I slumped in my chair. I never knew I had a crooked nose.

"And you," he said, turning to beautiful Sharon, "the same. But also your lips need work."

He took off his glasses and stood up. "That will be seven hundred pesos for today's visit, please. Each."

9

MY REPUTATION, WHEN IT COMES TO ENTER-
taining, is, shall we say, somewhat spotty. Though
I shine when it comes to the procurement part—
I'm the one who's always assigned to bring the
chips or the sodas for any get-together—my short-
comings, when it comes to dealing with an oven
or even a mixing bowl, are widely known. I try to
keep things simple. The one and only time I
volunteered to host Christmas dinner for the entire
family, including the in-laws, I knew better than to
attempt a roast turkey. But cooking spaghetti for
fifteen turned out to be a whole different matter
than doing it for four. Fortunately, the day was
saved by a secret dash to the gas station for their
famous fried chicken. Another time, when I
decided I wanted to try my hand at my own gas
station chicken, my tendency to get easily
distracted resulted in a kitchen fire, where everything, including the carpet, went up in flames.
Even in Kabul, at my own coffeehouse, I was told
in no uncertain terms that my one and only job
was to greet customers and stay out of the kitchen.

But on Carnaval Street none of that stopped me from impulsively inviting a few of my neighbors over one Saturday morning for a little get-together. Thank goodness for Analisa, who arrived early with a cake from Panama Bakery, along with her crucial bilingual skills. I put on the coffee. Pepe, the old man who lived on the other side of my bathroom wall, appeared at my gate exactly on time, with a tan fedora on his head and a bag of candy in his perfectly manicured hand. It wasn't long before Josi and her brother-in-law Jorge, who together own a building six houses down on Carnaval Street, arrived, Josi in her flip-flops and shorts and Jorge looking as though he were headed to a board meeting.

I'm not sure what I had been thinking. I picked at my cake while the four of them chatted away. Analisa tried her best to draw me in.

"Tell your friends how do you like living on Carnaval Street, Debbie."

"You know how I like it, Analisa. You go ahead and tell them."

Analisa rattled something off in Spanish. "Jorge wants to know if you have met the dead people yet."

"Excuse me?" I almost spit out my coffee.

"You heard me, Debbie. So *have* you seen them? The dead people?"

"Um, no."

"He says he knows lots of dead people. One who

lives in his building is a doctor." Analisa looked at Jorge and nodded her head, clearly impressed.

"Really," was all I could say. Who was I to judge? After all, I'd seen plenty of strange things myself in my own lifetime. Besides, there was no way I'd want to offend him.

"Yes," Jorge continued, "but he is a very nice and very peaceful dead doctor."

"That's good."

"Josi says she wish he would send the dead people to shop in her store." Analisa laughed. "Jorge says he does, but they don't need many groceries."

Jorge was full of stories. I had barely finished pouring a second round of coffee when off he went on a long, tragic tale about the people who used to live a few houses down from mine. The story goes that one night a young girl who lived there went out dancing with a friend. They met some boys, things turned ugly, and the girl was murdered. Her mother, inconsolable, spent two years mourning over her deceased daughter's clothes and locks of her hair, praying for her return. Then the girl did return, in the body of her twelve-year-old niece, who had been living in the house as well. One day the niece was normal, and the next she was howling like a wounded animal, suddenly with enough strength to throw tables and chairs and people across the room. She began attacking everyone around her. Jorge heard the commotion and went down to look, and caught sight of the girl growling. The doctor was called, but everyone quickly agreed that this was no illness—the girl was possessed. The street emptied as priests and pastors and ministers of all denominations came to perform an exorcism. The only noises to be heard for the next three hours were the screams of a young girl and the baying of dogs across the neighborhood. That was twenty-two years ago, and the last time anyone ever lived in that house.

"Ask him if he knows anything about my house," I urged Analisa, praying that I wouldn't uncover a grisly past to keep me up at night.

Jorge pointed to the street. Analisa translated. "Did you know that the Carnival parade used to start right here, outside your door? It went from here, down to the water. And the Carnival queens, many of them came from this street."

I had to smile, thinking of how I had been unwittingly following in the footsteps of bygone beauty queens every time I set out on those daily strolls during my first few weeks in Mazatlán. I was just about to chime in with some stories of my own when Analisa's phone rang, for about the fifth time since she had arrived. This time she excused herself and went into the kitchen to talk. An awkward silence filled the room as I refilled cups and passed around more cake. I was tempted to try out my Spanish, but how can you trust a language where potato, pope, and father are all the same word, where penis and comb are easily confused, and fart and dog sound suspiciously alike? I waited and hoped (the same verb, in Spanish) for Analisa to hang up and join us again soon.

"Ask Pepe what he knows about Carnaval Street," I asked when she did return.

"He says it is a good street. He lives here his whole life. He is ninety-three."

"Wow."

"He remembers a furniture store, and a shoe store where you drive up a ramp to get in. If you have no car, you had to use a ladder."

The irony of Pepe's early life didn't seem to have escaped him. Forced to quit school at fifteen after his mother became ill, he went to work to help pay the electric bills. His first employer? The power company, who had him climbing the poles to disconnect those who didn't pay. Mazatlán was pretty wild back then. But Pepe's mother, he told us, taught him to be respectful and honest, to stay away from trouble. "I had an invisible umbilical cord to her," Analisa translated with a smile.

"WHAT IS IT WITH MEXICAN MOTHERS AND their sons?" I asked Analisa later, while we were cleaning up in the kitchen. Her phone rang again. "And who keeps calling you? You have a new sugar daddy or something?"

"It's my son, Debbie. He just wants to know when I am coming home."

"Aha! See what I mean?"

"What? He takes care of me. He worries about me."

"He worries about his next meal. You spoil him, Ana."

"No. He is a good boy, Debbie."

"I didn't say he wasn't good. But he's already eighteen years old, and I'm just saying you shouldn't be a slave to him."

"I am not a slave to anybody! So what if I cook for him and wash his clothes?"

"And come running whenever he calls." I knew better than to pick a fight with Analisa, and I honestly had no business criticizing her parenting skills. But I had been battling with my own problems in that area recently and was feeling pretty raw. My son Noah, who, following our escape from Afghanistan, had left Northern Cyprus for the States after a couple of months with his brother, was struggling. Always a party boy, he was now a full-grown man with a serious drinking problem, a severe lack of funds, and the distinct possibility of homelessness staring him in the face. A series of bad choices had sent my son into a devastating downward spiral. My heart was breaking.

Noah had never been an easy child. His strong will and boundless energy always kept things lively, to say the least. Focus, when it came to schoolwork, was not a part of his vocabulary. He was a good boy, but suffered from the grass-is-always-greener syndrome to the point of resentment. That was the challenge of bringing up kids in a working-class family smack in the middle of a fairly upscale community. We weren't poor. I'd seen what poor was from my travels in India, digging wells with a humanitarian group, and I was determined to teach my kids to appreciate what they had. I worked hard to make sure we always had a nice home and a car and gifts under the Christmas tree, but we just couldn't afford the extras, like ski club or vacations in Florida. Noah wanted what he thought of as normal, but with a nontraditional mother living in a highly traditional community, he didn't stand a chance. Things just didn't fit in with his Hallmark image of how life was supposed to be. Zach, being younger, was more willing to go along for the ride. Case in point, our stint in the Bahamas. Zach embraced it as a wonderful adventure. I think Noah still resents me for it, to this day.

Things only got worse after Noah decided he didn't want to live by the house rules his father and I had set down in our respective homes. My mother took him in, let him run wild, and then bailed him out of every bad situation he managed to slide his way into. It was the worst mistake we ever made.

By the time I left for Afghanistan, Noah was already twenty-one, an age when most kids *prefer* that their parents live thousands of miles away. I really thought he'd come into his own. I had dealt with Noah and his drama for his entire life and was confident that he'd eventually find his way. But now, after years of him struggling and me joining in on the enabling, since I had naïvely come around to the idea that a little financial support might help him move forward, he seemed close to hitting rock bottom instead. As difficult as it might be, it was clear that my only alternative was the tough love route. Unfortunately Noah never had any minutes left on his phone, so our communication was limited to e-mail, and accusations had been flying back and forth between Chicago and Mazatlán for weeks.

Noah: Mom, I need to ask a favor. Can you wire me $200? I know that's a lot, but it would really help. I don't ask for much these days.

Me: I just sent you $250 a week ago. Do you not have a job anymore? No lies, Noah. Tell me what's going on.

Noah: Nothing really. Just need a little money. You know I hate asking shit like this.

Me: Giving you money doesn't seem to help you. There will never be enough money to keep you on your feet. You need more than money. As soon as you have money you spend it like it is the last day of your life.

Noah: I just need a little help with the bills.

Me: I love you, Noah, but I am not going to rescue you every time you are unable to pay your bills. It's clear you don't think you have a problem, and that's fine. Because you are the only one who can help you.

Noah: When someone has a problem you don't turn away.

Me: Noah, it's time you make the right choices. You can't guilt me into shit like you did when you were a kid.

Noah: So we are done. I didn't ask you for anything, just to be a mother, and you can't even do that. If you don't want to be part of my life, then don't. I don't need you.

Me: I am being a mother, but what you want is a bank account. Giving you money is not a mom's job. Making life easy for you is not a mom's job. It is my job just to love you. I do love you with all my heart and that's why I am going to be hard on you now. I am sorry about how this is going to feel for you. I may not have been the perfect mom but I do have a mother's heart, and I won't let you manipulate me.

Noah: I don't want your money, don't need your help. Someday you will look back and never forget this. You have no idea how I feel. All I wanted was a family. I will leave you guys alone.

Me: You have a family that loves you, try not to forget that.

Noah: I'm trying, and I'm just asking for some help. I can't do this by myself. We both know that. You've done everything you could have done to help me, I just seem to fuck things up no matter where I am . . .

Me: Noah, you are a wonderful human being and a good person.

Noah: I'm truly sorry about everything, I'm disgusted with the way my life has turned out. And know that I have no one to blame but myself. I just want to get out of here.

Me: Go back to Michigan and try to find some sort of work.

Noah: Can't I just come to Mexico with you and never come back . . . get away from all this shit?

Me: If you can't make it in the States, why would you think you can make it in Mexico?

Noah: I don't understand why you won't take me in. I'm your son! You would rather me be on the streets? I'm asking for help. This is not what people do to each other. God, Mom. This is going to end badly, I can already feel it. Please don't do this to me. I will end up in the gutter facedown, and you will end up with a phone call from the hospital.

Me: I refuse to play games with you, Noah. Nobody put you in this place. You put yourself there. It's time you take responsibility for your actions. I know it's hard. It's hard for me, too.

Part of me, the part that made my entire insides ache when I pictured Noah's impish smile, wanted to hop on a plane and rush to the rescue. But I knew that bringing Noah to Mexico was probably the worst idea of all. I'd seen sober people turn into drunks practically overnight in this town, a place where beer is cheaper than water. And the fallout from the violence surrounding the drug cartels was making jobs harder to find for everyone, let alone someone who didn't speak a word of Spanish. No, there were plenty of safety nets for Noah in the States. I just prayed he'd fall, gently, into one of them soon.

AS SOON AS I HEARD A HEALER WAS COMING to town, I knew I had to go. El Maestro Constantino would be here for five days, and between my own issues and my anxiety about Noah, I felt I could use all the help I could get. I called everyone I knew to invite them along. Most of them thought I was nuts, but I didn't care.

Now, though I consider myself to be a somewhat spiritual person, I wouldn't call myself a spiritual person in the way that people toss that term around these days. I know I'd never be able to keep quiet long enough to meditate—I don't have a whole lot of sit in me—and I'm really not the chanting type. Scrubbing floors in a cold monastery on my bare knees? Not a chance. Enlightenment is probably going to have to fall into my lap, preferably while I'm shopping or something, and my spiritual leader will probably be someone I meet while he's having a beer at the bar. But I don't close doors, because I do believe that anything is possible. If nothing else, I'm observant. Celebrations, ceremonies, rituals, and rites have always held a particular fascination for me. I'm pulled to them, whether it's Hindu body piercing in India, Shinto naked gatherings in Japan, or the Hungry Ghost Festival in China. They make me want to know more. What are these people seeing? What are they feeling? Personally, I do believe there is some bigger force, some higher being out there. And I'm not about to rule anything out. In that way, I have a lot in common with the Mexicans, at least the ones I have met.

But six o'clock in the morning is not my favorite time of day. The line outside the dance hall was already snaking around the block when I met up with Bonnie and Cheryl, my only two friends to live up to their promise to join me. We had just settled into our folding chairs when I heard Sharon's voice, yelling down from the terrace of Casa de Leyendas. "Ya healed yet, Deb?"

Very funny, I thought to myself. She'll be sorry she chose not to join me.

"Hungry, guys?" she shouted.

"Yeah!" I yelled up, just then realizing how hungry I was.

Fifteen minutes later Sharon was at our side with a trio of juicy sausage sandwiches and three steaming cups of coffee. I had just unwrapped mine and was starting to wrap my lips around it when a loud "Noooo!" rang out from behind. I turned to see a short, dark-haired man shaking his finger in my face. "Muy horrible. No puede comer eso!" He was staring at my sandwich.

A hefty woman behind him stepped out of the line. "You can't eat that. And no coffee. No caffeine, no meat, no eggs. That is what El Maestro believes. This is a spiritual healing, and you're polluting your body before you even begin?" She shook her head in disgust and went back to her spot. Bonnie and Cheryl sheepishly rewrapped their sandwiches and stuffed them into their purses, and I reluctantly followed their lead.

"Have fun," Sharon said, as she turned and left us there to starve.

But the four hours we had left to go in that line,

which was now snaking its way down the street and around the corner, were proving to be more than my willpower could take.

"Save my place, guys. I've gotta pee. Be right back." I could feel my friends' suspicious eyes following me as I trotted off around the corner toward the privacy of my friend Sonja's kitchen, clutching my purse under my arm and my coffee cup in my hand. And when I came back half an hour later with crumbs on my shirt, they were barely speaking to me.

We were finally herded into the hall, everyone abuzz, excitedly anticipating the arrival of this powerful man. There must have been more than two hundred people there. *Palms up, open your hearts, and breathe in,* we were instructed. So we did.

Suddenly the room fell silent. In walked a teeny bearded guy in white robes and combat boots. As he got closer I could see rings on every finger and a beanie covering his head. A white scarf tied around his mouth and nose made him look like a bank robber. Trailing behind Constantino were three women in long, flowy white skirts, all of them waving incense in the air. We stood as they formed a little circle in front of a makeshift altar watched over by images of saints and the Virgin and Jesus himself. Constantino and his women bowed their heads in prayer. Then he began to approach his eager followers. Over and over I could hear him ask the question, "Qué te pasa?" They would lock eyes, the healee would share whatever ailment they were seeking relief from, and then Constantino would poke them. *Really?* I thought. *He's healing with a poke?* And I'm not talking just a little nudge, I'm talking a full-force jab, one that had some people reeling so hard that those standing behind had to catch them to keep them from falling.

I braced myself as my turn approached. What should I say? What *wasn't* wrong? How could I describe it? My own wounds weren't visible to the outside world, at least not usually. There was no way to explain it all in one sentence, or even two. All I knew was that sometimes I felt like I was two people, and was living in constant fear that the functioning one could fall off a cliff at any moment and become the other one, the one who was needy, scared, and an emotional mess.

Then, before I knew it, the little guy was right in front of me. "Cuál es tu problema?" The room seemed to fall silent again.

One of the women in white repeated in English, "What is your problem?"

I could feel the entire crowd, including my friends, lean in around me. "My mind needs to be healed," I whispered.

"Mande?" Constantino barked.

"It's my head," I answered, a little louder this time. "I'm suffering from things that happened. I want to be cleansed of my past. I need to get strong enough to deal with the present. You see, I was in a war zone, I'm not sure—"

His two fingers were on my chest. "Look into his eyes," instructed the flowy-skirted woman.

And when I did, electricity shot through my body as if I had stuck my wet finger in a socket. I heard myself let out a wail like a cow in heat. It was as if everything I had been hiding inside since I arrived in Mexico had come rushing to the surface and was spewing out into the dance hall through the tears that poured from my eyes. The anguish of loss, the guilt about my girls, the shame of failure—all my grief about leaving Afghanistan seemed to come gushing out all at once. But Constantino didn't budge. He just stood there and pressed. Just when I started to think I'd faint, he pushed me into a chair and said, "It's finished. Your pain is finished."

I RETREATED TO MACAWS A LITTLE SHAKY. The whole healing thing had not been what I expected. I wasn't sure what being healed was supposed to feel like, and I certainly wasn't convinced that all my problems had disappeared in a poof. But I did sense that something inside me had shifted, as if the channel had been changed on my internal TV.

I checked my phone while I waited for Analisa to bring me a cup of coffee. Three more messages from Noah. I couldn't even bring myself to read them.

"What is the matter, Debbie? You don't look so good."

"Nothing. I'm just tired." I knew that Analisa was the last person with whom I could discuss my problems with Noah. She'd throw herself across a track smack in front of a speeding train if her son asked her to. She shrugged her shoulders and left me alone to stress. But it wasn't long before Sharon plopped herself down in the chair next to mine.

"Healed?"

"We'll see." I didn't quite know how to explain to Sharon what I had gone through. "But it was quite an experience."

"You do look kind of wiped."

"You go to the healer, Debbie?" Analisa asked from across the patio. "My aunt, she was there. Cancer." She looked down at the ground and shook her head.

"Does she believe in this stuff?" I asked, rubbing the spot on my shoulder that had been poked.

"Why not? You don't?"

"I don't know. I just thought with everyone being so Catholic down here . . ."

"Catholic, Mormon, what is the difference? If someone is healing, you must go get healed. Especially if it cost nothing."

I couldn't argue. But it did worry me that there were so many desperate-looking people in that hall asking for help, people who were in all probability, I now understood, lacking the resources to pay a doctor. The whole thing felt so sad. My phone vibrated with a little hop across the table. I was scared to look. What I should have asked Constantino for was a healing by proxy for my son, I thought. "Be glad your kids are the four-legged kind," I sighed to Sharon, reaching down with one hand to pet her wiggly Shelties.

"What's going on, Deb?"

"I'm just tired. Haven't slept very well for the past few nights."

"Well, I hate to say, but you look more than just tired. I think that healer guy must have really done a number on you."

I dabbed my napkin at a tear I could feel escaping from the corner of my eye. Though I was sure Sharon would be sympathetic, I feared that once I started talking I'd fall apart. Noah was a mess, and trying to help him by denying him help seemed to go against every drop of maternal instinct I carried around inside. Intellectually I knew it was supposed to be the right thing to do, but when my mind would go to that dark place where I'd imagine Noah squatting in front of a bank begging for change, or unconscious in a ditch, all bets were off. I went back and forth and back and forth from being angry to frightened to guilty to ashamed, and all that ricocheting around just left me feeling so overwhelmed that I admit I often found myself desperately trying to simply shut Noah and his problems out of my mind.

"So how did the Art Walk go?" I asked with a shaky voice, in a feeble attempt to change the subject.

Sharon kindly played along. "The Art Walk? Oh, it was good. More crowded than the one last month. We had good business that night."

As she went on about the pros and cons of running a business in the old part of town, I began to notice something happening across the street, behind Sharon's back. The city gardener at the museum was holding a huge iguana up by its tail. I could see its long green body squirming and writhing helplessly in one hand, as the gardener held a machete in the other. I kept waiting for the gardener to release the poor thing, but he just stood there. I tried not to look, and struggled to concentrate on what Sharon was saying. But suddenly I couldn't bear to watch this cruelty any longer, so I pushed back my chair, apologized to Sharon for the interruption, and ran, yelling, into the street. "Stop! Please!" Halfway across I watched as the gardener straightened his arm. That's when I noticed the red gash across the iguana's neck, so deep I could see the bone underneath. The gardener's eyes were moist. He shook his head sadly. I quickly looked away, as a million thoughts flooded my brain. *I should just walk away,* something was telling me, *back to Sharon and back to the comfort of Macaws. Don't get involved. If you look too closely, you'll have no choice. Once you really open your eyes, you open your heart. There's no turning away. You'll have to take responsibility for that poor animal. I don't want an iguana! I don't even like iguanas that much. What do iguanas even eat? Where do they sleep? Why am I even doing this?* But, as if my body had been taken over by some other, more benevolent being, instead I yelled as loudly as I could for Glen, who came and picked up the maimed lizard in his arms and marched it back over to Macaws. We placed it gently down on the bar and asked Cesar the bartender to call the vet. By the time he arrived the bar top was littered, thanks to everyone who was there that afternoon, with enough pesos to cover the emergency on-location surgery, right there between the bowl of limes and the pile of cock-tail napkins.

Later that night I called Noah, and made him a deal. Though he'd clearly be way more work than a crippled iguana could ever be, I opened the door for him to come down to my house on Carnaval Street.

HAVE I MENTIONED HOW MUCH I LOVE TO shop? I am so, so good at it. Just point me in the direction of a nice boutique or gallery or crafts fair, and I'll come out with my soul full, even if my hands are empty. And malls? They are just about my favorite places on earth. I used to fly from Kabul to Dubai just for the malls. I didn't even have to buy. Simply sitting anywhere among the Sephoras and Victoria's Secrets and Bath & Body Works and Sunglass Huts of the world, sipping a coffee, people-watching or reading a book, is to me what being on a yoga retreat is for other more disciplined, more flexible women. I relax. But in Mazatlán, shopping has its limits. No decent sheets, not one affordable lamp, and forget about those size-nine shoes. Apparently drag queens were the only ones wearing pumps that big down here. By now I was well versed in every item to be found in Centro, and was itching to move on.

So when Sharon suggested I join her on a road trip to Pátzcuaro in search of Catrinas, with a stop at the mall at Morelia, I had to hold myself back from kissing her on her pale pink lips. So what if I didn't even know what Catrinas were, and who cares if it was a ten-hour drive? I was in.

We left the following Thursday in my Mini, looking like a couple of shoplifters who had scored big-time, our clothes bulging with the cell phones we'd stashed in our bras, the wallets we'd hidden in our underwear, and water bottles we'd stuffed in our pants. We weren't about to take any chances. Some friends of Analisa's had just been carjacked the month before. The banditos took their purses, their jewelry, everything, leaving them stranded on the side of the road in the middle of the desert. The only thing they were left with was a warning: Walk away, hand in hand, and whatever you do, do not turn around.

So we were prepared, at least physically. It was an early departure from Mazatlán, which is always an interesting process. We had just braked for the first stoplight when a snot-nosed kid in cowboy boots flung himself onto the hood of the car. A splash of dirty gray water hit the windshield. "Go away!" Sharon yelled, as she lunged to turn on the wipers in an attempt to minimize the damage. The kid laughed, the light turned green, and he jumped off the hood, the early morning sun bouncing off his enormous silver belt buckle as he held out his hand for a tip. Sharon stepped on the gas, only to find herself trapped by the next stoplight, victim to the next window washer on the strip. "No!" I wagged my finger out the rolled-down window. No was no in Spanish, right? "No!" I yelled, even louder. We drove on to the next light with an even muddier windshield, and so it went, block after block, until we finally reached the highway barely able to see the road in front of our faces. But we were on our way.

You can get to know someone pretty well over ten hours inside a locked vehicle. Sharon and I talked about everything, probably divulging more than we would have had we not been relying on the fast-paced chatter to help keep our nerves from falling prey to the dangers of the Mexican roads. At least we were in the Mini, which I figured was too small to appeal to banditos. Really, how many of them, *and* their drugs, *and* their guns, could fit inside one of these things? There was no way they'd get my car up those steep mountain roads, and it was too small to run a roadblock. Not like my friend Carolina's SUV, which was used in ten murders before the police returned it to her, with advice to sell.

But some of the personal horror stories we shared that day made the drive down Highway 15 look like a game of Candy Land. The two of us were one-upping each other like a couple of bragging kids in the schoolyard. And I have to admit, even though I was pretty confident I could easily top Sharon when push came to shove, she did have quite a story. I had just finished my own tale about being trapped in an elevator in Pakistan with a lecherous policeman when she took over.

"Well, did I ever tell you about my creepy first husband?" Sharon settled into the passenger seat with a can of Pringles. It was my turn to drive.

"Um, no." I figured this one had to be good for at least fifty miles.

"Yep. I was only eighteen when I moved in with him. Wouldn't allow me to work, would barely allow me to even leave the house. We didn't even have a phone."

"Are you friggin' kidding me?" I had dealt with a couple of control freaks myself, but I doubted I ever could have survived that kind of situation. I would like to think I would have walked right out, but then again, I was well aware of just how complicated things can sometimes be.

"Nope. He was crazy jealous of everyone, my family, my friends, even strangers on the street. I always had to wear my shirts buttoned up to the top, and forget about a bathing suit. He bought all my clothes. I never went shopping."

"Why the hell did you marry him in the first place?"

Sharon laughed. "*You* are asking me that question? Miss 'I Do, I Do, I Do'?"

"Okay, okay. But seriously, you so don't seem like the type to—"

"Deb, I was so insecure back then that it didn't

even occur to me that the situation wasn't normal. And you know what finally woke me up? He actually accused me of incest. Incest! Can you imagine? One afternoon he walked in on me and my brother watching TV from the couch, and just lost it."

"Jeez, what a wack job!"

"Uh-huh. I am just so grateful I met Glen."

"So you just met Glen and that was that?"

Sharon lifted her bare feet to the dashboard. "Oh, it was a lot more complicated than that."

Thank God for those complications. They managed to keep me awake and entertained for the rest of my shift, all the way to Guadalajara. Sharon hadn't managed to fully extract herself from her marriage until two long years after that afternoon with her brother, and it had been her creepy husband's own mother who introduced her to Glen, who wooed her with flowers and walks in the park, something she had never, ever before experienced with a man. The relationship did have its fits and starts. But one night, after a long separation, Sharon walked into the bar where Glen was playing. The music stopped. Glen handed over his drumsticks to a friend and took Sharon in his arms. They danced, and lived happily ever after. Well, at least from my outsider's point of view happily ever after, but I was pretty sure theirs was a good marriage. They were a real team when it came to their commitment to Casa de

Leyendas and Macaws, and I loved the way Sharon's blue eyes sparkled when Glen made her laugh. I wondered if I'd ever find that in my life.

Sharon was already familiar with some of my stories, but she didn't really know all that much about Noah or Zach, at least not before this trip. But by the time we switched places again, half-way to Morelia, she was well up to speed.

"Wow. You've got quite a dilemma, Deb," she said with a sigh.

"Tell me about it."

"You know, there are times when I wish I had had a kid, but then again . . ."

"Yeah, they can break your heart. And even worse, they'll give you gray hair while they're at it."

Sharon laughed.

"So why didn't you guys ever have kids?" I asked, a little worried that I might be crossing the line with the question. But so far nothing had seemed off-limits in this conversation.

"Just didn't happen for us."

"Yeah, that happens," I said, imagining what a good-looking kid Sharon would have had.

"You know, Deb, I was pregnant once."

For once I stayed silent, giving Sharon the space to continue, or not.

She dug under her seat for the Pringles can. "Actually, I can't believe I'm telling you this. It's a story I haven't shared with anyone down here."

She paused and looked out the window for a minute. "It's so strange. You're probably not going to believe it."

"So try me."

Sharon hesitated, then began. "You know, when Glen and I moved down to Mazatlán, it wasn't the first time I'd been there. Forty-five years ago, my mom brought me down to Mazatlán for an abortion."

"But you must have been just a kid!"

"I was. And abortion was illegal in the States back then. I remember coming through town in a taxi in the middle of the night. The Golden Zone didn't even exist yet. I think the Playa Mazatlán was probably the only hotel out that way at that time. We came to Centro. And I know the doctor's house was somewhere in our neighborhood, right around Casa de Leyendas."

"Are you kidding me?"

"I told you it was a strange story. It was a beautiful home. I can still remember the inside. If I walked into it this day, I would know it right away."

"I can't believe that happened right there."

"I'm sure it was within walking distance of Macaws. I have a feeling it's one of those little houses right around the corner from us."

"Oh, Sharon, I'm so sorry." It killed me to envision a frightened, teenage Sharon being forced into such an ordeal.

She shrugged her shoulders. "I survived. But isn't it an amazing coincidence?"

How lonely she must have felt, I thought, in a totally foreign place, vulnerable, in the hands of a stranger. I doubted I'd ever be able to return to the scene of that sort of horror. To me, the odds of Sharon choosing to live right there, out of the blue, seemed pretty slim. Coincidence, or not? What is it that really drives us to make the decisions we do? I wondered, and not for the first time.

IT WAS JUST AFTER SHARON TOOK OVER THE wheel again that things started to get a little dicey. First she insisted on giving what little food we had left in the car to a skinny dog at the gas station. Granted, it was just a bag of Cheetos, but still. At least she left me with a box of Red Hots, and she respected the line I drew when it came to our water supply. Then, before we had even traveled a mile, we were pulled over by two guys in military uniform. I grabbed my bra, hoping to God these men were the real deal. Sharon pulled over and rolled down her window.

"Dónde está la hierba?" growled the taller one.

Sharon looked at me. I shrugged my shoulders. She turned back to the officer.

"Dónde está la hierba?" he repeated.

"Lo siento, mi español es muy malo. Por favor, habla despacio." Sorry, my Spanish is very bad, please speak slowly. Sharon seemed to have that line down.

"Dónde está la hierba?" he said again, this time very slowly.

"Deb, I know that word. I use that word. I think it's the word I use to tell Pedro to pull the weeds. Why would he be telling me to pull the weeds?"

I leaned over Sharon's lap and yelled out her window. "We have no fruit!"

"Fruit? I don't think it means fruit, Deb."

"I know. But it has worked for me before. *No fruit!*"

The officer waved us through with a big sigh.

"Grass! I just remembered. It does mean weed, Deb. They're looking for drugs. Ha!"

"Well, that doesn't seem like the smartest way to find them. *Oh, the pot? Here it is, Officer. Is this what you're looking for?* Sheesh."

The next incident was even more confusing. Now it was a pair of cops pulling us over. This time I rolled down my window. We seriously had no idea what they were saying, but I did think I heard the word for coffee somewhere. I turned from the one cop to his partner, who simply nodded his head in agreement.

"Café?" I asked, thinking that perhaps I had been hearing things.

The officer nodded yes. Coffee? I thought. Why would they want coffee, and why on earth would they think I'd be traveling with an extra cup? My eyes went to the cup holder, where I spied a can of Red Bull. I gamely offered it through the open window. The cop rolled his eyes, and once again we were waved through. It wasn't until we returned that Cesar, the bartender at Macaws, explained. "The police asked you for coffee?"

"Yes! Wasn't that weird?" Sharon asked. "We offered them Red Bull, but I guess they really wanted that coffee."

Cesar laughed. "No, it's not that. When a cop says can you give me a little something for coffee, it's their polite way of asking for some money. You know, a bribe."

We were very close to making it to Pátzcuaro when, unfortunately, we took a wrong turn. I was driving again and had put Sharon in charge of the GPS.

"Just enter Pátzcuaro," I told her, GPS pro that I was.

"P-A-T . . . oh shit. I pressed the wrong button." Sharon dug in her purse, searching for her glasses.

"Hit the back button."

"P-A . . ."

"No! Just hit it once. Don't start all the way over."

"Okay! Relax! A-R-O. Now it says country."

"So spell it." I could feel my heart rate increasing with every wrong mile we drove. The roads were becoming narrower and windier and bumpier by the minute. "What does it say? Can we get there this way?"

"It keeps coming up with Canada."

"Canada? Just type in country."

"I am! And I'm telling you, it keeps saying Canada."

Sharon was punching the glass GPS screen so hard I thought it was going to shatter.

"It's a *touch* screen, Sharon! Stop hitting it."

"Stop yelling at me!"

"I'm not yelling!" I yelled. "You're getting us more and more lost by the minute."

"Calm down, Deb. You're stressing me out."

"I'm stressing *you* out? You're stressing *me* out!" I pulled over onto a narrow turnout, leaving barely enough room for a donkey to pass. The steep hillside below was littered with tires and rusted car parts. "I can't drive like this!" I yelled, turning to look Sharon in the face.

Sharon crossed her arms. "Well, I can't ride like this."

"Really? Really, Sharon? Is this the way this weekend's gonna go?"

"Yeah, I guess it is!"

"Really? Well, then, I'm going home." I started to unlock the door.

"Ha! Go ahead. Let me just type in country and see if it will help you get there. C . . ."

"Sharon, Mexico starts with an M."

As our laughter rocked my little car, I realized,

with delight, that we'd had our first fight. Sharon and I were now officially best friends.

THE MINUTE WE PULLED INTO THE TOWN OF Pátzcuaro, my head began to whirl. At first I chalked up my wooziness to the long drive or the altitude or my empty stomach, or maybe even the sensory overload from the little shops lining the streets, windows filled with handwoven sweaters and blankets and hats and hand-carved furniture and so much folk art I couldn't even digest it all. But I had a feeling that this might be something different.

"Wow," was all I could manage when we first walked through the doorway of the B&B. Casa Encantada was as enchanted as its name implied. It felt as though we had entered a special secret world. The sun-dappled courtyard was lush with exotic flowers and plants, calmed by the sound of water cascading down the tiered fountain with a refreshing splash. On our left, a covered dining area was lined with heavy wooden tables and chairs, every inch of wall space crammed with tapestries and candelabras and pots and plates from all over the world. Cynthia, one of the owners, suddenly burst out from behind the office door, two little Yorkies following closely at the heels of her black boots. "Greetings! Long drive, eh?" With her spiky silver-blond hair, twinkly eyes, and tiny, athletic build, Cynthia reminded me of some sort of badass sprite. There was something about her that seemed to immediately draw me to her, though for the life of me I couldn't explain what it was.

Sharon and I were shown to our rooms, which were just as impressive as the courtyard: huge arched fireplaces built from stone, beamed ceilings so high a giant wouldn't have to stoop, and wide beds so inviting that I was tempted to snuggle right in. Instead, I unpacked a little and joined Sharon and Cynthia on the patio for a glass of wine.

"It's so beautiful here it's giving me goose bumps." Indeed, the hair on my arms was standing straight up.

Cynthia nodded. "This house is truly magical, as is all of Pátzcuaro."

"You must really love it here," Sharon said, craning her neck to take note of the details.

Cynthia smiled. "In the old days they said that people like us, those who can feel the power of this town, have drunk from the lake. Which meant that somehow we've been bewitched, and can't leave. Sort of like drinking the Kool-Aid, eh?"

"Who would ever want to leave a place like this?" I asked.

"Exactly." Cynthia ran her hand across the top of her cropped head.

"Just how old is this house, anyway?"

"Old. The oldest stone that we excavated was

marked from 1784. You can see it over in the back patio. And that's considered young in comparison to the other buildings on the plaza. Before that, the land was used as an orchard for the Sisters of Catherine of Siena."

"And how long have you had it?"

"I convinced my ex to turn it into a bed-and-breakfast about ten years ago."

"And you guys still run it together?" Sharon asked, no doubt trying to imagine how she and Glen would handle that sort of situation themselves.

"We do."

"Wow. He must be a lot more civilized than any of my husbands were," I said.

Cynthia laughed. "She owned the house for ten years before we met. I've always operated the business, and she spends the bulk of her time doing her art."

"It must have been a ton of work renovating this place," Sharon said.

"Uh-huh. It was a trip. Funny story. When we first started doing work on the house, people would always be asking us if we'd found the gold yet."

"Gold?" I asked, imagining some sparkly, overflowing treasure chest.

"Yep. Back when the house was built, there were no banks, and people buried their money in the ground or hid it in the walls. So these days, whenever a worker doesn't show up for a job, or if construction is halted for a day, people say they must have found the gold. God forbid you're a contractor who takes a sick day, eh?"

"If these walls could talk, right?" I asked, draining my glass.

"Oh yeah," answered Cynthia. "There's a lot more going on than meets the eye around here. Trust me. You'll see. You'll feel it."

"I think I might know what you're saying, but right now I mostly feel hungry." We hadn't had a proper meal since we left Mazatlán.

"You two must be famished!" Cynthia stood and whistled for her dogs. "Señorita! Max!" She took our empty glasses from the table. "Hey, I need to run some errands around town. If you head out with me I can point you in the right direction for a bite."

Later, as Sharon and I wandered around working off our sopa tarasca and carnitas, I couldn't help but think about Cynthia and what she had said about Pátzcuaro. Walking up and down the cobblestone hills, past the low red and white adobe buildings stretching all the way down to the lake, the bizarre sensations I had experienced earlier in the day came back with a vengeance. Strolling through the Plaza Grande, I felt the hair on the back of my neck stand up. Passing under the arched doorway of the basilica made my face flush with heat. I couldn't remember reacting to anything this way in a long time, if ever. This was a Debbie with a whole other something going on.

Now, I am well aware that I possess a decent sense of intuition. I've always been able to get an instant read on places and people, though it seems I'm much more attuned when emotions, or marriages, aren't at stake. And I used to be much better at it before I got to Afghanistan, where life was so chaotic that I sort of began to lose touch. In California I was just too broken inside to tap into anything. But here, in Pátzcuaro, I could feel a similar, yet broader, type of power flooding back, stronger than ever. I didn't know how to explain it. It was as though I were Alice in Wonderland, right after she went through the looking glass. The only way I can describe it is that I could feel a force, not an evil one or a dark one, but one that was good and full of light, a light that was pulling me in and filling me up with an energy so pure that I couldn't drink in enough of it. And it was there for me whether I wanted it or not.

I was reluctant to mention any of this to Sharon. She seemed like such a practical, no-nonsense person in so many ways, and here I was going all Shirley MacLaine on her. But I couldn't help myself. There was just too much going on inside not to acknowledge it out loud. And when I did, Sharon simply looked at me, lowered her lids, and nodded, a knowing smile crossing her face like a ray of warm sunshine.

THE NEXT MORNING, AFTER AN INTENSELY fitful night, I was interrupted mid-bite in the dining room by a ponytailed man with a guidebook tucked under his arm.

"Encounter any ghosts last night?" he asked, as he slid his chair in between Sharon and me. I hate ponytails on men. And nothing was about to keep me from those fluffy, cheesy egg enchiladas.

"Ghosts?" Sharon's eyes widened as she pushed her bangs aside. I shot her a look.

"Stop scaring my friends," chimed in Cynthia, from the kitchen. But as soon as we were done eating, she graciously offered to satisfy Sharon's curiosity with a tour.

"In this room, there is an Indian chief, and also a woman, Pluma Blanca, who was a cook for the nuns who used to live in the house," she told us as she unlocked one of the heavy wood doors circling the courtyard. "They're happy spirits. We let them stay."

"How do you know? You've talked to them?" I obviously needed more coffee.

"What's the matter, Deb? You don't believe in ghosts?"

I had to laugh. "I don't know. In Afghanistan, they blamed everything on the jinns."

"Afghanistan?" Cynthia raised her eyebrows and lowered her chin.

"Yeah. I lived there for a while. A few years."

"Really?"

"Yes, really. So, anyway, jinns are supposed to be sort of like genies. Over there, they say that the jinns were responsible for winning wars in the old days. They'd make the enemy's eyes see way more advancing warriors than were actually there, so that they'd retreat in fear of being outnumbered."

"Smart cookies," Cynthia said.

"And my girls, my students over there, they'd point to the jinns whenever a glass would break or a door would slam. Everything I thought was the wind, they thought was a jinn."

"Yours sounds like a story I want to hear, girl."

"Oh, Deb's got a story, all right," Sharon piped in.

"Well, we don't do jinns here in Mexico, but we do have what they call duendes, sort of like gnomes. I've never personally seen one. We did have a curandera come visit."

"A what?"

"Curandera. A spirit cleanser. They clean the spirits from your house."

"They do that?" Though so far I had only felt good vibes from my house on Carnaval Street, I wondered if these people might be able to apply their skills to other parts of a person's life.

"They do. The curandera actually went into trances while she was here doing the cleansing, the limpia. She's the one who told us the spirits were happy. And she isn't the only one who has seen them. Some of our guests have encountered Pluma Blanca, always in a white nightgown, always calm. Men sometimes think it's their wife getting up in the middle of the night, but then they turn over and see their wife still in bed."

Again I could feel those goose bumps start to crawl up my arms. What was up with that?

"We plant roses for her," Cynthia continued. "The curandera told us she'd like that. And then there's the little boy, who we think arrived hurt and hungry, and was taken in by the nuns. We asked the curandera what would make him happy, and since he had been hungry, he wanted us to feed people. We started holding fund-raising dinners for charity, to please his spirit wishes."

I must have shuddered out loud.

"What's the matter Deb? Am I creeping you out?"

"I'm good!"

"I warned you." Cynthia laughed. "Strange things can happen, do happen, here in Pátzcuaro."

CATRINA SHOPPING WAS ON SHARON'S AGENDA for that day. Her plan was to create a little boutique inside Casa de Leyendas, to take advantage of all the hoopla surrounding the Day of the Dead. Sharon, like everyone else with a business in Mazatlán, was searching for backup plans, as the tourist economy had barely started to recover from a swine flu outbreak when the sensation-hungry press turned its attention to the violence. Some claimed it was only a matter of time before the cruise ships took note, which would be a disaster for local businesses. So Sharon was stocking up.

To me, the Catrina figures I first came across in Pátzcuaro seemed a little morbid. Skeletons all dressed up with nowhere to go. Skeleton dogs, skeleton cats, doctors and dentists and brides and grooms made of bones. We even saw a ceramic school bus filled with little skeleton children. But when we took off in a rattletrap truck with a hundred-year-old guide who never stopped talking, but who knew exactly where to look, the whole idea started to grow on me. Our first stop was in front of a trio of roadside shacks, so dark inside that I doubted there was even a lick of electricity. Once my eyes adjusted, I began to see that the Catrinas were actually quite beautiful. The only problem was that they had no heads. "Where are their heads?" I asked as the old shopkeeper tried to fit a tiny skull onto a giant Catrina torso.

"Dónde están las cabezas?" our guide translated. Saturday, was the answer. The Catrinas would have their heads by Saturday. This being Mexico, we weren't about to bank on which Saturday that might be, so we decided to move on to the next stop.

Now I had to have a Catrina. When I thought

about it, what was so creepy about bones anyway? We all had them inside us, albeit some buried under more padding than others. These dead women looked so poised, so joyful, so alive. As our guide explained in a long-winded speech, I began to understand the story behind the Catrinas.

It was the artist José Guadalupe Posada who they say popularized the Catrina figure, with his etchings of high-society women and their desire to glom on to everything European. Back then, in the early 1900s, the Catrina was a symbol of revolution, a jab at the inner emptiness of the upper class. But in Mexico, images of women and death go way back to Aztec mythology, to Mictecacihuatl. Try saying that one out loud. Anyway, she was Queen of the Underworld, and her job was to watch over the bones of the dead. It wasn't until after Christian beliefs got mixed up with Aztec traditions that Catrinas became symbols of the Day of the Dead, an expression of the Mexican willingness to laugh at death, and a reminder that everyone is equal, in the end.

In the little town of Capula, we hit pay dirt, a Catrina co-op, offering thousands of Catrinas from hundreds of artists. At first glance, they all looked alike to me, with their delicate bony fingers and gaping grins. But up close I could see that no two Catrinas were the same. They wore their wide-brimmed plumed hats, earrings, strings of pearls, aprons, and ruffles with the attitude of a woman strutting her one-of-a-kind designer outfit at an opening-night gala. Each parasol, every bright bouquet, every little purse, each hand-crafted appliqué on every lavish gown had its own unique design. Even the poses they struck and the expressions on their skinless faces seemed to all be different. I shopped for hours.

The first Catrina I chose was dressed all in black, with one bony leg suggestively poking out from a slit that ran from heel to hip, her ribs exposed down to her waist by a wide, pink-edged neckline. And she had wings. Black wings. She seemed funny and naughty, sort of like the way old friends who knew me well saw me way back when.

The next one had an elegance about her that reminded me of my mom, an elegance that I always strived for yet never seemed to be able to achieve. Her strapless yellow gown cascaded down her skinny frame as if it were made from silk instead of clay. The matching hat perched atop a head held high by her long, graceful neck, like an ornate bloom on a reedy stem. She was perfect. No, I was more the naughty black angel type. But I added this one to my purchases anyway. One can dream, right?

The gun-toting Catrina spoke to me in a faint voice from a distant past. With two ammo belts crisscrossing her puffed-out skeletal chest, she was the rough-and-tumble girl with traces of her parents' Arkansas blood pumping through her veins. She was the tough one who took no nonsense patrolling the prison yard, who survived living with a hot-tempered wannabe warlord, who will defend anyone, and who isn't scared of anything.

Masked Catrina was the one who was afraid to let anybody see who she really was. Strong and confident on the outside, but inside not so much. Faking it until she was making it, as my mom always advised. Her sequined eye mask hung around her vertebrae at the ready, and though her black boa and leg garter suggested a masquerade party, I chose instead to stick with my own interpretation.

I fell in love with the Frida Catrina the moment I spotted her. Adorned with the long dark braids and the birds and flowers I recognized from some of Kahlo's self-portraits, this one's face was unmistakable in its determination to appear strong no matter how deep the hurt. I knew that face.

My final purchase was the butterfly Catrina. Not only was her deep blue gown sprinkled with a handful of the dainty orange and silver creatures, but she was, herself, a butterfly, with strong, broad wings fanning out from behind her back and two sparkly antennae sprouting from the top of her cranium. Her cocoon long gone, she was a Catrina who had proudly morphed into a beautiful being, the one who had always been there deep inside, just waiting for her chance to shine.

IT WAS THE NEXT DAY THAT EVERYTHING
came crashing down on me with a thud so loud
you could have heard it all the way back in Kabul.
We were in the mall in Morelia. I was trying on
sunglasses at a kiosk, and when I turned around,
Sharon was gone. Vanished. She had simply
disappeared. The spot where she had been standing
just one minute before was now an empty hole. I
took off the glasses and scanned the area on all
sides of the kiosk. No Sharon in sight. I dug out
my phone and I dialed her cell. No answer. It
didn't even ring. She must have wandered into
one of the stores, I thought. I also thought about
what my mom had always told me: If you ever
get lost, just stay where you are, and I will find
you. So I stayed. But Sharon didn't find me. I sat
down on a bench and tried her phone again, only
to get that message you get when someone is out
of range or their phone has been turned off. I
could feel my breath quickening. Keeping one eye
on the area where I had last seen Sharon, I stepped
into the doorway of the Liverpool department

225

store to see if I could spot her inside. No dice. I wandered in a little farther, trying to convince myself that I'd sooner or later run into her over the sales racks or at the cosmetics counter. But my brain just wouldn't let me go there.

A normal person would use logic, as in *she's probably in the restroom,* or *she went to get a soda.* But no, not me. My mind immediately went to me being stranded in a strange town where I didn't know my way around and where I didn't speak the language and where I didn't know a soul. No matter that I was the one with the car keys and the GPS. In my mind, I was stranded. And Sharon? Where was she? Was she having an asthma attack somewhere? Kidnapped, held against her will at the back of the Mac store with a black bag over her head? Bound and gagged in a storage closet behind the escalators, her purse (with cell phone) on its way to Mexico City? Images from every terrible documentary I'd seen about human trafficking flashed through my brain. A terror had come flooding over me, as if I had witnessed the bloodiest of bloody sights right before my eyes. I was frozen, shaking, gasping for air, and sobbing like a five-year-old. I was completely, totally, utterly out of control, way beyond caring who was witnessing the spectacle of my breakdown or what they thought. Until, through my tears, I saw Sharon approaching with a cup of steaming coffee in her hand.

"Oh my God, Debbie! What happened? Are you okay?" Sharon quickly put the coffee down on a bench and rushed to my side.

"I have to go home. We need to go. Now." My heart was racing.

"But what happened?"

I just shook my head. How could I explain?

"Just tell me if you're hurt. Did someone die? Did you get a call or something?"

I willed myself to stop the tears, to no avail. For a moment I was tempted to make something up, some story about twisting my ankle or losing my wallet, anything to make it sound as if I had a real reason to be shaking and sobbing, anything to make it sound as if I weren't crazy. I was mortified that this had happened in front of Sharon. I felt blindsided, never having dreamt that something as major as my breakdown in Yosemite would ever happen again. Especially in a mall!

But here is the most amazing thing. Sometimes, when you are very, very lucky, life steps up with exactly what you need, precisely when you need it. Or, as Cynthia put it later that day in Pátzcuaro, my angels were guiding me. When we returned to the B&B that evening, Sharon headed toward the kitchen, where Cynthia was waiting, and I retreated swiftly to my room. As I fumbled for the key I could overhear them talking.

"Did you guys have fun?" Cynthia asked eagerly.

"Well . . . sort of. Deb had kind of a rough day."

"Really? What happened?"

"I'm not really sure. She seemed to have some kind of a meltdown. Something freaked her out, and I have no idea what it was." Sharon lowered her voice. After that, all I could make out were a few words here and there, but I could definitely tell they were still talking about me.

The next thing I knew, Cynthia was knocking on my door. "Want to join me for a cup of tea?" Her eyes locked onto mine in a way that told me I couldn't, or shouldn't, say no. Behind her I could see Sharon tiptoeing to her room, a much-needed glass of wine in her hand.

Cynthia gently led me upstairs to the patio outside her own room, into an overstuffed armchair that swallowed me up in its soft, warm embrace.

"Relax. Breathe. I'll be right back." As Cynthia headed back down to get the tea, I forced myself to close my eyes and willed my muscles to soften. By the time she returned I was sort of in a half daze.

"Sharon told me you had a strange incident today," she said as she handed me my cup. "I just want you to know that I think I have an idea of what you're going through."

"Really? You do? Because I sure don't."

"Ya know, Deb, you and I aren't as different as you might think we are."

"In what way do you mean?"

"I suspect we've *both* been through a lot in our lives." Cynthia patted her lap, the two dogs leaping at the invitation.

"That's for sure; at least I know it is in my case. But I honestly have no idea what that has to do with me falling apart in a mall."

Cynthia ripped open a bag of chips. "Do you know what I did, Deb, before I moved down here from Canada?"

I shook my head.

"I was a licensed clinical psychologist."

Here we go again, I thought. Though I was remarkably comfortable in Cynthia's presence, I had to admit that my first reaction was not a great one. No, sir, no more glowworms for me. The visit to that overpriced charlatan in Napa certainly hadn't been my first encounter with a shrink, but I was pretty determined for it to be my last. But then again, Cynthia seemed so different. Maybe she *was* different. When I thought about it, it was usually when I actively sought out help that things seemed to fizzle or backfire. But help that had fallen into my lap often seemed to be something of a different sort. Indian Larry was a chance encounter, and who knows what good fortune could be chalked up to the little santo around my neck, now joined by a little silver Hand of Fatima, just for good measure. Maybe there was a reason that I just happened to tag along with

Sharon for this trip, a reason that I freaked out in the mall, and a reason that I was now finding myself face-to-face with this little powerhouse of a woman who could somehow so effortlessly put me at ease. I just wished whoever or whatever was pulling the cosmic strings would do me the courtesy of letting me in on the plans. These surprises were wearing me out.

"My specialty was trauma," Cynthia continued.

Bingo. I could almost hear the bells go off.

"Yeah, weird, eh? Has anybody ever talked to you about trauma?"

"Sort of," I answered tentatively. "I was told that I might have PTSD. But I'm still not sure if that's true or not. And even if I did have it, I thought it was gone by now. I thought I was pretty much over it."

Cynthia took off her glasses and rubbed her eyes. "If only it were that easy. It's not. Trauma is something that's often hard to pinpoint and acknowledge, and even then it takes a whole lot of work and a whole lot of time to overcome."

"But I sat!"

"Huh? What are you talking about? You sat? How about if you back up just a little?"

So I did. And once I started, everything just came pouring out, as if someone had opened the faucet full force. Cynthia literally seemed to be drawing the words out of my soul and into the warm night air that filled the space between us.

When I finally stopped talking, Cynthia took a deep breath. "Wow. You *do* have some story, girlfriend."

"But I don't get it. Why now? Why the mall? I think I'm going crazy."

"You're not crazy." Cynthia reached over and gave my hand a squeeze. "You know, Deb, I quit the therapist racket a long time ago, but if you want my opinion, I'll give it to you."

"Please. Be my guest."

"Okay. But remember, you asked for it." Cynthia tossed a chip into her mouth, chewed, and swallowed. "First of all, it wasn't the mall. It was the frame of mind you were in before you went to the mall."

"But I was so jazzed to be there!"

"I'm sure you were jazzed. And I'm sure you were also relaxed. Panic attacks happen when you're gearing down. People who have experienced trauma tend to stay on alert. But you let your hair down, you let your guard down. You felt safe. Then something happened."

"But nothing happened! That's what I'm telling you."

"Something did happen, to your body. You were startled by Sharon's absence, and it triggered an adrenal reaction. It's like a rush, like a drug. Your body is acting as though you've put yourself into what we call unreasonable risk."

"But I'm really good in risky situations! I swear!"

231

"I have no doubt about that. You seem like a tough cookie. But that's when you're on alert. You're ready, you're pumped, you can handle it." I sank back in my chair with a sigh.

"I know. This is heavy-duty stuff." Cynthia poured us both more tea.

"You're telling me. But how does not being able to find Sharon have anything to do with anything?"

"Well, think about other times you've had panic attacks. What were the situations?"

"They were all kind of different. But a lot of times they seemed to have something to do with getting lost. I have this huge fear of being stranded. I used to force myself to drive in Afghanistan, but I was so afraid of being lost and alone. Being lost over there means you could be killed or kidnapped. You were warned every day against doing normal things like walking or driving. But I used to do those things all the time, just to feel like my so-not-normal life was just a little bit normal."

"And how were you about that before you went to Afghanistan?"

"I know I had some issues, as a child, about being lost, but what kid doesn't? I was always that kid at the supermarket courtesy desk, waiting for my mother to be summoned by the lady on the PA system. I do remember, I think I was around four years old, how I used to fall asleep calling out to my mom, over and over, just to make sure she was there. Being an only child, I had this huge fear of something happening to my parents, of being left all alone." Cynthia nodded and waited for me to continue. "But it seems like any fears I had going into Afghanistan became even scarier during my time there. I'm just now beginning to realize I was probably sort of a mess before I even went to Kabul, and came out of there even more of a mess. I felt like I had been chewed up and spit out. And by the time I reached California I didn't even know how much of a mess I really was!"

Cynthia shooed the dogs off her lap and leaned forward. "You know, Deb, it sounds like Afghanistan probably wasn't your first offender."

"Well, then, who was?"

Cynthia shrugged her shoulders. "I'm not a psychic."

"I know, I know. It's just that it wasn't like I was abused by my parents or anything."

"Honestly, Deb? I have no idea what your relationship with your parents was or wasn't. But many of us have had times in our lives when we've felt trapped or manipulated, either emotionally or physically." A sudden shift in Cynthia's eyes told me she knew, firsthand, what she was talking about. "And I'm sure that you, like me, have witnessed and experienced things that have made you realize that there are humans out there who are not good people, who don't believe in the 'do unto others' system. We'd like to believe everyone operates that way, but they don't."

"That's for sure."

"You must have seen a lot of ugly stuff go down in Afghanistan. And in a trapped situation," she went on, "it's not always you who's the one being assaulted. Sometimes it's just the act of witnessing an offense that causes the most pain, that causes a spiritual wounding. A person who has been a witness to any kind of an assault gains a deep awareness of what human beings are capable of doing to one another. To the outside world it looks as though they came away unscathed. But that's far from the truth." Cynthia paused, and propped the earpiece of her glasses on the edge of her lip.

My head was starting to fill up with so many thoughts and questions and hazy memories that it felt like it might explode. Half of me wanted Cynthia to stop, but the other half was excited by all these new ideas.

"You know," I said in a quiet voice, "I've tried all my life to hide my issues from other people. Everyone always thinks *Debbie's just fine, Debbie's so strong*. Nobody knows that sometimes I'm afraid. Nobody knows how much I hate elevators, how I have to take Xanax just to step on a plane, how I have panic attacks that come from nowhere. No one would have a clue."

Cynthia had given me so much to think about. She seemed to have my number, even if she, or I, wasn't entirely aware of all the details. "So now what do I do?" I asked her. "Never go shopping again? I don't think I could bear that."

Cynthia smiled. "Just us talking is a good thing. But if you want, I can give you some tools that might help you next time you feel this kind of thing happening."

Cynthia's words were music to my ears. I loved tools. Like my mother and her whole family, I could fix anything and everything with the proper tool. I carried a deluxe Swiss Army knife in my purse at all times, just in case.

"Here's the phrase I want you to remember: *That was then, and this is now.*"

"That was then, and this is now," I repeated, feeling like a Girl Scout taking the oath.

"So, like today. You think Sharon has vanished. But this is the Morelia mall, and chances are she's getting some coffee."

I nodded.

"You have to think to yourself, 'I assume the worst-case scenario because I'm aware of what the worst-case scenario can be. But that was then. And this is now. And now the chances are that, for instance, Sharon has just gone to the restroom. Or Sharon is getting a cup of coffee.' You can't just rely on other people to calm you down. Someone else telling you it's going to be all right will never work. The words, and thoughts, have to come from within. Do you think you can do that?"

"I can try. I'll try anything not to feel like such a crazy person ever again."

"Stop it. You're not crazy. But I'm not saying it's not going to happen again. Though at least now you have some tools to work with, a way to start coping with the PTSD."

"I hate that label."

"I understand. And honestly? Trauma has become sort of an overused term these days. But it is good to have a name for it, because it's hard for people to explain an injury that's invisible. And I suspect that it may not be the classic war-zone syndrome, the one that legitimized the diagnosis for the rest of the world, that you're suffering from. What happened over in Afghanistan did leave you raw and exposed, and for certain paved the way for a whole host of issues to come back and bite you in the ass, hard."

"I guess I can buy that. But I still can't believe what happened here today. And I'm still blown away that I met you. It's all so weird."

"Not so weird. It's all a part of the magic in this area. It draws that energy out of you. The trauma will eventually stop controlling you, just maybe not as quickly as you'd like." Cynthia stood and held out her hands to pull me to my feet. "Sleep well, my friend." She hugged me with a strength a girl her size had no business having. "Meet me downstairs at breakfast. I have something I want to show you."

I headed wearily down to my room. Appreciative as I was for all Cynthia was trying to do for me, it was a lot to digest, and I still really wasn't sure what I believed. But I couldn't get the thought out of my head that meeting Cynthia was somehow meant to be. And maybe, I was beginning to think, moving to Mexico was meant to be. Despite my implosion at the mall, there was no denying that I was feeling a little more like the old Deb, in the good way, every day. Mexico seemed to be giving me something I desperately needed. I was genuinely grateful, and looking forward to the day when I could figure out how to give back something in return.

"GOOD MORNING, MARY SUNSHINE," CHIRPED Cynthia the next morning as a cup of steaming hot coffee seemed to magically appear in her outstretched hand. "Sleep well?"

"Arumph," I mumbled, my tongue seeming to have stayed behind in that nice cushy bed.

"Take a slug and follow me," she ordered. I dragged behind as Cynthia marched toward the far back wall of the courtyard. "I wanted to make sure you saw something before you went home."

"It's a wall, Cynthia. And I'm gonna need some more coffee."

"Suck it up. You'll get your coffee in a sec. And I'll have you know it's not just a wall."

"Okay," I said, anxious for that refill.

"People often tell us they get odd sensations here at Casa Encantada, but especially in this spot. They say it's the same feeling they get when they're out visiting the pyramids around here."

"Huh. Interesting."

"It is interesting. The pyramids often seem to leave people in a state of high energy, an other-worldliness. It's all positive—not scary, just different."

"That's kind of cool," I had to admit, remembering how my skin tingled that first night, when Sharon and I were walking around town.

"It is cool. We wonder if there might have been a pyramid at one time on top of the hill behind us, where the basilica is now. It's all speculation, but from what's been excavated it's clear that this is not a 'natural' hill."

I have to say that when I reached out to touch the orange surface, I did feel more than just the bumpiness of the adobe against my palm. It was sort of like a little jolt, as if I had brushed up against an electrified fence or had been jolted by one of those dog zappers. But who knows, I thought. The power of suggestion can be a potent thing.

Cynthia must have read the doubt on my face. "We had a guest once, a guy who worked for

NASA. Even he kept telling me he felt funny every time he approached the back of the house. A scientist! He also explained to me about the vortex. You've heard about the vortex, eh?"

I shook my head.

"They say Pátzcuaro is a vortex. Some say there's an energy flow that interacts with your inner self, that facilitates prayer, meditation, and healing. Most places in the world have a certain amount of vibration, but here it's outrageously intense. The NASA guy told me he wished he had brought his equipment with him, to show us. He said that butterflies and birds feel the natural vibration; they're drawn to this spot, almost pulled into it."

I didn't say that I did sort of feel the same way, personally, about Mexico in general. "So why is that?"

"It's the pyramids. You know about the power of pyramids, eh?"

I shrugged my shoulders, making a note to myself to read up on that later. Cynthia continued. "A lot of people believe that the purpose of building the pyramids was to harness the cosmic energies. Think about it. If the interiors of the pyramids could be fresh and energized, the mummies would be well preserved. *Pyra* means fire, so think pyramid, fire in the middle. The pyramids harness the fire, or energy, and preserve it within. There have been tons of experiments showing how pyramids can keep food fresh longer, make razor blades sharper, even bring sick plants back to life. So of course it makes sense, as so many have claimed, that exposure to pyramid vibrations can alter your mental, physical, and emotional states. It's all about the aura."

As I've said, I am far from a woo-woo type of person, but the fact was that the slight dizziness I had felt as soon as we arrived in Pátzcuaro had still not gone away, and I was beginning to wonder if it had anything to do with what Cynthia was talking about. It wasn't a bad feeling, it was just a strange one, like having permanent butterflies in your stomach and an extra beat in your pulse. Whatever it was, it was not to be denied. Nor was the feeling that my encounter with Cynthia was meant to be. I didn't know quite what to make of it all, but I did know one thing: I would be making the trip to Pátzcuaro, and Casa Encantada, again, soon.

12

AND THEN A FEW THINGS HAPPENED THAT I never saw coming.

Noah had gone back to Michigan and was working hard to live up to his end of our bargain. He had stopped drinking, on his own, cold turkey. I was proud, and extremely relieved. But now that it was time for me to step up to the plate, I seemed to be dragging my feet through the Pacific beach sand. I had offered Noah a three-week temporary visit. I really looked forward to seeing him, and was hopeful about witnessing the change that, he swore over and over, had come over him. On one hand, having family nearby sounded truly wonderful. And yes, Mexico seemed to be the great do-over spot, the perfect place to start fresh. And we all knew Noah needed that. The problem was that I was still worried about his ability to stay sober here, and was concerned about the challenges of earning a living, should we agree that he could stay longer. But there was something else that was fueling my reluctance. Here I was, trying to get my own act together, trying to build a new life for myself, on my own. Did I really want my empty nest invaded by a full-grown duckling?

Cynthia and I had been talking regularly by phone. One thing we had recently discussed was the idea of moving from surviving to thriving, something she assured me was totally possible for those suffering from trauma. I was so ready to thrive it was killing me. Just being in Mexico had caused something to shift inside me, and I did feel like I had changed even a little more since my return from Pátzcuaro. After a lot of effort devoted to thinking about everything Cynthia and I had been talking about, I thought that maybe I was beginning to understand myself better. Between our frequent conversations and e-mail exchanges (hers always ending with the sign-off "Love and Light") things were slowly starting to make a little more sense. Was it really such a smart idea for me to take on the responsibility of caring for Noah when I was just beginning to learn how to properly take care of myself? Even on airplanes they tell you to secure your own oxygen mask before putting one on your child. But a deal is a deal, and down he came.

I wasn't sure what to expect when he got off that plane. The last time I had seen Noah, about a year earlier, he was not a pretty sight. His clothes were dirty and worn, and I had to hold myself back from throwing him in the shower and scrubbing him down. Imagine my relief when a trim young man in a crisp white shirt came bounding through customs with a huge grin on his face. I just prayed, for both our sakes, that the new leaf he seemed to have turned over was more than skin deep.

It wasn't long before Noah fell in love with Mexico, and with a Mexican woman. Martha was Sergio's sister-in-law, and Sergio and his wife, Teresa, had introduced them within days of Noah's arrival. I was good with that. Noah needed to hang out with people closer to his own age, and besides, Sergio was the only guy around who never touched a drop of alcohol.

During those first few weeks all of us had been walking around on tiptoes, drinking water and sodas with Noah, quickly stepping away from any social situation that we feared might turn into too much temptation. But Noah was pretty amazing. Nothing seemed to faze him, and he was just so happy soaking in all that Mazatlán had to offer (minus the booze) that I began to relax. But watching Noah as he tried on life as a sober person turned out to be exhausting. He ran every day, despite the ninety-five-degree heat and one-hundred-percent humidity. Then it was off to the gym. And those were just the mornings! In the afternoons he'd wander by foot, alone, through the streets of the city, just as I had done not that long before. He'd come home happy, with descriptions of places he'd been and stories of people he'd met. I was in awe of his ability to adapt so easily to a new life in a new country. For him, it was more than that.

"People down here just accept me for who I am," he explained to me one night over dinner. "At home I felt like such a failure. I know I disappointed you, and everyone else."

"Oh, Noah . . ."

"I know I did. You don't have to deny it. I felt like it got to the point that everyone, including myself, expected me to fail."

"We knew you'd be okay, eventually."

"Well, to me, it felt like everyone was always looking at me and thinking 'loser.' Here, I'm not a loser. I'm just Noah."

It wasn't long before Noah started looking for a job. If he wanted to stay, that was to be part of the deal. He grabbed the first thing he found, a gig as a time-share salesman, where he was urged to go hang out at the cruise ship terminals or in front of the hotels, luring innocent tourists into a sales presentation. Not ideal, but he was trying. Then Martha told him she was pregnant. The deal was sealed.

Noah had always been attracted to the notion of family, and now he was starting his own. I knew all too well that a cross-cultural relationship was a hard tree to be climbing. Now both my sons seemed to be following in my footsteps. Zach had married a Persian woman he had met while in school in Northern Cyprus. With her high expectations and relentless pushing, she was good for Zach, in the long run. But his wife held on tightly to her family's ways, where even a hundred-year-old grudge was something one was bound to honor. Let's just say that avoiding a quarrel was something Zach was becoming quite adept at. And Noah was about to be put to the test by the paradox that was the Mexican female. Martha and her sister Teresa were fiery women. And I had been a target of Analisa's hair-trigger temper more than once, like when I teased her about her picture in the paper next to a foul-mouthed old lecher I knew from around town. She flew into such a rage that I thought her head was going to fly right off her neck like a rocket from a launching pad. Any of these women could rip you a new one in a nanosecond. And from what I had seen, Mexican women had very conflicting expectations of their boyfriends and husbands—they complain about their men carousing too much, yet don't respect them when they're not macho enough. They'll put up with all sorts of crap, but in the end, they, the women, are the ones who run the show. I feared my Noah might be way too sweet for this world. Even the toughest of men don't stand a chance with a Mexican woman. Usually the men's way of coping is to just ignore their wives' mouths, and go off to the cantinas with their pals or meet up with their mistresses. That's sort of normal down here. And there are plenty of men who even have whole other families outside the home. Martha once caught her best friend's husband down at the mall, cradling an infant, a baby that clearly didn't belong to her friend, in his arms.

I admit I was nervous when Noah set out to make his first visit to Martha's house, straight up the donkey-trail streets to the top of The Hill, a neighborhood with the best view of the city, yet one that nobody I knew had ever dared to visit. Generations of Mazatlecos had made their home up there for years, with houses passed down from parents to kids, and cousins and nephews and in-laws taking up residence so close to one another that if anyone sneezed their entire street would echo with their family's *salud*s. It was cheap, way back when, to buy on The Hill. And it wasn't a bad place to live. But by now the old neighbor-hood had become the turf of a bunch of small-time drug dealers, who unfortunately at times neglected to pay up, and who unfortunately at times could find themselves in big trouble. Handcuffed guys tossed into the back of a truck were a common sight at the bottom of The Hill, though you never could tell who it was behind the wheel.

But I had to laugh when Noah described that first evening at the house—all of Martha's six brothers and sisters and various spouses and children, including Martha's own three-year-old, Derek, all talking at the same time. Except for Martha's mother and father, who hadn't spoken a word to each other in more than twenty years, their communication limited to the bird her mom flipped her dad every time they passed in the hallway.

I was going to be a grandma. And as horrified as some people my age might have been hearing news like that, I, on the other hand, was struck with wonder. A new life! Though it probably could have waited a little bit, I was determined to be supportive of Noah, just as my parents were of me and some of the more questionable turns I had taken in my life. And I do believe that everything happens for a reason. It wasn't just about me coming to Mexico anymore. Any second-guessing I had put myself through about the move down here was over the minute that baby was announced. A whole new human being was going to come into this world, and if I hadn't been restless and unsettled and unable to submit to the allure of the California lifestyle, this, in all probability, never would have happened. I crossed my fingers that it would be a girl.

Of course, I loved having my boys. I can still picture Noah gleefully climbing every vertical object in sight, and Zach crawling around in the dirt hunting frogs and bugs. But deep down I also wanted a girl. Someone I could take shopping for little ruffly skirts and sparkly shoes, who would watch in the mirror as I put on my lipstick and beg with pursed lips, "Me too," who would some-day share her secrets and hopes and dreams—that's what I ached for more than anything.

Now suddenly every little girl on the street drew me in like a magnet. I began to picture those beautiful big brown eyes and that shiny dark hair belonging to the girl I imagined growing inside Martha's belly. I smiled as they poured out of the school gates in the afternoons, dressed in identical pleated skirts and white blouses, peering up and down the sidewalk for their mamas, and laughed as they squealed at the sight of the balloon man in the distance. But, of course, along with that I became even more struck by the sadness of the girls who lived the other life, who spent their time on the streets desperately trying to bring home enough change to keep their mother or father or whoever was pushing them out that door day after day, night after night, satisfied. I was particularly disturbed by the same young flower girl I'd been seeing since I first moved to Mazatlán, who I now seemed to come across every time I turned a corner. I started buying enough flowers from that girl to fill a mausoleum. It did cross my mind that I actually might not be helping her. Who knows what that money was going for? And seeing how much she was bringing home, whoever was making her work would probably just raise the bar, and start expecting that poor girl to sell out her inventory each and every day. It just seemed so hopeless for all these girls. Even if they had a parent around, the kids were simply doing all they knew how to do, the only thing they saw around them. And if they were left to fend for themselves, what else could they do? There had to be some way to shore up the banks of that slippery slope, though for the life of me I couldn't figure out what it was.

THE NEXT THING THAT HAPPENED TOOK ME even more by surprise. I had stopped by Macaws to say hi to Analisa on my way to the first meeting with my new Spanish teacher. I was just getting ready to leave, bolstered by Ana's words of encouragement, when a couple of guys came barreling in, mouths first. You couldn't ignore these two, with their booming laughter and eager expressions. It was clear they were new to Mazatlán, they just seemed so damn excited about everything. The big one, who had the broad face of a Pacific Islander or something, ordered a couple of beers as his pal, a snowy-haired Japanese man, started chatting it up with everyone within earshot. I remained at the bar to eavesdrop, curious to know who these two characters were, tourists or snowbirds or what? When I overheard the Japanese guy say something about how he and his partner just got a home in the Marina, I put one and one together. Partner, plus a home in the Marina—a very chichi area—equaled gay. I loved these two guys. Funny and happy and loud, they were so entertaining that I was tempted to skip class. Instead I stood and offered the little Japanese guy my seat.

He smiled, which made me smile back. Behind his back, Analisa gave me the local sign for "rich," her thumb and index finger held far apart, as if an invisible fat wallet were sitting in between. I ignored her.

"New in town?" So I'd be late. Hopefully the lesson ran on Mexico time, where it's ten until it's eleven.

"Just got here yesterday."

"I could tell."

"It's that obvious? My name is Denis."

"Debbie." I shook his cool, smooth hand.

Denis nodded toward his big friend. "Bill and I both just retired. Came down here to start a whole new life."

I toasted him with my empty coffee cup. "Well, then, good luck to you. I've been starting a whole new life down here myself."

"How's that working for you?"

"So far so good."

"Any words of advice for the new guys in town?"

"Yeah. Don't drink the water. And if you do,

bring your own toilet paper. That, and you should know that all tacos are not created equal."

Denis laughed so loud I'm sure they could hear it all the way down on the Malecón. "I'll try to remember that. But seriously, I'd love to get some tips on where to go, what to see. We're open to anything."

I started to share the names of some of my favorite restaurants and shops with Denis, until I realized that if I didn't leave right away I'd definitely miss class.

"Shoot. I've gotta run. But it was a pleasure to meet you two."

Denis stood and shook my hand. "Likewise."

"You have an incredible head of hair," the hairdresser in me blurted out, running her hand through his thick white mane. "Has anybody ever told you that?"

Denis laughed again, unfazed by my boldness. I scribbled my phone number on a cocktail napkin and rushed off to class, hoping I wouldn't lose track of this guy in the gringo shuffle. But on my way I had a brilliant idea, and dialed Analisa immediately to explain the plan.

"Listen, Ana, you know those two guys who just walked in before I left?"

"You mean the cute Chinese men?"

"Whatever. Anyway, don't waste your energy thinking you've found yourself a new meal ticket. They're gay. But I'm thinking that maybe we

251

should ask them if they want to join us when we go shopping in Guadalajara. They're new here, they'll need stuff for their house, right? And I'll bet you they love to shop." I knew that Analisa was nervous about taking the trip. The violence in the area seemed to be exploding, and besides, even in the quietest of times Mexican women do not just take off on a midnight bus for a twenty-four-hour shopping spree in a strange town without an entourage, like we were going to be doing. For me? After a bus ride through the Khyber Pass, this seven-and-a-half-hour ride on a Mexican highway seemed like a first-class journey on the *Orient Express*. Back then, I had convinced my son Zach, who was staying with me at the time, that a trip into Pakistan to pick up a much-needed facial machine would be a wonderful adventure. We'd travel just like the Afghans did, and for safety purposes we'd even look just like Afghans, Zach with his curly hair slicked down flat, and me in a head-to-toe black burqa. We kept our conversation to whispers as the bus rattled its way around the steep hairpin turns, slowly making its way through the rocky landscape lined with poppy fields and abandoned, overturned semis and old tanks, bombed-out cars and trucks, in plain sight of the Taliban fighters who were known to fire down on military transports from their nearby mountain hideouts. I was actually relieved when our covers were blown, just as we were leaving

Afghan territory. Showing our passports caused all sorts of excitement, along with the enforcement of a Pakistani government requirement that we accept the escort of an armed guard for the rest of the journey across the border zone.

Even though I knew the odds of anything happening on a trip to Guadalajara were slim by comparison, the thought of having two men accompanying us as a deterrent to anybody who might want to try something stupid was an appealing one. There were plenty of other men we knew in town whom we could invite, but that invitation would have been taken to have, no doubt, a few benefits attached. So these guys appeared to be a perfect solution, even if they didn't seem like the type to jump in between us and the barrel of a bandito's pistol. Besides, I thought, how nice would it be to develop a friendship with a gay guy down here? It would be so great to have a man to hang out with, especially at night, when I never felt totally comfortable traveling around alone. I told Analisa to hand her phone to Denis.

"Hey, Denis, it's Debbie. The Debbie you just met there at Macaws."

"Hey there!" he answered in a voice so loud I had to hold the phone away from my ear.

"You know, I was just thinking. Have you ever been to Guadalajara?"

"Can't say I have. But Bill and I have been

looking forward to doing some traveling around Mexico."

"Well, here's a thought. Analisa and I are doing a twenty-four-hour trip, leaving Friday night. You guys want to come with?"

"Just the two of you?"

"Yep, just the two of us."

"Hey, Bill, want to go to Guadalajara Friday night?"

I could hear Bill's voice coming through loud and clear. "Whatever you want, little buddy!"

"Count us in."

I told Denis to give me a call later in the week to confirm, but seriously wondered if I'd ever hear from him again. Bar talk is sometimes just bar talk, forgotten even before the tab is settled and the tip paid. But the very next morning Denis's voice was exploding through my phone with his own invitation for me to join him and Bill down at Panama's for breakfast. Thirty minutes later we were chatting over runny plates of huevos divorciados. We met at Panama's the next morning as well. When Bill heard me mention that my washer was on the fritz, he insisted I bring my laundry over to use theirs. We stopped by my place, then headed over to the Marina and their home—an over-the-top drug lord palace with pillars and a pool.

"Decorate this yourselves?" I asked, eyeing the chandeliers dripping from every ceiling.

They both laughed. "No, it came this way," Bill assured me, as he wiped some invisible dust off the dining room table.

In the tradition of the expats I had first met down here, we kept our initial conversations pretty much centered on the here and now, in a sort of don't ask, don't tell kind of way. I really didn't feel like prying, nor did I have any interest in going down the Afghan road with Denis and Bill, or whining to them about my time in California. And they were just so happy to be in Mexico that it was all they really seemed to want to talk about. I was able to pick up on the fact that they had both been truckers. I had a hard time imagining Denis as a Teamster. To me, he looked more like a science or math teacher. In fact, Denis did tell me he had a degree in education, but was expected nevertheless to join his family's landscaping business in the Pacific Northwest. In the end, he had opted for trucking, and the solid paycheck that it would bring. The other thing I learned that day was that Bill was the most phenomenal laundry folder I'd ever seen.

WE MET THE GUYS AT THE BUS STATION ON Friday night with our blankets in tow. Denis didn't seem to be his usual chipper self, and Big Bill looked like a deer in the headlights. "I don't do buses," muttered Bill when I asked what was wrong. He was clearly terrified, shooting a look of *you owe me big-time* at Denis as we boarded together. Analisa just looked tired. After a double shift in high heels, she was ready for some sleep, and so was I.

The next day started early in the Tonalá area of Guadalajara, where we shopped our way through town with a joyful vengeance. The stalls at the Mercado seemed to go on forever, their tables covered in handmade pottery and glass, textiles, ceramic masks. Bill and Denis were good sports, to a point. When I stopped at what was probably my twentieth stall to chat (via Analisa) with the women who were weaving the most amazing little purses out of long, colorful strips of straw right in front of my eyes, the two of them pleaded for mercy and headed to a shady bench to wait me out. Which was fine by me, as I had become completely awed by the sea of goods surrounding me, and enamored with the people behind it all. These people were artists. I learned that much of their merchandise was created in living rooms and back alleys. Whole families were put to work painting and embroidering and sculpting and carving. But it was the women I was drawn to most, and my rapidly emptying wallet became a testament to just how far my admiration went.

After hours of dragging everyone through street after street, shop after shop, I finally succumbed to the temptation of a cool table in the tree-lined courtyard in the middle of town, and the huge ceramic bowlfuls of sweet, strong punch that Analisa ordered for us off the menu. By now we were all giddy with exhaustion, too tired and silly to protest when we caught her slipping little shots of tequila into our bowls whenever one of us turned away. The evening flew by, and before we knew it we were weaving our way back to the bus, pushing and joking and teasing like a pack of schoolchildren. I settled in next to Denis and pulled my blanket around me, comforted by an intense feeling of familiarity that, at this early stage of our friendship, I had no business feeling. My eyes slid shut before we were even close to the highway, the bumpy road rocking me into submission. But suddenly, from within that fragile place between watchfulness and dreams, I thought I felt the unmistakable sensation of a pair of cool, moist lips pressing against my own. My eyes flew open as a loud gasp escaped from my mouth.

Denis looked even more surprised by my reaction than I was by his kiss. "What?" he asked.

"What are you doing?"

"Kissing you."

"Why?"

"Why not?"

"What about Bill?"

"What about Bill?"

"You know."

Denis's brows furrowed in confusion. "Bill's on his own."

"But aren't you and Bill, I mean, aren't the two of you . . ." Denis remained silent. Why wouldn't he help me out here? "C'mon. It's cool with me that you two are gay."

"Who's gay?" shouted out Bill from behind.

I couldn't tell whether Denis wanted to laugh or cry. "Well, this is a first," he said, straightening up in his seat. "Bill, do you think our ex-wives know about us?" Now Denis did laugh. Bill did not.

"How long were you m-married?" I stammered, stunned at this sudden shift of fate.

"Thirty-three years," Denis answered softly.

"And how long have you been divorced?"

"One month today."

I sighed, silently vowing to keep my distance. Behind me, Analisa was sound asleep, her head resting on Bill's broad shoulder. I'd wait until tomorrow to pass on a warning, to both of them.

BEFORE I EVEN GOT HALF A CHANCE TO contemplate sitting back in a rocker and knitting some baby booties, Analisa and I got invited out on a double date. Denis and Bill had asked us to join them for a dinner dance at the Playa Mazatlán Hotel. And I didn't have a thing to wear.

"Put on something nice," was all Analisa advised when I asked her what people down here wear to these sorts of things. Mexican women dress up to go to the supermarket. You never see them walking along the Malecón in anything but high heels and bright, tight dresses or pants, no matter what the time of day.

The long black dress I bought, with a plunging neckline and millions of rhinestones, was, in my opinion, pretty spectacular. It was my first evening gown, and slipping it on made me feel like a teenager heading to the prom. My hair was swept up into a loose, wispy bun in defense against the heat. I could only hope that the glue holding the eyelashes onto my lids wouldn't melt over the course of the next few hours. The rhinestone-covered heels were the icing on the cake, twinkling like Cinderella's fated slippers as I turned and twirled in front of my bedroom mirror. I rushed out the door to pick up Analisa so we could head over to the Golden Zone together to meet the guys.

Analisa climbed into the taxi and we quickly gave each other the once-over, then said our hellos. Her casual white hip-huggers looked like they had been painted on, and her green strapless top was showing off her chichis to their max. Had I totally misunderstood the dress code? We remained unusually silent for the rest of the ride, me tempted to tell the driver to turn around and go back to my house so I could change. But instead I just prayed that Analisa was the one who was inappropriately dressed, and not me.

The long circular driveway at the Playa Mazatlán was jammed with cars when our taxi pulled up. I breathed a huge sigh of relief seeing the full range of attire that filled the arched walkway leading to the hotel's entrance, and was reminded once again just how much I loved this place where even a fifty-year-old wannabe prom queen doesn't cause the slightest raised brow or blink of an eye. Denis and Bill were waiting for us right where they said they'd be—in front of the apparition of the Virgin of Guadalupe.

"Can you two see this thing? I can't seem to find her. Denis says he can, but I don't believe him."

Bill was shifting back and forth in front of the shrine, squinting at the cracked mirror where, just a few years earlier, a desperate hotel maid had seen the vision appear in answer to her prayers for her troubled family. At first she had thought it was a spot of dirt, and tried every type of cleaning solution at hand to wipe it off. After she realized what she was seeing, priests were called in to verify her claims. Whatever they decided, the apparition became a huge draw for both the pious and the curious. And the maid's prayers were answered, thanks to the hotel management, who stepped up with the funds to help.

"Of course I see it!" Analisa lifted the cross suspended in her cleavage and gave it a kiss. "What is wrong with you, Bill? You don't believe?" she added, playfully swatting his shoulder.

"Wow, you look great, Debbie." Denis hooked his arm through mine. "Shall we go in?" His black pants and matching shirt blended in seamlessly with my prom dress, and, I had to admit, set off his white hair quite nicely.

I had been spending quite a bit of time with Denis since our crazy shopping trip to Guadalajara. Mostly we'd meet for breakfast by the beach, watch movies, take walks, and once I even tried to cook dinner for him. Thank goodness for Sergio, who, much to my surprise, was standing on the other side of the door holding the pizza I was forced to order in defeat. How many jobs did that guy have, anyway?

My neighbors seemed strangely wary of Denis. I finally figured it out one day after he and I stopped by Josi's store to pick up some eggs on the way to my house. I could see the Spanish version of my book, which I had given her a few weeks earlier, on the back counter. Josi nodded to me as Denis leaned over the dairy counter. "Sam?" she mouthed silently, her brown eyes wider than wide.

I couldn't stop laughing as we headed outside and up the block.

"What's so funny?"

"Josi thinks you're a warlord!" I managed to say, and cracked myself up all over again.

In fact, Denis caused quite a stir wherever we went in Mazatlán, where apparently Japanese people were a pretty rare sight. "Mr. Miyagi!" shouted out a voice from across the street one day, where we turned to see a big, burly guy striking a karate pose. Of course that became Denis's instant nickname. Mr. Miyagi. Sometimes people would bow down to him on the sidewalk, and waiters would speak especially loudly and slowly so the Japanese man would understand. The funny thing was that Denis, being a third-generation American, didn't really think of himself as Japanese. *I* was more Japanese than he was, having traveled there four times, as opposed to his never. But in Mazatlán, he was the Japanese Guy. He was like a rock star, and everyone came to recognize his raucous laugh a mile away. I know that whenever I heard it, it never failed to bring a smile to my own face, no matter what kind of mood I was in.

That night at the Playa Mazatlán folks were dancing under the stars to a full mariachi band. Denis and I watched while Bill and Analisa sambaed and mamboed their way across the floor, the sweat slowly seeping its way across Bill's Hawaiian shirt, turning it into a deeper shade of blue as the dampness spread across his back. The two of them finally wore themselves out and joined us at the surfside table, panting like a couple of tired dogs.

"I don't know about you, but I've worked up an appetite. Anyone ready to join me?" Bill pointed to the buffet tables, heaped with platters of excellent-looking food.

"I'm with you, buddy. Girls?" Denis stood and bowed a little, gesturing the way with his upturned arms.

"Just bring back a plate and we'll share. I'm good with that for now."

"Me, too," echoed Analisa. "I am good, too."

I could see Analisa's eyes following Bill as he walked away from the table. "He's a nice man, Ana. Don't be leading him down a bumpy path. He's not just some fat wallet on two legs."

Analisa shot me an icy look that told me I had crossed the line. I put my hand gently on her arm. "All I'm saying is be careful."

"You be careful yourself, Debbie."

We sat in silence until the guys returned to the table, their plates overflowing. I had just helped myself to a shrimp when the first pop echoed through the still night air, quickly followed by another and another, until the sound of the surf was completely drowned out by a deafening symphony of explosions.

"Ooh, fireworks!" Analisa was beaming from ear to ear. I, on the other hand, was fighting an urge to dive under the table.

I had so far succeeded pretty well in hiding my issues from my new friends, except, of course, Sharon. Luckily any weirdness they'd noticed had gone unmentioned, like when I refused to sleep in that bedroom Bodie had built on my roof, as it had bars on the windows and a door that required a key to get out. He graciously changed all the locks without question. I was determined for this not to be the night where I would be nominated as the poster child for PTSD.

I felt a hand on my shoulder. "Hey, are you okay?" What, could he see my heart pounding through my gown or something? I prayed that my makeup wasn't melting under the sweat I could feel trickling down my face. I nodded and took a deep breath. Denis handed me a glass of water.

"You're shivering. You can't be cold in this weather. Are you sick?"

It's just fireworks, I told myself. *In Mexico. A celebration. Nothing more.* I tried hard to remember everything Cynthia had taught me. *That was then, and this is now. That was then . . .*

"Want to go down to the water?" Denis stood and pulled out my chair. I slipped off my shoes with a shaky hand and silently followed him down the staircase to the beach, the sound of the fireworks crashing through my ears. As we stood at the surf's edge to watch the light show overhead, I forced my breath to slow in unison with the rhythm of the tide. *Am I trapped? No. Am I lost? No. Am I afraid? Well, yes. But that's okay. It will pass.*

The flashes were multiplying into a frenzy of color. I could see the light bouncing off the waves as Denis stood beside me in open-mouthed awe, entranced by the spectacle above. Suddenly the entire sky exploded all at once, with a roar so loud its echo bounced back and forth and back again against the hotel wall. I took a deep breath and planted my feet firmly in the sand.

And then it was over.

BEFORE I KNEW IT SEVEN MONTHS HAD PASSED, and Christmas had come to Mazatlán. It sort of snuck up on me, because Christmas is really the last thing you expect in eighty-degree weather, at least for someone from Michigan. The first things I noticed were the lights in the Machado. They seemed to have multiplied overnight, creating a glow that could practically be seen all the way from my house. A huge tree had sprung up in the center of the square, its frame built from metal rods and Coke bottles, and a roped-off sand sculpture of the Three Wise Men appeared in front of the theater. The whole town seemed to be buzzing with excitement, the streets taken over by pedestrian traffic, the shop windows bursting with anything and everything that might be considered a gift, the street vendors hawking every moving, flashing toy a kid could dream of, and the stores crammed with shoppers running up months' worth of wages on their credit cards. And just when you thought there couldn't possibly be room for one more note of music blowing through the Mazatlán breeze, there it came— "Feliz Navidad" in the restaurants, "Ave Maria" from the church, "YMCA" behind some sort of holiday talent show in the street downtown, and Frank Sinatra seeping through the walls from my neighbor Pepe's house. Everyone was celebrating, in their own way.

Me? I got into the spirit by dressing up my car as Rudolph. Analisa couldn't stop laughing when I picked her up in the little Mini decked out with antlers on top and a huge red nose on the hood. Together we headed down to the Marina to meet up with Denis and Bill. Analisa and Bill had, by this point, progressed into a "relationship-relationship." And though there was no question that Denis and I were becoming closer and closer, I struggled with myself daily to keep him a short arm's length away, determined to fend off a visit from the ghost of relationships past.

That night we decided to cruise the El Cid neighborhood to check out the holiday decorations. It being a gated community, one that you could sense was shifting from an expat safe haven into a moneyed-Mexican showcase, we had to take a creative approach to talk our way onto the grounds. I was volunteered for the job.

"We're going to our Spanish teacher's?" I yelled out the rolled-down window. Denis let out a huge guffaw. I had recently fired the teacher I had found online, a sketchy-looking gringo who had instructed me to read the newspaper to see how many words I recognized—basically anything with an *o* at the end, as in *perfecto*, *exacto*, *rancho*. Then he told me to buy a slang dictionary and learn as many swear words as I could.

The guard eyed the antlers on top of the Mini and turned his expressionless gaze to me.

"Profesor de español," piped in Analisa from the backseat, with her perfect Spanish, before anyone could stop her.

The guard bent down to my level. "Cuál es el nombre de la persona . . ."

"I'm sorry. I don't understand Spanish." I flashed my widest smile, and waited.

"A quién están visitando?"

I shook my head and shrugged my shoulders. The barrier arm lifted. We were in.

"OH MY GOD! LOOK!" ANALISA WAS HANGING out her window, furiously snapping photos from her cell phone. The stucco mansions lining both sides of the wide road were decked out to the max. There could have been an entire HGTV special shot right there on that street—*Extreme Mexican Christmas*. We weren't just talking lights, of which there were more than plenty, lights of every color and shape and size outlining the balconies and roofs and windows, endlessly flashing and blinking and twinkling. These people had created entire scenarios using their homes as the stage, crazy mixed-up worlds where Mickey Mouse and Santa, teddy bears and polar bears, snowmen in scarves and tigers in elf hats all lived together in complete holiday harmony. One house was wrapped in polka dots with a sign proclaiming it the Casa de Santa. And there he was, right on the front porch in his sunglasses and Hawaiian shirt, toasting us with an upraised glass.

Then there were the inflatables. Maybe I had been away from the mainstream too long, but since when did blowup dolls become a Christmas staple? Analisa snapped away as we passed more than one inflatable Santa escaping up a tree while getting pantsed by a mischievous dog. But my absolute favorite was Inflatable Jesus, standing next to a huge penguin carrying a gift, like a tuxedoed arctic Magi cradling his offering under the palms.

I loved it all. Christmas was always big in my house growing up in Michigan. My rotund dad was custom-made to play Santa, which he did year after year. Junior "June Bug" Edward Turner came alive at Christmas, when *he* became the child who couldn't wait until morning to rip open the presents. Even my mom would join in, dressing up as Mrs. Claus. A tacit truce would come over the household, and for a few days we'd operate as a unified trio. It was the one time a year we'd both manage to see my dad as the lovable, jovial life of the party everyone else saw him as, instead of the villain in the black hat he was to my mom, and therefore to me.

As an adult I did my best to keep the Christmas tradition going, renting elf costumes for myself and whomever I was married to that year. I'd replace all my everyday towels and plates with the holiday variety, and would string enough lights on my house to put Chevy Chase to shame.

When I saw what Sharon had done to Casa de Leyendas it was all the proof I needed that we truly were long-lost sisters. She is a total Christmas freak. Back in the States, Sharon used to transform her entire household into a wonderland, including switching out the pictures on the walls, the spreads on the beds, and the curtains in the windows. She'd start her decorating in September, beginning with the assembly of a miniature village complete with a hundred and fifty teeny homes, a pond full of skaters, and fountains and lights, arranged piece by piece until it took over her entire dining room. The five themed floor-to-ceiling trees would come later. Before she and Glen had moved down to Mexico, she told me, they had to purge two whole storage units' worth of Christmas paraphernalia, including more than four hundred and fifty poinsettias that they sold at a garage sale, as they'd heard the holiday wasn't that big south of the border. But that didn't stop her from starting all over again once they got here.

This year she was hosting a Christmas Eve gathering. That afternoon the town had turned into a bundle of energy, the streets jam-packed with last-minute shoppers and early revelers pushing their way through the crowds under a cacophony of Christmas music blaring from every store. After a long nap, I headed over to Casa de Leyendas by foot under the starry sky, feeling secure that the streets would still be buzzing. But it was eerily quiet when I rushed out of my house. Until I hit the corner of Carnaval and Constitution, where I ran into what appeared to be a little parade. As the leader of the group, a man holding a bright paper lantern, came near, I backed into a doorway to allow them all to pass. Behind the man was a young woman on a donkey (who looked as if he'd rather be anywhere but there), followed by a procession of little boys and girls carrying poinsettias in their arms. Shepherds and angels and a group of musicians brought up the rear. I slid out of the doorway and followed behind as they wound their way down the street. I practically crashed into a tuba player when the whole group suddenly came to a stop in front of a large wooden door. In unison, they broke into a sweet verse, of which the only word I understood was *esposa*. Wife. The door swung open. From inside came another chorus of voices, answering back with their own verse. Then the outside people sang again. Another answer rebounded from behind the door. This went on a few times before I understood what was going on. It was Joseph and Mary, seeking lodging. In Mazatlán. I was tempted to tell them to follow me to the B&B, but thought better of it and instead continued to follow them as they made their rounds. I knew I'd be late for Sharon's party, but this was just way too cool to miss.

Finally there was room at the inn. I watched from the street as the entire procession was welcomed into a courtyard jammed with partiers of all ages. White lights had been slung across every branch, eave, and beam, illuminating a huge piñata that hung from a tree smack in the center of it all. Because, of course, that's what Mary found when she came to the inn. A giant piñata.

WHEN I FINALLY ARRIVED AT CASA DE Leyendas the party was in full swing. In the foyer, a spectacular tree stretched practically all the way up to the twenty-foot ceiling, and a life-size wooden nutcracker stood guard at the foot of the garlanded marble staircase. Every inch of the B&B was stuffed with some sort of holiday thing. It was a true winter wonderland. I was envious. My own little house remained dreadfully Scrooge-like. But it had just seemed a little silly this year to invest in a tree and all the trimmings, when I still barely had enough furniture to seat myself and Noah. This year all I had was a measly sprig of mistletoe hanging in the archway leading to the dining table.

Everyone was there at Sharon and Glen's. Except for Noah, who hadn't stood a chance of prying Martha away from her family on The Hill on Christmas Eve. Bodie and his girlfriend, Wendy, were there with Bodie's dog, Snickers, by their side. Barb was there, holding on to her husband, Art, as if he were one of those wobbling clowns that might topple over at any moment. I saw Bonnie and Bob, all duded up Texas-style, and a festive Lisa all dressed in red. Pete was acting his usual gentlemanly self, escorting

Cheryl by the arm, and Sonja was bouncing around like a Mexican jumping bean, waving her arms in an animated conversation that Barry, Donna, and Rob were silently trying to follow. Analisa had the night off and was already home with her family, even though their party wouldn't even begin until midnight.

"Where's Denis?" I asked, pricking up my ears to locate his unmistakable laugh.

"He was here earlier," Glen assured me. I could feel my heart sink a little. "He set up the hot buttered rum. Went to run an errand. He'll be back." Glen offered me a steaming cup.

"Got any ice?" I could already feel the sweat trickling down the back of my neck.

Glen laughed, handed me the drink, and walked away. I wandered out to the patio of Macaws, which had been taken over by a giant fir tree sagging under the weight of dozens of little white envelopes hanging from its boughs. Curious, I picked one off to see what it was. Inside was a card showing a photo of a small boy with a crooked grin.

Carlitos is 7 and in the 1st grade at a school for kids with disabilities. He had TB when young, resulting in weakened lungs. His wish list includes a bike, a soccer ball, and clothing size 8 or small, and shoes size 20.

"Would you like to participate in our angel tree?" came a voice from behind my shoulder.

"Sure," I answered, not really understanding what this woman was talking about. "My name is Deb. And your name is?"

"Connie. Pleased to meet you. All you have to do is sign your name here." A clipboard seemed to magically appear at her side. "Then just bring your gift for Carlitos down here to Macaws by Friday, and we'll take care of getting it over to the home."

"The home?"

"It's the boys' orphanage. They take in boys from the streets."

"That's wonderful." I added my name to the sheet. The generosity of the expats down here, when it came to devoting energy or money to local causes, was awesome, and their tradition of giving was one I was eager to be a part of.

"I'm curious," I said. "Is there anything like that for the girls down here?"

"Well," Connie responded after a little thought, "there are a few I know of. One is a sort of safe house for neglected or abused girls. It's over by the Pacífico Monument. I know they're always on the lookout for help. They do such an amazing job with those girls. You know how hard it is to keep girls on track down here, what with the pregnancy rate so high, and legalized prostitution and all." She scribbled the name down on the back of my little envelope, and I tucked it into my purse.

Denis had still not arrived. I scanned the room

for Sharon, and was anxious to deliver the gift I had stashed in my purse. I had fretted for days over what to get her. What do you get for the woman who seems to have everything, or if she doesn't, goes out and buys it herself? It seemed so fruitless. I had had no problems shopping for my other gifts. Noah was getting some new jeans and shirts and sneakers, things that he desperately needed. And there were the tiny pink blankets and little soft hairbrush I couldn't resist buying, now secretly stashed away at the bottom of my closet for when the time came. For Cynthia, I had found the perfect present to send. It was a fairy god-mother with wings, all dressed up quite chicly in a sheer black sequined gown and silver crown. And for Denis, I had painted a large canvas with a scene of old Centro that I couldn't wait until Christmas to give him, so I didn't. He loved it, but if I had to listen to him complain one more time about not knowing what to get for me, I thought I'd scream.

For Sharon, I decided to repurpose something I already had. I settled on a beautiful scarf, pure silk, handwoven, and one of the few things I still had to my name that were from Afghanistan. I had given it to my friend Karen in Michigan during one of my visits back to the States from Kabul. The first time we saw each other after I had left Afghanistan for good, with nothing to my name, Karen returned the scarf to me.

"What's the matter? You don't like it?" I asked Karen as she handed it to me.

"I love it, Deb. It's just that I think that now, you need it more than I do."

I was touched, and it was beautiful. But now I wanted to share it with Sharon. However, when it came to wrapping it, I found myself hesitating. Into the gift bag it went, and out of the gift bag it came. Another scarf went in in its place, then out again. This went on for two days, the thought of parting with anything related to Afghanistan causing so many emotions to flood back that I was simply paralyzed. I had finally, that evening, with a burst of resolve, stuffed the scarf into the bag and shut my door behind me.

"It's gorgeous!" Sharon rubbed the silk against her cheek. I could feel the tears welling up, but I was happy. I knew she'd look beautiful in it.

"Ho ho ho!" I couldn't mistake the sound of Denis's voice booming from the back of the room.

"Ho ho ho!" Glen shouted back, as he threw a thin package toward Denis's outstretched arms. Seconds later I heard his laughter roll across the B&B. Wendy and Bodie had made Denis his own little Mr. Miyagi paper doll, a generic flat body topped with a Pat Morita head. Genius.

"Hey, little girl, want to sit on Santa's lap and tell him what you want for Christmas?" someone whispered lecherously into my ear. I turned to see Denis suddenly behind me, empty-handed.

"You're on your own there, bud."

"Later," he promised, dragging me out to the patio of Macaws.

It was just after midnight when Denis walked me home. By now the streets had taken on a whole different feeling. It was like a Saturday afternoon, the neighborhood teeming with kids shouting and hollering as they tried out their new toys. Little remote-control cars circled our feet as we scrambled to dodge the shiny soccer balls flying overhead.

"Thanks," I said to Denis as we reached my front door. "And Merry Christmas."

"Mind if I just come in to use the bathroom for a sec?" he asked, playfully jumping up and down on the sidewalk.

I unlocked the gate and swung open the door. And there, smack in the middle of my living room, was the most beautiful Christmas tree in the world. I had never seen anything like it. Wait, or had I? Come to think of it, I had seen this tree. This *exact* tree. It was while I was window-shopping with Denis. At Fábricas de Francia, probably the most expensive store in all of Mazatlán. I remembered admiring the display. It was a white-flocked tree, my favorite kind, just like my mom always got. Denis must have gone back and plunked down a fortune to buy that display, ornaments and all. I was, for once, speechless.

"You like it?" he asked, his hands coming to rest gently on my shoulders.

I nodded.

"I'm glad." He steered me around the tree toward the dining room, and pointed like a little boy up at the wilted green leaves suspended by Scotch tape, hovering above. Of course we kissed. And kissed again. Then he turned toward the door. "I know you may not be ready, but I'll wait for you, Debbie. You can count on that. I'm a poker player, and I know you're a one-in-a-million shot. But trust me, I can wait."

And with that he was gone. It was going to be an interesting new year.

"SHIT! TOO COLD!" SHARON'S SCREAMS bounced across my patio.

"Oops." I laughed. "My bad. Forgot to test the water first. Rookie mistake." I poured the rest of the bucket over her upside-down head. The soapy water swirled around the drain, leaving an orange residue I hoped wouldn't turn into a stain on my beautiful Saltillo tiles.

"Jeez, Deb. Do much hair lately?" Sharon pulled a dry towel around her shoulders and parked herself on a stool.

"You know the answer to that. And don't forget, I'm doing you a favor, right?"

In fact, I was breaking one of my own cardinal rules. When I was growing up in a professional salon, the idea of a kitchen beautician just didn't fly. My mother had always warned me about going down that road. I really hated doing hair in my house.

"You really should open a salon, Deb. I mean it."

"Not gonna happen. So stop asking. You and

Sergio, I swear, you're going to drive me up a wall." Sergio had been slyly encouraging me to open a salon practically from the moment we met.

First it was "Teresa used to have a salon."

"Really."

Next it was "Her sister is a massage therapist and aesthetician." What *doesn't* this family do? I thought. Then it was "Teresa really wants to read your book." So I gave Sergio a copy in Spanish. Two weeks later he said, "Teresa really wants to meet you." So meet we did. And she was nice, if not a little shy at the time, but I was beginning to see where Sergio was going with this, and I knew I'd better nip it in the bud before it went any further.

"Sergio," I told him one day while he was refinishing a table for me, "I have absolutely no interest in opening a salon here in Mazatlán. As we say in the States, been there, done that. And not gonna do it again. I'm retired." The truth was, despite my protestations, I did miss a lot about salon life. Just as some people get their warm fuzzies from the taste of a dish their mom used to make, or from hearing a familiar song, my memory senses are triggered by the aroma of perm solution and nail polish remover. I had been trying hard to ignore my destiny, but the funny thing about destiny is that it really doesn't take too well to being ignored. I'd find myself sitting in a beauty shop, having my hair done or getting a mani-pedi, and the sound of the Mexican girls joking and laughing with each other would bring on a kind of profound homesickness. But it still wasn't enough to make me want to jump in and do it myself, again.

"So if you're so opposed to a salon, Deb, what *are* you going to do?" Sharon chimed in as if she were reading my mind. She knew I was antsy, and she assumed, correctly, that eventually I'd need to generate some sort of income. When I first came down to Mazatlán I was so focused on literally getting my house in order that I shoved the thought of working way back into the dusty corners of my brain. Sometimes I'd engage in some wishful thinking that what little money I had might last forever. I'd do the math. I figured that if I only spent, say, three dollars a month, what I had in the bank should last for like a hundred years. Or I'd look at it the other way: I'm good, if I make sure I only live until around sixty-three. I never was that great with numbers. But there was more to it than just the money. I was too young to retire. I hated playing cards. I wanted to live a normal life in Mexico, and to me, normal meant working. Maybe that's why I was so attracted to hardworking Sharon.

"I don't know what to do," I told her. "I do know that I'm not made for the nine-to-five thing. I tried that once, the prison gig. It's just not in my blood, I guess."

"Yeah, me neither." Sharon laughed. "But that didn't mean I had to be a Playboy Bunny like my mom. Maybe you should try something different. I'll bet you could do anything you put your mind to." Sharon's words brought back a picture of my mother's beaming smile as I would twirl clumsily around our living room in my too-tight tutu. "You're no Pavlova, so get out of the way of the TV," my dad would growl. "You'll see," I'd growl back. We always did have sort of a rocky relationship, especially when I started to have my own opinions, or maybe when I started parroting those of my mom.

But funny enough, in my family, it was my dad who was the dreamer, and my mom who was the doer. Dad was always looking for the next deal. He fancied himself as a mover and shaker, and was a serial risk taker, much to my mom's dismay. One of his nicknames was Windy, and for good reason. He talked his way into buying bakeries, dress shops, apartment buildings. But it was Mom who always ended up doing all the work. She just wanted security. Like when he bought that bakery. A German bakery. We didn't have a drop of German blood in us. And of course *he* didn't know how to bake. So who stayed up all night making bread and doughnuts and turnovers before heading out the door, exhausted and resentful, at 7 A.M. to do hair? But I have to give my dad credit for always seeming to come out ahead, even if it was thanks to my mom for blocking some of his crazier schemes, and for her willingness to have his back at the ones that did fly. For a cotton picker from Arkansas, I'd say he did pretty damn well.

Between my dad with his big ideas, and my mom's can-do attitude, my entrepreneurial spirit kicked in at a very young age. By the time I was seven I was melting crayons onto my dad's discarded beer bottles and selling them as candle-holders for ten cents apiece from the side of the road. Sometimes, if I ran out of empties, I'd secretly uncap and pour out whole bottles of my dad's Budweisers to up my inventory. I'd even sell food from my own house if I could make a profit. Our apples and candy bars would disappear at an alarming rate. A little while later I learned how to knit, and sold scarves to the captive audience at my mom's salon.

"It's just really hard for me to even think about doing hair down here!" I shouted to Sharon over the noise of the blow dryer. What I didn't share with her that day was a notion I had been thinking about, one that had been bubbling up in my brain for the past few weeks, but one that in no way was I ready to act on. It came to me, of course, at a beauty salon. I was getting my hair extensions done, an endless process that requires me to sit still for hours longer than I'll sit still for anything. I watched with horror as client after client came through for their pedicures, each and every one subjected to poking and prodding from the same wooden pedicure wand. Seven pedicures, all with the same, unsterilized tool. They'd dip it in a little cold water between each job, but that was it. For me, it was appalling. Afghanistan, where even the air you breathe is full of fecal matter, was the harshest environment anywhere for keeping things sanitary, but I made sure we did it. In Mazatlán, I felt like I was playing Russian roulette with my feet every time I sat down in that chair. I'd give anything to get a good, clean pedicure, I thought. And then I sort of laughed out loud a little, because suddenly my mind went back to Afghanistan, where I said the same thing about a good cup of coffee, and ended up opening the Kabul Coffee Shop just so I wouldn't have to drink Nescafé.

BUT MY MOST PRESSING TASK, AT THAT TIME, was planning Martha's baby shower. Though the baby (a girl!) wasn't due for another few months, I just couldn't wait, so I took the opportunity of the post-holiday calm to claim the date. Of course, in Mexico there really is no such thing as post-holiday calm. There always seems to be another celebration on the horizon. Right after Christmas and New Year's, we had Kings Day. The Mexican tradition for this day is to share a sweet wreath of bread with candied fruit sprinkled on top and a little plastic baby Jesus baked inside. Now, where I'm from, people are raised to believe we have Jesus in our hearts, but not so much in our cake. My grandmother would have loved this holiday. She had Jesus everywhere in her house, gifts from her fourteen children and millions of grand-, great-grand-, and great-great-grandkids. Pillows, figurines, bedspreads—if Jesus could be printed, sculpted, or cast, Grandma had him in her house. I even made her a paint-by-numbers Jesus one Christmas, which hung proudly over her mantel. But a cake? One bite and you're choking on the Almighty. It should come with a warning.

Whoever chomps down on the baby Jesus during Kings Day becomes the designated host for the next holiday, Día de la Candelaria, or Candlemas, which falls on February 2, forty days after Christmas. And of course, that year, that person was me. I've heard all sorts of interpretations of how this day is celebrated. In the States it's also the day we call Groundhog Day, because it comes at the midpoint between the winter solstice and the spring equinox. For Catholics, it's "Feast of the Purification of the Blessed Virgin." According to Jewish law a woman was considered unclean for forty days after giving birth, so the custom was to bring a baby to the temple after forty days had passed. That would have been the day Jesus was taken to the temple. In Mexico, the most traditional families have their own Niño Dios, a baby Jesus doll. Some of these dolls have been handed down through generations, and sometimes godparents are even chosen for them. The lucky godparents then become the ones responsible for hosting all the celebrations between Christmas, when the doll is placed in a manger, and Candlemas, when the doll is presented to the church, dressed head to toe in a brand-new outfit that often costs more than the families' flesh-and-blood children's entire ward-robe. In some parts of Mexico they celebrate with bullfights and parades. I chose to go with the simple, yet time-honored, tradition of having people over for tamales.

Just one week later, it was the start of Carnival time in Mazatlán. This being my first Carnival, I was jazzed. But it was clear that it was going to be a challenge finding people to join me for the celebration. There had been a lot of chatter about a threat of violence, something about a rival drug cartel out to make a big statement, to hurt Mazatlán during the city's biggest holiday cele-bration. The beach had been completely blocked off, and there was a rumor spreading that a major cache of weapons had been found in a cave.

"Be careful, Debbie," said Analisa as she declined my invitation to the parade.

"Cuidado," warned Martha after she demanded that Noah stay home.

The last parade, on Sunday, was scheduled to

come down toward Centro, my neighborhood, right past Olas Altas. Denis and I, along with a handful of friends, got to the patio in front of the Hotel Belmar early, to grab a front-row seat right up against the little cement wall that separates the café from the road. Though the sidewalks were soon lined with people peering with anticipation down the wide, empty street, everyone was commenting on the fact that it was way less crowded than usual. We watched as the federal police stood guard by the temporary gates that had been set up, patting down the men and searching through the women's purses. The marines were already stationed down by the water, their huge boats patrolling back and forth along the shoreline. But apparently the parade wasn't going to start before dark, so we settled in for a long afternoon. Lucky for me, I could easily pass the time with a little tableside bargaining, thanks to the army of eager vendors who were out that day. One Oaxacan woman, with an adorable pigtailed baby strapped to her back, an infectious laugh, and perfect English, became my pal that day as she passed back and forth tempting me to buy. Carmelita was a pro, and soon I had yet another new purse I probably didn't need.

It wasn't until hours later, when the sun finally melted into the Pacific, that we first heard the bottle rockets that, fortunately, I had been warned were simply a signal that things were getting under way. I could see the lights sparkling in the distance as the floats approached. The first one arrived, a spectacular rolling temple in the moonlight. Everyone oohed and aahed at the revelers on board as they passed, with their brightly feathered headdresses and shimmering jewels. Then came the second float, a twisted, giant sea creature with fiery eyes, even more magnificent than the first. Then nothing. Everyone was straining and squinting into the distance to spy the next float heading down the Malecón, but you could have shot a cannon down the street and not hit a soul. "What's going on?" I asked nobody in particular. Nobody answered. The crowd became eerily quiet.

Then, all of a sudden, I turned to see a wall of people thundering toward us. Parents were grabbing their babies, strollers were flying through the air, street vendors were flinging their wares right and left. It was raining jewelry and cotton candy all around us. Everyone was running, screaming, diving under the tables on the patio, and pushing their way into the restaurants. It was just like one of those old horror movies where the monster or giant wave is coming. Sheer terror. But I had no idea what everyone was running from. The stampede seemed to be a mile long, and it wasn't ending. The only thing I could imagine was that there had to be an army of gunmen, shooting wildly into the crowd, behind it all.

By now I could see boatloads of people pressed shoulder to shoulder against the restaurants' plate glass windows. "Get behind the wall! Dive! Dive!" I shouted to my friends. But the ground beneath our table was already crammed with more panicky people. "Get down!" I yelled at Denis as I pushed his head toward the pavement. "Everyone duck! Keep your heads down!" I shouted from my own spot flat on the cement. "Just wait this out. Don't move!"

After a couple of minutes, the commotion seemed to end. All we could hear were crying children. It wasn't long before more rumors started to fly, fueled by the cell phones that were lighting up all around us. The one that seemed to be gaining the most momentum was that the Carnival Queen had been shot.

By now, all the floats were coming through, but without a soul on them. As I stood and brushed the dust off my skirt, I found myself next to a familiar-looking woman frantically dialing her phone.

"Mi bebé! Mis hijos!" She was sobbing.

It was my purse lady, Carmelita. "Where are they? Dónde?" I knew a desperate mother when I saw one.

She turned her tear-streaked face toward me. "They are lost! My son and daughter were with their aunt, and I tried to find them, and the baby was pulled from my hand!"

I turned to search the street around me. It

seemed like everything was moving in slow motion, as if hours were passing instead of minutes. As Carmelita desperately combed the sidewalks calling out her kids' names, I heard someone knocking on the restaurant window behind me. A man inside pointed to a woman standing next to him, who was cradling the pig-tailed toddler safe in her arms. I gathered up the baby and stayed put right in the place where Carmelita had left me, where, thankfully, she eventually returned, with the rest of her family in tow.

LATER THAT NIGHT, AFTER I HAD SHUT THE door to my little house on Carnaval Street behind me, I gave Cynthia a call and filled her in on what had gone down that day.

"What the hell is it with me that I can go all commando when everyone around me is freaking out, but when the most threatening thing around me is a steep escalator or a freshly mopped floor I'm the one having a total melt-down?"

"You know the answer to that, Deb. We've talked about it. Today was a perfect example of a situation where you were on high alert." I could hear Señorita and Max yapping in the background. "And by the way, what *did* happen? Why the stampede?"

"I have no idea. Either nobody's talking, or nothing really happened. But honestly, I didn't really think anything *was* going to happen. There were just a bunch of rumors going around."

"I understand that. Maybe your head had doubts, but your body was in high gear. And when everyone else started to panic, you jumped into action, because you know how to act in a situation of unreasonable risk."

This wasn't the first time Cynthia had talked about that. "So, what, if I just stay on alert all the time things like what happened in the mall won't happen again?"

"That's not the point, Deb. You really don't want to live your life like that. You don't want to walk around all pumped up like a Green Beret all the time, do you?"

"I guess not. So what can I do?"

"You're already doing it. Look at it this way. The body has a natural impulse toward healing, a resilience. Acknowledging the trauma is the first step. And you've come further than that. I hear it in your voice. I see it in the choices you are making, the people you're surrounding yourself with, your relationship with Denis." Cynthia paused, the sound of crunching chips unmistakable through the phone. "And by the way," she continued, "you were already on your way when you made the decision to move down here. That Indian guy up in Oregon was on to something, Deb. Trust me on this one. That time in California was good for you."

"But I've told you how miserable I was there," I whined.

"Yes, you were miserable. But you allowed yourself to tune in to your own feelings, maybe even for the first time in your life. Whatever those feeling were—disconnection, isolation—you felt them. And you knew that place just wasn't right for you."

"That's for sure," I said, laughing.

"And buying the house in Mexico was another sign of your evolution."

"I do have to admit it was one of the more practical decisions I've made in my life. But it didn't really feel so practical at the time."

"It's true, it was sensible. But don't discount that 'pull' you talk about as well. There is a sort of spiritual part of the healing process, a part that can only be accessed when you unclutter your-self. After you get rid of unhealthy behaviors and relationships, that's when you start to get your answers from a deeper place."

At first blush Cynthia's words sounded a little like mumbo jumbo to me. But then I remembered the feeling of those powerful sensations that seemed to engulf me in Pátzcuaro, and suddenly I felt shivers go up my arm.

"Cyn?" I said in a quiet voice. "I'm going to come visit again. Soon. As soon as I can. Is that good with you?"

"Anytime, sweetie. Anytime. You know you're always welcome here."

WHEN THE DAY CAME FOR THE BABY SHOWER I arrived at Cahoots early, eager to get everything set up before the first guest arrived. Though I had been under the impression that Teresa and I were to be sharing the hosting responsibility for this event, she had been totally missing in action, so I was on my own. And I was nervous. What did I know about Mexican baby showers? I didn't really know Martha's mom or her other family members, and I was anxious to make a good impression. All I knew was that showers were normally large affairs, and usually held in a restaurant. So I invited everybody, including all of my friends, who had become quite fond of Martha and Noah and were excited about the baby, seeing as how there weren't too many of those crawling around in our circle down here.

I PLACED MY OWN PILE OF GIFTS UNDER THE arch of pink balloons I had purchased from Amigos Dulcería that who else but Sergio had already delivered. When I had told Denis I was going shopping for things to decorate the baby's room, he laughed. "Just like when you did Zach's?" He loved the story I had told him about when Zach, at nineteen years old, had come to Kabul to stay with me. He had been going through a rough time in Michigan, so I got him a job flipping burgers on a military base. I thought it might be nice to fix up his room before he arrived, to make him feel welcome. I was waiting for Sam at a job site, a lot where a new hospital was being built, when I came across a bunch of discarded old bombs that had been dug up and placed in nice, neat rows along the side of a shipping container. Zach would love these, I thought. He always had a thing for collecting anything old that looked like it had a story to tell. These would be great for his room. I could put a little shelf across them, and there was one really big one that would make a perfect lamp. One was just interesting to look at, with its little whirly-bird thing on top. They would be so unique, so Afghanistan.

"Here, grab these!" I shouted to the driver who was waiting by the car. I started tossing big ones, little ones, noticing him jumping and ducking as he strained to catch each one before it hit the ground. "Just throw them in the trunk," I told him.

On the long drive home, the driver's snail's pace was beginning to irritate Sam, who started to berate him in Dari.

"What are you saying?" I asked.

"I told him his mother was a donkey's ass." He scowled, sighing loudly as the driver slowed even more to avoid one of the hundreds of ruts and potholes in the road.

I had to agree that the guy *was* driving like an

old woman (though I never did understand why mothers always had to be dragged into these kinds of insults). By the time we got to our compound Sam stomped off into the house in a huff. I asked the driver to unload the trunk and bring everything inside.

"What the . . ." Sam pointed to the rusty canisters the driver was cradling in his arms like a baby.

"They're pretty cool, right?" I said. "I found them by the shipping container, all used up. Perfect for Zach's room. He'll love them."

"All used up? What were you thinking?" He gestured to the driver, who gently placed the bombs on the salon floor. Sam bent down to take a look. "Some of these are still live. What is the matter with you?"

Needless to say, Zach ended up with a more traditional room, and my grandbaby would as well.

EVERYONE ARRIVED AT CAHOOTS LATE, AND all at once, crowding in through the doorway of the restaurant like a bunch of chattering hens. I saw Martha's mother, and rushed over to say hello, which was about all we *could* say to each other. Martha quickly came to our rescue, kissing her mom and bending over, not without some difficulty, to pick up the scarf her mom had dropped.

"What's that?" I asked.

"A scarf?" Martha replied.

"No, not that. That." I lifted Martha's shirt a little and pointed to the red cord, with a safety pin hanging from it, tied around her swollen waist. She and her mother looked at me as though I were nuts.

"What?" I asked.

"You don't know what that is?"

I kind of thought it might be some sort of thong underwear, but I doubted she'd be wearing that at this stage of her pregnancy. I shrugged my shoulders.

"It's for the moon. It's to protect the baby."

"The baby is in danger from the moon?"

"Do you mean the eclipse tonight?" Bonnie suggested, seeing the look of utter confusion on my face. She pantomimed two circles, one passing in front of the other, with her hands.

"Yes, of course." Martha's look dared me to mess with her.

"Oh, I know about this," Lisa chimed in. "The Mexicans believe that if a pregnant woman is exposed to an eclipse, the baby will be born with a cleft lip. It's an old Aztec superstition. They thought that an eclipse happened when a bite had been taken out of the moon. If a pregnant woman viewed an eclipse, a bite would be taken out of her infant's mouth. They used to put knives on the women's bellies before they went out at night, to protect them. Nowadays they just use safety pins."

I nodded as respectfully as I could, suspecting that this wouldn't be the last time I'd come up against a cultural challenge when it came to my grandchild. I turned around to see the two big tables filling up, my guests separating like two teams on opposite ends of the field. Mexicans and foreigners. English versus Spanish. My heart sank a little. An awkward vibe had taken over the room, but thank goodness I had a little something up my sleeve that I hoped would warm things up.

Now, I don't do games. I've always hated those showers where they make you balance a balloon between your legs or guess how big the mother-to-be's tummy is. No, it was my party, and we were going to do things my way. And when the five Trannies of Mazatlán came prancing into the room, you could almost feel the ice melting. These guys were amazing, and really quite beautiful, if not a little worn, in their sequins and silk. It wasn't long before they got everyone hooting and hollering with their act. The Mexicans were clapping and chanting, and my friends had tears rolling down their cheeks, they were laughing so hard, especially when a platinum blond with boobs almost as big as mine lassoed Noah with a pink boa and pulled him up onstage for a dance. Martha was clearly having a blast. Fun is fun in any language, but I did worry a little about how this all was going to look in my granddaughter's baby book.

CHANGE WAS DEFINITELY IN THE AIR. THE cruise ships had stopped docking in Mazatlán, in reaction to the overblown reports of violence in the area. It was true that there had been a couple of stray incidents, the circumstances of which remained a little murky. And there was that shooting that happened down in a Golden Zone parking lot, unfortunately in front of a slew of tourists. But according to my friends, the exclusion of Mazatlán from the ships' itineraries was an unfair and unwarranted blow, and some thought the move was no doubt financially motivated, a result of a battle over docking fees. "Hell, the crime rates against tourists in the Dominican Republic, Jamaica, and Cuba are all higher than Mexico's," Bodie told me. The travel advisory issued by the State Department didn't help, either. "I don't see any travel advisory for Tucson," Glen pointed out, referring to the recent shooting that left six people dead and a dozen others, including Congresswoman Gabrielle Giffords, gravely injured.

I thought the whole thing was crazy. All you had to do was spend thirty minutes in front of the big-screen TV at Macaws, watching the news from Detroit, to realize how ludicrous the finger-pointing at Mazatlán was. I swear Glen and Sharon deliberately chose to point to the Detroit satellite feed in order to make their B&B guests feel safer where they were. A fierce pride had sprung up among all us expats, eager to defend our city against the fearmongers and rumor junkies. A volunteer army of "Blue Shirts" was quickly formed to patrol the streets, assisting whatever tourists there were with directions and helpful advice, in an attempt to convince them that it was okay to venture out from the resorts. But for some, like Glen and Sharon, it was more than pride. It was survival. As word got out about the cruise ships, business started to drop like a rock. I worried about Noah and his ability to support his growing family.

I could also sense a change happening inside me, though this change was definitely for the better. Denis's patience had paid off, and in fact became one of the many characteristics that made him, eventually, irresistible to me. It was clear to me that Denis was different from most of the men in my life, but it also was becoming clear that I was a different person from who I had been with those men. While I was wide awake one night analyzing my past relationships, one after the other after the other, after the other, my own special version of counting sheep, I came to the revelation that the relationships all had something in common. They had all started up during periods in my life when I was feeling particularly weak. I'm really not sure if it was my weakness that compelled me to seek a partner, or if the partners were drawn in by my vulnerability, but either way, it was, inevitably, a deadly combination.

But by the time I was getting to know Denis, I was actually feeling relatively good about myself. And a relationship born from strength was turning out to be a whole new experience. That night in bed I ticked off the differences:

1. Denis and I don't fight. Well, if we do, it's usually just me doing the fighting.
2. Denis is low-maintenance. I love that. Except for the times when I hate it, and feel like I need to put a mirror under his nose to see if he's still breathing.
3. Denis does not thrive on my adventure. For most men, instead of being arm candy, I'm more like arm TNT. Maybe it was because they were looking for some vicarious thrills, or some secondhand drama. I don't think Denis really has any interest in going along for that ride.
4. Denis doesn't want to rescue me. And by the time we met, I guess I really didn't need a whole lot of rescuing, thank you very much.
5. And then there is that laugh. No man I ever

knew before could light up a room the way Denis does, simply by opening his mouth and letting the joy burst out. That man can find humor in anything, he is such a good sport. Well, almost anything. He didn't laugh much the time I accidentally hit him right between the eyes with a cardboard Christmas ornament, as if it were a Japanese throwing star. I swear I didn't mean to chuck it that hard, but I had been trying everything in my power to turn his attention away from the television—I yelled, I waved my arms, I got up and danced a little—I couldn't believe this man was not noticing me just two feet away. No, Denis wasn't tickled by that particular incident. But I sure was, once I realized he wasn't hurt.

Given my track record, I should have been giving up on men by now. But honestly, I love having a partner. Hell, I loved being married. It's just who I am. But I do believe that *everyone* can be stronger with someone by their side, whether it's a husband or a lover or a friend, as long as they're both on the same team. And it looked like, for Denis and me, it was finally time to play ball.

ANOTHER CHANGE WAS DEVELOPING, ALMOST without me really noticing. I kind of blame the whole thing on Sergio. Though he had been trying to put the salon bug in my ear long before Noah came down to Mexico, by now the final move in his playbook had been put in place. When I think back on it, Noah had barely gotten his luggage off the plane when Sergio brought Martha by. Lucky for Sergio, they hit it off. Martha was the only girl left in her family who didn't have a man, and since she and her sister were so close, Sergio had become the man responsible for both of them, driving Martha to and from work, pitching in when her son, Derek, needed a male's guidance. He was tired of taking care of his sister-in-law and needed somebody else to take over. Noah was his golden opportunity. And now Martha was family, *my* family. And, as I knew, Martha had been working as a masseuse in a spa, just like her sister.

Early on in their relationship, Noah had asked me to drive him to pick up Martha at work. All I will say is that the conditions were appalling. The place looked like a flophouse, dark and dingy and crammed with run-down lawn furniture. Then I saw a couple of drunk crew members head in from port, looking for massages.

"We have to get her out of there, Noah," I whispered as we hurried back to the car.

"I know, Mom, but what's she going to do? Martha needs to work, and loves to work, and this is what she knows."

At the time I didn't have a solution. But now I was starting to think it was all meant to be, all part of a plan belonging to some higher being . . . or Sergio.

"I don't know what I'm thinking," I confessed to Sharon one morning over coffee at Macaws, as I told her about my idea. "It's overwhelming, with the language barrier, working seven days a week, constantly having to deal with clients and staff."

"Yep," agreed Glen as he passed by with an armload of plates.

Sharon nodded knowingly.

"And I swore I wouldn't do it again after what happened in Kabul. It was just too painful. Why am I even thinking about this? I feel like a homing pigeon. No matter where I go, or what I want to do, my homing device pulls me back into the salon whether I want to be there or not."

"Sergio *is* handing you your staff on a silver platter. It's a start. And trust me, finding the right staff down here is no easy feat."

"Yeah, *his* golden opportunity turned into *my* silver platter."

Sharon laughed. "You should just go for it. You know you can do it."

"I know." I sighed. "How can I not do this? It's what I do, who I am."

"That's not a bad thing, Deb."

"It isn't a bad thing. And honestly? I know it's

the right thing. Think about it. I'm a teacher. And I know I could train Martha and her sister to help me build a kick-ass salon. We could specialize in manicures and pedicures. It could be great."

"Are you trying to convince me, or convince yourself?"

"No, it's true. I think I'm okay about this. I'm actually more than okay. If only I could find a place to rent before I change my mind."

Glen stopped dead in his tracks and pointed to a little storefront right across the street from Macaws. "That place is empty. Been empty for a couple of years."

"Are you serious?" I never did know when to trust Glen's sincerity.

"He's not kidding, Deb. There's nobody there."

My heart started racing a little, but in the good way. I was going to open a salon. A family salon, where Noah could run the office and the baby could be with her family. There's no better place to grow up in than a salon. Look at me! I was never lonely as a kid, even though I had no brothers or sisters. And my own kids never had a babysitter who wasn't like family. I'd bring Noah and Zach to the salon every day after school. They'd do their homework there, play games on the sidewalk in front, eat gas station chicken in the back room for dinner. It was home.

And then I thought about Kabul, and for the first time in a long time the image of the beauty school brought back a flood of positive memories. How I loved joking with the girls once we started understanding each other's language a little, and enjoyed joining in on the teasing that went on as they got dolled up to go home for "Happy Thursday," the start of the weekend for them. My awe at their determination, the satisfaction that came from seeing them develop their skills, and the joy of being a part of something that gave them the power to become breadwinners, that gave them hope for the future. Suddenly I was overwhelmed with the urge to get things going as fast as I could. I was ready to do anything. Anything but hair.

TIPPY TOES AND BABY ITALYA ARRIVED AT almost the same time. Italya's birth was a real family affair, with Noah and me and Derek and Teresa and Denis all cramming into the car to drive Martha to the clinic for her C-section. It was all rather calm and matter-of-fact, as if we were simply popping down to the supermarket to pick up some chicken for dinner. That's the way they do it here. Women are given the choice, well before their due date, between C-section and vaginal delivery. It seems as though many of them choose the former, to avoid the pain and gore of doing things the natural way. I guess in Mexico it's just not posh to push.

The Mexican medical system remained as baffling as ever. The receptionist didn't even bother to turn her gaze away from the TV hanging on the wall when Martha approached the desk, belly first.

"Estoy aquí por mi bebé," she announced.

The woman briefly shifted her eyes. "Bueno," she replied, turning her attention back to the TV.

Noah took out his wallet and began counting out the seven thousand pesos he'd been instructed to bring along.

"Mi bebé?" Martha repeated, a little louder.

"El brazo," ordered the receptionist, her eyes still glued to the television. She held out her hand for Martha's arm, attached a cuff, and took a blood pressure reading without missing a word of her telenovela.

The clinic was BYOB, as in bring your own blanket, along with pillow, food, *and* caretaker. You even had to rent a bassinet for the baby. Derek played happily with his toys on the tile floor of the sparse room as his mother, and the rest of us, waited. I had my doubts that Denis had any clue about what he had signed up for, but he was a trouper nevertheless. After a while he got antsy and headed up to the roof for a smoke, then came back later with a wild story of witnessing a weapons exchange on the street below, right in front of the hospital. I was tempted to go back up with him to check out the action, but just then a nurse came in and silently rolled Martha out of the room. Thirty minutes later, like clockwork, she was wheeled back in. Only this time there was a little blanketed bundle with her, cradled in the nurse's arms. It was bizarre. One minute no baby, the next minute, out of nowhere, she's here.

The nurse handed the baby to Noah, and that's when it hit me. My son had a baby! My son, the same kid who had driven me to hell and back, was a father. That's *his* baby he's holding. *His* daughter. And then I started to think *don't drop the baby, watch out for the baby, don't forget the baby,* until I had to remind myself that wasn't my job anymore. By the time Noah handed the baby over to me, I could barely see her tiny pink face through the tears that seemed to have bubbled up straight from my heart.

Within what seemed like minutes, it was standing room only. Every aunt, cousin, sister, and niece seemed to have appeared out of thin air, each of them vying to be the next in line to hold the baby.

"Qué linda nene!" cooed Martha's mother as she stroked Italya's forehead.

"Preciosa," echoed Teresa, poking the baby's arm.

"Bonita," added a young cousin, reaching under the blanket to squeeze my granddaughter's toes.

"Hey, guys! I know she's adorable, but let's give her some space, okay?" I asked, as gently as I could. "Denis, could you get the hand sanitizer from my purse?"

"It's the evil eye, Debbie," came Martha's groggy voice from the bed. "When you say something nice about the baby, you have to touch her."

I held the baby closer. The nurse pointed to Italya, then to me, and back again. "Como abuela." Everyone smiled and nodded.

"What?" I asked.

"I think they're saying she looks like you," Noah suggested.

"Como él también," added another of Martha's relatives, pointing at Denis, laughing. A blushing Denis held out his palms and shook his head.

"What?" I asked. "They think she looks like him because her skin is pale?"

Teresa rushed to my side. "El hilo rojo!" She gasped, suddenly pulling a thin red string from her pocket. I didn't dare move as she began to tie it around Italya's tiny wrist.

"The evil eye again?" I asked. Martha nodded and closed her eyes. Just then the nurse reappeared and gently took the baby from my arms. "Where's she going? What's the matter?" Thinking the worst. She looked healthy to me. Mix-up? Wrong baby?

"Now she must go get her ears pierced."

TIPPY TOES' BIRTH WAS A BIT MORE COMPLI-cated. Starting a business from scratch in a place where you can't buy anything wholesale, or locate the necessary equipment anywhere within hundreds of miles, is, needless to say, a challenge. I was down to my last five hundred dollars by the time I was ready to open.

Bodie and Sergio were putting the finishing touches on the remodel when they gave me a call. "You do want a water hookup in the back room, right?"

"No, don't need one back there. What we have is fine."

"But you're going to want to do hair, shampoos, right?"

"Tippy Toes, Bodie. Get it? It's not called Happy Hair."

"C'mon, Deb. What if you change your mind?"

"Not going to."

"But let's just say you do. It will be expensive to bring the water in later. If we do it now, it'll be a breeze."

"No more money?" I asked, wincing at the thought of my bank balance.

"Nope." I could hear Sergio in the background urging him to just do it.

"Okay. And Bodie? Tell Sergio to keep his opinions to himself. He's done enough damage already."

But of course it was mostly thanks to Sergio that my staff was in place—Martha and her sister, Teresa, their niece Luz, plus their friend Daniela from up on The Hill, and Selena, a girl I had inherited from a shuttered Golden Zone salon. Training began amid the elaborate paint job I had commissioned for the inside of the salon. I wanted something different, something that said beachy and fun, so an airbrushed wraparound mural with a surfer theme was in progress. My friends, enlisted as guinea pigs, arrived two by two for the free services I offered as incentive. It was important to me that my staff become comfortable working with foreigners, and I hovered over the girls as they followed, step by step, my carefully choreographed manicure and pedicure instructions. I admit to being a taskmaster, but I was determined to make the experience a memorable one for my customers, including the presentation. Most of all, I wanted to ensure consistency, a level of comfort that comes with knowing you're walking into something familiar, especially in a foreign country. Sort of like going to McDonald's when you're in, say, Bulgaria, but better.

I had, by now, decided to branch out a little from just doing nails. So when my scheduled test subjects showed up, either for a morning or afternoon session, they had to take whatever service they were offered. If we were practicing facials, they got their pores steam cleaned. Massages? Lucky stiffs. But Lord help the ones who showed up at waxing time. More than one woman of a certain age turned and ran out the door before we could attempt a Brazilian, much to my girls' relief. I couldn't help but think of Kabul, about the time when a young aid worker asked if we could do a Brazilian. Sure, I said. Of course we could. My girls were mortified at the thought, as this just wasn't the kind of thing that was done there. Maybe it was something your mother or sister might help with, at home, but it certainly wasn't a procedure done by strangers, in a public place. The aid worker knew this, and was nervous putting herself in the hands of novices. I assured her it would be fine. I'd do the job myself.

It was dark in the salon the afternoon she showed up for her waxing. It was dark there every afternoon, as the windows were cemented up to block us from the street view, and the electricity wasn't turned on until four o'clock. That day my top student was enlisted to help me get started as soon as the lights came on. The woman's blond hair would have been tough enough to see in any lighting, but when the power went out halfway through, we were doomed. "Light!" I yelled to the rest of the girls outside the door. "We need light! Hurry!" A minute later they all marched in, with miners' lamps on their heads and flashlights in their hands. I still don't know who was more embarrassed, the nervous, spread-eagled customer or my painfully modest girls.

It was proving hard to find volunteers for waxing in a retirement community. At first I had the girls practice on Noah, but when he started resembling a hairless Chihuahua I had to put a stop to that. I managed to find a couple of other guys to come in, but when one asked for a back, crack, and sack wax, Martha almost puked and threatened to quit. Luckily he was just kidding. Another victim came in looking like a gorilla. I felt so sorry for him, with the pain he had to be going through getting all that hair ripped off his back, that I ran to Macaws and got him a double shot of whiskey with a straw, which one of my girls held under his face while Teresa yanked the strips off, one by one.

It was finally showtime. Martha, Teresa, Luz, Daniela, and Selena were all good to go. Five girls, just like I had in Afghanistan. Sometimes, when I'd listen to them giggling about a customer who'd just left, or hear them complaining about a tip, picking up just enough of the language to understand what was going on, I'd almost forget where I was. But there was no mistaking Mazatlán for Kabul when it came to how my girls showed up for work. With their low-slung pants and skintight shirts that ended well above the belly button, all I could see were stretch marks and the crack of an ass when any one of them bent over to do a pedicure. At first I tried to tease them out of their fashion habit by sliding a ten-peso coin into an exposed crevice every time I saw one, or by tickling their bare belly rolls, which those who had had babies wore like a badge of honor. Then I bought aprons to cover their tummies. Eventually I had to take the drastic step of bringing in longer, looser shirts from the States.

Noah took to his role managing the salon like a fish to water. It was in his blood. Both my boys had gained experience in the field over the years—I had sent Noah to beauty school at one point in his life, and Zach had pitched in during his time in Afghanistan by doing pedicures for embassy workers while I did their hair. Of course, now he was on a different track, selling kidnap and ransom insurance, another career choice no doubt inspired by his mother. But Noah had fallen closer to the tree. Sometimes I felt sorry for him, the lone man plopped into a bevy of highly emotional, high-strung, hormonal women, most of them related, which gave them even more of an excuse to fight and cry at the drop of a hat. Especially after they had all worked together long enough for their cycles to become coordinated.

Noah's home life was only slightly less tumultuous. From that very first day in the hospital, when Teresa and her relatives, including Martha, dug their heels in to insist that Noah could not possibly be the one to stay overnight on the skinny Naugahyde couch—*You can't change her diaper. She's a girl! You don't know how to feed her. You're a man!*—he had been struggling to stake his claim as a father, an involved father, in a country where that has traditionally been far from the norm.

"You don't know how to do any of this," Martha would tell him.

"I can learn."

"Well, you're not going to learn on my baby," she'd answer.

"She's not your baby, she's our baby," he'd reply.

When they were released from the clinic the next day, Martha was planning on taking the baby up to The Hill to her family's house, so the women could care for Italya while she recovered from her surgery. Noah refused. And when it became clear that he was going to stand his ground ("over my dead body" were his exact words, as I recall) the entire family came down from The Hill to them. Fifteen people, crammed into Noah's little apartment across from my house, for days on end. At any given time you could find at least seven women sitting on the bed watching telenovelas, passing the baby around like a plate of cookies as Martha tried to sleep.

But Noah wouldn't budge. When the noise and the cooking smells and the stifling summer heat (*you can't have the baby in air-conditioning!*) became too much for him, he'd hoist a cranky Italya over his shoulder and escape to my place. But not before the aunts and cousins and sisters bundled her up like an Eskimo for the seven-yard trek.

"No wonder she's fussy," I'd say, as we pulled off the sweaters and mittens and booties to give the poor child some air. I marveled at the way Noah was with his baby, calm and confident, always attentive. He had a knack. And when he'd bend over to kiss her chubby cheeks or smooth her little curls, I swear I could feel something melting inside. It wasn't long before he became known in the neighborhood as that guy with the baby permanently attached to his chest. And it also wasn't long before he became the only one who could comfort his fidgety child.

His wife was another matter. He'd begrudgingly replace every one of those layers of clothes on poor Italya before he'd head home, knowing there would be hell to pay should the baby let out even the tiniest of sneezes. I was glad he was learning to pick his battles, as I was sure there would be many more to come.

My own crash course in Mexican culture continued at Tippy Toes. One day, not long after we had opened, Martha arrived at the salon and plopped Italya into my arms as she headed toward the bathroom.

"What's up with the baby?" A huge red spot had appeared smack in the middle of Italya's forehead. What kind of terrible Mexican insect had bitten my poor girl?

"She has the hiccups!" Martha yelled from the back of the building.

"No, I mean what's up with her skin?"

"She has the hiccups!" Martha repeated even louder.

I looked over at Noah, who just shrugged his shoulders. I put on my glasses and held the baby up to the light. On second glance the dot looked man-made, more like a little Indian bindi than a bug bite. I dipped my finger into a manicure bowl and rubbed gently at Italya's forehead. Martha was suddenly at my side, first frowning at the inky smudge, then scowling at me.

A week later, when I tried to gently point out to Martha that it might be time to cut the baby's nails, unearthing a pair of infant scissors I had bought months before, she grabbed Italya right out of my arms. It wasn't until Analisa explained to me later, that you don't cut a baby's nails before they're a year old or they'll have bad eyesight, that I understood. Sort of.

And there were plenty more things I apparently didn't know. One day I brought in some fresh orange slices from home and offered them around after lunch. Everyone looked at me as though I were serving up arsenic. "What?" I asked, looking from face to face. Teresa pointed at Daniela, who had been blowing her nose for days. I held out the plate toward her, and she backed away. "Vitamin C!" I insisted.

"No fruit. She is sick!" Martha explained. And there was a lot more I learned about fruit. Pineapples mean good luck. But never eat an avocado when you are mad or fighting, because if you do you'll wind up with a terrible stomach-ache. And limes? I actually got a pretty useful tip from Analisa about them. In a pinch, just squeeze the juice under your armpits. It makes an excellent deodorant.

By now I felt that my Spanish language skills

were improving, even though I had quit going to my second teacher because she insisted that I speak only Spanish in class. Why would I even be there if I knew how to speak Spanish? Besides, she was mean. I thought that I had picked up quite a bit just from being around the girls, but you wouldn't know it by their reaction. "Baño no está limpio," I complained one morning, repeating the exact words they'd taught me just the day before. The bathroom isn't clean. The girls just looked at me blankly.

"Baño no está limpio," I repeated, slower.

"No lo entiendo," Teresa claimed, shrugging her shoulders and turning to the rest of the group for an explanation.

Frustrated, I marched over to Macaws and pulled Analisa back across the street with me.

"El baño no está limpio," Analisa told them.

"Ah, no está limpio!" they all echoed, standing and heading for the buckets.

I fared a little better with the sign language they shared with me. "Okay" was said with repeated crooks of the index finger. Talking about being boiling mad? Shake both hands over your shoulders, which I had witnessed Analisa doing plenty of times, though I had never known what it meant. And say you want to tease someone who is trying too hard to impress. Just make the shape of an eye with your thumb and index finger and place it over your own eye. It's sort of like saying, "Oh, look at you!" My favorite was when the girls wanted to let each other know that someone was a cheapskate—they'd simply whack one elbow with a palm of the other hand. For people who relied heavily on tips, this was a handy one, though that gesture was usually reserved for the snowbirds, who have a notorious reputation down here. I guess they aren't used to living in a culture where everybody—gas station attendants, supermarket baggers, self-appointed traffic cops who, sometimes with disastrous results, take it upon themselves to help you back out of parking places—expect a little something for their trouble. Me, I've always been one to be generous with a tip. Maybe it's because I've been on the other end of that stick.

We had a fair amount of downtime in those early days, which gave us plenty of opportunity to get to know each other, or rather for me to get to know them. One quiet afternoon, after I'd been wondering if my girls were happy in their new jobs, I started a conversation about what they'd do if they could do anything at all. Martha wanted to be a nutritionist. Selena a nurse. Luz dreamed of being a tattoo artist, Daniela a teacher. Teresa joked that she just wanted a rich old man.

"So what's keeping you?" I asked, ignoring Teresa's crack. "You're all smart, capable women." This wasn't like Kabul, where the women were risking their reputations, and sometimes their lives, for the privilege of working for a living. All these women, except for young Luz, had been working for years.

I thought I pretty much knew what the story was for Martha and Teresa. In their crowded household, there was clearly not enough to go around for seven educations. But when Teresa told me she had dropped out of school at age twelve, I was surprised.

"Our dad said all the girls in secondary school got pregnant," Martha explained. "He made Teresa stop going."

"Did she want to go to school?" I asked.

"Of course," Martha said. "Always. But then there was no time, and no money. That's just the way it is."

As it was, Teresa was eighteen when she gave birth to the first of her three children. After twelve years with a cheating, abusive man, she finally packed them up and left. She did everything she could to support her kids, eventually following a lead for training as a massage therapist. Then she met Sergio.

"If you could change anything in your life, would you?" I asked, anxious to know what made her tick.

Teresa shook her head at Martha's translation. "Not now. Now I am happy. It would be nice to have more money, but I know I can take care of myself. Sergio treats me good. My life is good."

By the time Martha was growing up, their father had relaxed a little. She was the only one in the family to make it through the twelfth grade. After graduation, she worked as a receptionist in a dental office by day, and studied English by night. Mazatlán was teeming with tourists back then, and it wasn't long before Teresa helped her get a better-paying job as a receptionist in the spa where she was working. There Martha was trained to do facials and massage. Then she got pregnant, by a guy who wanted nothing to do with her or the baby. Any dreams she had about continuing her education were gone. Now it was all about having enough money to take care of her child.

Daniela's story wasn't much different, pregnant at fifteen, such a young age that her father refused to believe it was possible. Why, she didn't even have a boyfriend! Or so he insisted. They could use some serious birth control around here, I thought. But who was I to judge? These women all loved being mothers. And they would do anything for their kids.

"What made you want to work here, Luz? Why not a department store, or one of the big resorts?"

Luz pointed to her earlobes, which hung low down her neck, heavy with the huge silver gauges that were creating two holes practically big enough to swallow a couple of grapes. Of course, in most places around here, sweet Luz would be labeled as a rebel. The truth was, despite her badass look, Luz was painfully shy. A dropout by sixteen, she was living on The Hill with her mom and siblings in Martha's mother's house along with everyone else, spending most of her time drawing. It was Noah who saw something in her and encouraged me to take a chance on a novice. My first impression was less than stellar. But I trusted Noah, and after Luz complied with my request that she remove some of the lip and eyebrow bling, tuck the nose ring up into her nostril, and pull the straight black hair out of her eyes, we were good to go. I figured if I could train women who had been held captive in their homes for years by war and the Taliban, I could certainly train Luz. If only she'd learn to speak up.

Selena I knew little about, her being the only "outsider" in the place. I was aware that she had a young son, and it was clear she was not much more than a child herself. I learned that her mother had been a beautician and did not want Selena following in her footsteps. Interesting. After a short time in nursing school, courtesy of an aunt with some money, she had to drop out. The money had dried up. Her options were few. Apparently she had never married the father of her child, a guy with more psychological problems than she could have, or should have, tried to handle. Her home life, with her mother, was tumultuous. But her sister watched the boy while she worked, and that was just how life was. Right?

For many women in Mazatlán, their dreams remain just that—dreams. Money is tight, especially since the cruise ships stopped coming. And that's why some, my girls told me, turn to the one profession you need no experience to enter.

"You know Samantha, yes?" asked Martha. I couldn't recall anyone by that name.

"She's the one you've seen hanging around Martha's family," Noah explained. "The one with the really, really short skirts? They say she's a prostitute."

"Are you kidding me? A hooker? She looks like a kid!" I remembered noticing her when she dropped by Noah's to pick up an old stereo he no longer wanted—she was a scrawny-looking thing with braces on her teeth.

Just then Analisa came through the door and settled in for her weekly manicure.

"Who is a hooker?"

"You mean a hooker-hooker? Or just someone who sleeps around a lot to get her phone bill paid?" I asked the girls. Analisa repeated the question in Spanish.

The girls nodded rather nonchalantly. "Sí, es una profesional," said Teresa as she started removing Analisa's polish.

"Why would she do that?" I asked. Teresa rattled off an answer.

"She had to take care of her family," Analisa translated. "She was twelve and her mother left for the States, her father had no job, and she had younger sisters."

"That's terrible," I said, bouncing a wiggly Italya gently in my arms.

Teresa continued telling her story to Analisa, who repeated it to me. "When she started she was a teenager, and only had one client, a narco who paid for everything, including her boobs. Then he was killed."

"So what happened then?"

"She wanted to go back to school, but she could not make enough money in a regular job." Analisa turned to me. "You know, Debbie, there are lots of girls who do this here. Girls who also work in normal jobs. So many jobs only pay you fifteen hundred pesos every two weeks. They have a secret life. It is too hard to take care of your family on so little pay, especially when your husband leaves, or when your family does not help."

I did some quick calculations in my head. That was only about fifty-nine dollars a week. Granted, the cost of living was lower down here, but it would still be impossible for a woman to live on her own on those wages in Mazatlán. I had struggled with the question of what to pay my girls. It was important to me that they earn a decent living, but I felt I had to be careful not to overpay, as I had seen firsthand the effects of overinflation. It happened all too often in Kabul, where, say, a doorkeeper who might overnight go from making a hundred and fifty dollars a month to an unheard-of salary of a thousand dollars, thanks to the arrival of a foreign company. Six months later, that company leaves town, and leaves the doorkeeper with the burden of a whole new lifestyle he can no longer afford.

The girls went on to explain the hierarchy that exists in the profession. The Velvets girls, and those like them who were working at the night-clubs where you could get absolutely anything you wanted for a price, make the most money. They said most of those girls, or "dancers," are from Colombia or Brazil, or sometimes Russia. Then there are the ones who work parties or in brothels, and on the street, who have "agents" managing their careers. At the lowest rung on the ladder are the cantina girls, with their painted, upside-down V-shaped eyebrows and their shirts even tighter than the ones my girls preferred. Not all girls serving at cantinas are prostitutes, but the ones who do turn tricks don't get much in return.

"Ask Teresa if Samantha's family knows what she does," I urged Analisa.

"She says of course not. They would kill her if they find out. She has a boyfriend who doesn't know, too."

What was going to happen to her in five or ten years? What if she wanted to, or needed to, get out? Could she? Did she have a backup plan?

Things could turn bad, and turn bad fast. I knew. Then I thought about the little flower girl, and all the other young girls I saw wandering the streets hawking their wares. How many years away might they be from having to make a decision like this?

"There is a woman on my street," Analisa continued, "she had to go to Tijuana and work for a company when her husband left her."

"What did she do? What kind of company?" I asked, knowing that there was money to be made closer to the border.

"You know, a company that hires girls."

"You mean she was a stripper?"

"No. She does the same as Samantha. She had to feed her babies."

"So her husband left her with nothing?"

"There was no law, Debbie. Now Mexico is getting the laws for the fathers to pay for the children. But Mexican women are strong. We fight for everything we have."

There was no arguing with that. But still, I couldn't stop myself from wanting to do something. What really got to me were the stories my girls told me about abusive husbands and fathers who would smack their daughters at the drop of a hat. I had witnessed it right on Carnaval Street. One evening, from my roof patio, I heard the unmistakable sounds of a domestic battle. "You are nothing but a cockroach! Get out of my house or I'm going to kill you!" At least that's how I interpreted the words. The man continued to rant, his intensity rising by the minute. The woman was silent. "I'm going to beat you until you are dead!" he screamed. My heart racing, I peered over my balcony to see if my neighbors were reacting to the commotion, to see if anyone was doing anything. But they were just going about their business, with one ear cocked toward the shouting. I had to call the police before this poor woman was murdered! I grabbed the phone, suddenly realizing that there was no way I had the vocabulary to handle this in Spanish, so I dialed Martha for help.

"Oh no, Debbie. We don't do that in Mexico. That is a family thing. That's just the way it is." Martha warned me that it might not be safe for me to intervene. The whole thing made me sick to my stomach.

I kept my eye out for the woman over the next few days but never caught sight of her. I was used to catching a glimpse of her every day or, if not, hearing her sing as she washed and cleaned. A few days later, a terrible stench began to fill my house, like old garbage . . . or decaying limbs. I began to picture the poor woman's body in a plastic bag, dumped in the empty lot out back. As the days got hotter and hotter, the smell got worse and worse. I was just about to ignore Martha's advice finally to call the police when

María arrived to clean the house. She wrinkled her nose, pulled me into the bathroom, and pointed to the drain. "Rata."

OKAY, SO MAYBE WE DODGED A BULLET, SO TO speak, with that one, but if I had to hear *that's just the way it is* one more time, I thought I'd scream. Even though violence against Mexican women was an issue that was routinely swept under the carpet, or worse, deliberately kept from public awareness, anyone with half a brain knew it existed, big time. How could it not in a machismo culture where women were so overtly considered inferior citizens, where education was often not an option for girls? I had heard somewhere that close to seventy percent of Mexican women have experienced some form of violence, most of it in their own homes. I thought about all that my Tippy Toes girls had told me about their own lives, and all those stories about the women they knew. And most of them were the lucky ones, relatively speaking. I thought about some of those street vending girls I had seen acting way too familiar with foreign men while their mothers intentionally looked the other way. I also thought about my brief conversation with Connie under the angel tree at Sharon's Christmas party.

Kids! The kids were the ones who needed the help, who needed someone to show them a way to take control over their futures, before their futures were stolen from their grasp. I knew I couldn't change hundreds, or more likely thousands, of years of cultural norms, or pull everyone out of the cycle of violence and poverty, but I knew there was something I could do.

I was lucky to have a mom who once told me I could be a princess. Maybe the girls around here needed someone to tell them they, too, could be a princess . . . or a hairdresser.

BEFORE I KNEW IT, MY LIFE HAD BECOME SO busy I barely knew if I was coming or going. The word of mouth on Tippy Toes had spread like freshly brewed gossip, thanks to those guinea pigs who had bravely taken one for the team. I'd run back and forth from the salon to Macaws, which I'd turned into my personal office, twenty times a day between appointments and paperwork and checking on my girls. And yes, despite my protestations, I had started doing hair.

Here's the deal. Once you decide to do hair, you commit to doing more than just a job. You become The Hairdresser, which comes with a certain level of expectation and responsibility that you just can't walk away from, and I really wasn't sure if I wanted to go there, once again. At first I took advantage of the water hookup Sergio and Bodie had insisted on to take care of the handful of friends I had previously been working on in my kitchen. That was fine. It was much more con-venient and comfortable for all of us. Then the disasters started to come through the door—blondes with brunette streaks, baby-fine curls brittle with bleach, hair so black it was blue—victims either of communication problems or of local beauticians lacking the proper training. People were begging for help, and I was there to perform triage. I even considered, at one point, marketing myself as The Hair Doctor. For a while that's all I did. And then, before I could stop it, my appointment book was drowning in ink. I just didn't know how to say no.

My days were starting way too early, gulping down a fast cup of coffee at Macaws as I watched the Tippy Toes girls parading down the street to work in their matching hot pink polos, a sight that never failed to make me smile. Noah and Martha would arrive with Derek and the baby, and I'd rush over for a morning cuddle before she'd be driven up to The Hill to her other grandma's. We'd settle in to work, Noah cranking up the music and switching on the coffeepot, the girls trotting out the mops and buckets and brooms. Soon Denis would arrive with stacks of fresh, clean towels before settling down for a smoke in the Adirondack chair on the sidewalk outside, perfectly positioned to greet the world as it passed him by. It couldn't help but remind me of my dad after his own retirement, going to work as a greeter at Walmart to keep himself occupied. But for Denis it was just a comfortable perch on a friendly street.

All of Mazatlán seemed to gather at Tippy Toes. Those plate glass windows were a magnet for passersby. A friend inside getting a pedicure? Perfect excuse to pop in for some chitchat and a cup of coffee. And most people didn't even need an excuse. The buzz of those early days cost me at least one good Trip Advisor review. As one of my rare disgruntled customers wrote, *I went expecting a relaxing two hours . . . it was a constant barrage of well wishers and friends having lots of conversation.* Sheesh. I guess we were just a little too *Steel Magnolias* for that one's taste.

For me, it was all good. It felt like home, and the days would go by in a heartbeat, with the setting sun reflecting off the windows across the street before I even had a chance to realize how busy I had been, or how hard I had worked.

My time off became precious. A long lunch, an afternoon of shopping, curling up with a good book—those were now distant memories. Especially now, with new family added into the mix. You see, around here, a lot of the time it's all about the children. Among my expat friends, I was the odd woman out on that score, as none of them had family around. At first it took some getting used to, I have to admit. *Everything* seemed to revolve around kids. There's even a special holiday for them—Children's Day—when every mother in town demands the day off to shower her offspring with love, attention, and of course, presents. Me, I thought that's what birthdays were for. And then there's Guadalupe Day, the holiest day on the calendar in Mexico. That day, everywhere you turn there's a pint-sized Indian, as this is the occasion for parents to dress their kids up in traditional Mexican clothing. Even little babies wear wide-brimmed straw hats, and for the girls, long black braids woven with red and green ribbons clipped into their hair. Martha had already started a search to buy a lighter-colored pair, to match Italya's dirty-blond locks. On Día de la Marina, they all dress up as sailors. On Mexican Army Day, as soldiers. There's always some street party going on. I can't tell you how many times I've had to squeeze my way around one of those big bouncy trampolines smack in the middle of a blocked-off, music-filled, piñata-strung Carnaval Street.

One Sunday Denis and I had to excuse ourselves early from our traditional brunch with the gang at Macaws. It was Derek's birthday, and we had been invited, for the first time, to a party up on The Hill. I have to admit I was a little nervous. "You don't want to go up there," Martha had said to me every time I expressed a curiosity about seeing where my grandbaby was spending her days. Even Noah was told not to go up there alone, and never to go up at night, back when he first started seeing Martha. I knew it was dangerous.

And I also really, really wanted to see those killer views of the ocean that had to be up there.

The long way around is the preferred, or to put it more bluntly, safest way to get to Martha's mother's house. Since that means parking at the bottom and doing the rest by foot, Denis and I locked the doors of the Mini behind us and started up the wide path, arm in arm. Noah met us at the top of the first staircase.

"Is it a long way up?" I asked, my heel slipping off the top of my four-and-a-half-inch wedges as I stumbled on the rubbled cement. I knew it was a stupid choice of shoes, but I wanted to look my best for the occasion.

"It's not bad. But you just missed all the excitement. There was another raid."

Noah had told me this happens a lot on The Hill. Masked men with big guns storming through the rabbit warren of little houses in search of drugs, weapons, and money. Apparently it's so common that the folks who live up there barely look up from their breakfasts.

Gringos aren't usually seen on The Hill. But by now everyone knew Noah, and knew I was his mom. And Denis? He just stuck close behind. Indeed, as we made our way through the maze of graffitied façades, the purples and greens and lemons and tangerines and aquas all crashing into each other in a crescendo of color, nobody blinked an eye. Not the woman leaning wearily on her elbows on the sill of a cutout window high above the street, a string of potato chip bags for sale behind her head, not the trio of kids banging on an old arcade game crammed against a cinderblock wall, not the two women parked in plastic chairs, the backs pushed up against their facing front doors, their knees so close they could almost touch. Only the dogs seemed on edge, barking wildly from behind locked front gates as we passed by.

By now we had turned off the main path and were following Noah in a convoluted route that had us weaving smack through people's front rooms. I kid you not. It was impossible to tell where one home ended and the next one began. You'd pop in and out of slivers of sunlight, one minute with a spectacular cliffside view of the ocean on your right, the next minute nodding politely to some guy watching TV from his sofa.

"That's where the lookout sits," said Noah, pointing to a dirty velour couch perched on a roof.

"What are they watching for?" I innocently asked.

Noah rolled his eyes. "Federales, or military, of course."

This is where my granddaughter spends her days, I thought to myself, peering down a precipitous garbage-strewn drop that ended practically all the way down at the fancy shoreline homes.

"Want to meet one of the neighbors?" Noah

asked facetiously, as something in the dirt rolled over and moaned.

"Is he sick?" I asked, watching the man wave his arms in the air, his baseball cap falling off to one side.

"No, he's just a drunk."

A rooster gingerly led his family around the slowly gyrating body, as if it were simply a part of the landscape.

"Pleasure to make your acquaintance!" Denis called out. I punched him in the shoulder.

"We're almost there," Noah assured me. "See, there's Daniela's mother's house, right up there." I followed his gaze up to a clothesline hung with trousers blowing gently in the breeze, to underneath, where a gnarly-looking mutt was patrolling from the roof. "Martha's mom lives right next door."

I could hear music and laughter floating through the open door. From the look of what was going on inside, the kids must have already consumed liters of Coke and gobs of candy. They were bouncing around like rubber balls, the girls swiveling their little hips in perfect time to the beat, the boys waving invisible lassos above their heads. Even the ones who were just learning to walk had all the moves. I couldn't help but burst out laughing myself.

"Where are all the guys?" I asked, after greeting everyone.

"Guys?" Martha handed the baby over to Noah. "My father is here, in his room. The men, they don't come to these things." Denis shrugged and helped himself to a plate of ceviche. Teresa and Daniela shot me a look.

"What?" I asked, looking around the room.

"In Mexico, we never let the man get his own food at home or at parties," Martha explained.

"Seriously?"

"It shows they respect us, they know we know what is best."

I had to think about that one for a minute. Then I silently vowed to try it out on Denis sometime. I'd serve him my personal favorite—red wine and Pop-Tarts.

"And it shows other people that you love him." Martha bent down to listen to a little boy who was tugging at her shirt. He pointed at Denis as he whispered in her ear. "He wants to know if Denis is a real Chinese person."

Everything seemed to stop for a moment as Denis's laughter ricocheted off the walls of the little house. Then Teresa's son Alex arrived with his boyfriend. Teresa hugged her boy, pushing the clump of fuchsia bangs off his face as they separated. Alex had recently become the latest addition to the Tippy Toes family, and I was beginning to adore him. Being a gay man in Mexico was a tough row to hoe, and Alex had faced his own share of the difficulties that come with the territory. I remember first seeing him when Sergio was working on my house, a sweet boy with hair hanging down over his eyes, who was way too slight to be lifting the four-hundred-pound chimney I was having hauled to my roof. I realize now that what Sergio had been trying to do was man him up. Later I heard more about his situation through Noah. Sergio, unable to reconcile his stepson's sexual preference with his own machismo mind-set, was becoming increasingly tough on the kid. Teresa loved her son, but she just didn't want him to be gay. Her concern was his future. Being an "obvio"—an outwardly obvious gay person—would put a lot of jobs out of his reach. A gay police officer in Mazatlán? Probably wouldn't fly. A construction worker? Not so much. Maybe it might work in Guadalajara or Mexico City, but not around here. Sergio and Teresa agreed on two things: Alex's "gayness" was a phase that needed to end, and they were the ones who had to make that happen.

They began withholding privileges, and even material goods. One Christmas he was the only one in the family to receive no gifts. He had refused to cut his hair. No haircut? No Christmas. He sat silently as everyone else at the party opened their gifts, then retreated to his room, cranked up the music, and tried to dance the pain away. There was a soft knock at his door. When he opened it, there stood his grandmother holding out a cardboard box. "It was the ugliest shirt in the world," he later told Noah. "But it was the most beautiful gift I've ever received."

But Alex still resisted his parents' pressure. "This is our house, these are our rules," they insisted. He rebelled by dropping out of school, and began to hang out on the streets. And the battle continued.

In a society where gender roles are so highly defined—men are expected to appear dominant and independent, and women are supposed to seem submissive and dependent—any man who doesn't obviously "act like a man" is considered to have committed a great offense. Of course, this whole notion cracked me up, as I was well aware that most of it was for show. I knew that even up here, on The Hill, it was the women who were the ones in control. But Mexican women know how to be strong, "like a man," without making their men feel weak. It's truly an art, and I was beginning to think that maybe I should try tearing a page from their book.

But for a man in a machismo culture who dares to let his feminine side show, like Alex, there's very little tolerance. Alex had been taunted, and worse. Some gay men are physically attacked by members of their own family, some are committed to psychiatric clinics, and some are downright rejected. People will do anything and everything to "get the gay out" of you.

A lot of people down here seem to have a complicated relationship with the notion of being gay. They love their drag queens, but if it's someone in your family, you just don't talk about it. You figure they'll simply grow out of it. In fact, there is a weird code word that's used—"forty-one." At first I thought it meant you had until turning forty-one years old to be considered actually gay. But I later found out that it, in fact, goes back to a society scandal that took place in 1901, when the police raided a male-only dance where, out of the forty-one people in attendance, nineteen were dressed as women. But nobody seems to be aware of the origin of the "forty-one phobia," so some believe that men are at their greatest risk of becoming sexually attracted to men when they reach that age. It's a big joke among men and boys around here, and it's apparently a number to be feared and avoided at all costs. Kids will yell out, "Not it!" if the number forty-one falls upon them in a schoolyard count. There is no forty-first division of the Mexican Army.

Once, when I had complained to Analisa that it hadn't rained in a long time, she replied, "Too many gays."

I shot her a look. "What?" she asked defensively. "That's what they say down here."

Not quite believing her, I tried it out on the car-wash guy. "Why hasn't it rained in so long?" I asked in an innocent voice.

"Too many gays," he answered without a blink. As did the cop who patrolled the area around Tippy Toes, as did the guy repainting my house, as did the man repairing my shoes on the sidewalk at the Plazuela República. Go figure.

At twenty years old, Alex was a survivor. He had sought refuge in his grandmother's house, and Noah had been helping him out, paying Alex to watch Italya for a few hours a day while he and Martha were at the salon. I saw firsthand how sweet he was with the baby, so kind and gentle. And I could relate all too well to his pain. Yes, it was Sergio and Teresa's house, and it was Sergio and Teresa's rules, but what Sergio and Teresa just didn't get was how their relentless demands about Alex's hair, about his clothing, the touch of mascara he sometimes wore, were tearing his soul apart. They may have wanted what they thought was best for him, but to him it felt like a complete rejection of his very identity, a refusal to love him for who he was. My own mom didn't like me fat. She thought being skinny would be best for me. But that just wasn't who I was. And Lord, did that hurt.

There was another reason compelling me to open the door of Tippy Toes to Alex. During my hairdressing days in Michigan, I became acquainted with a sweet nineteen-year-old boy who used to frequently come into the salon for makeup tips and eyebrow waxings. I suspected that his appointments were often just an excuse to talk. In conservative Holland, I was a rare friendly shoulder to lean on. One day, he was my last appointment on the books, and he was late. After half an hour of waiting, I left to go home. Apparently he showed up shortly after, but refused to let anyone else do the job. He only wanted me. That night, he committed suicide.

I knew Alex well enough to know he, in all probability, wasn't a candidate for suicide, but the memory of the boy from Michigan was one that had haunted me for fifteen years. And the two of them did remind me a bit of each other, with their love of makeup and their flamboyant clothes. And I did worry that Alex might be taken advantage of by the wrong people. So into Tippy Toes he came. He was family, and that's where he belonged.

I LEFT DENIS AT THE FOOD TABLE, WHERE HE was deliberating over some puffy round things with hot sauce on them, and picked my way through the dancing kids and through the open door into Martha's mom's room, where Luz was sitting on the bed, tuning out the ruckus under a large set of earphones.

"Whatcha drawing?" I asked, gesturing to the pad on her lap. Luz smiled shyly, turned the page around, and held it up for me to see. A swarm of those wide-eyed, mop-headed Japanese comic-book characters stared back at me. "That's really cool! Muy bueno!" Luz's smile grew a little bit broader. "You really could be an artist."

At Tippy Toes, Luz was finally starting to shine. At first things were iffy, she seemed so afraid, refusing to look the customers in the eyes. I'd ask those I knew to talk to her, engage her, in English or Spanish or whatever, anything to help her connect. But it wasn't working. Luz just couldn't seem to get the feel for the job. My head was telling me I had to let her go—my business was too new to jeopardize relationships with the customers. But my heart kept telling me to give her a chance. So I called in the cavalry, and they went into overdrive. Martha would park herself next to Luz, counseling her step by step as she did a pedicure, while Noah would distract the customer with a little chitchat. As Luz tended to get a little heavy-handed with the polish, Teresa would sweep in the minute it was time to open the bottle, and take over the job. Then Selena would push Teresa out of the chair, and paint on a design. They were like runners in a relay, passing the baton. Soon customers were requesting Luz, who by now would grab their feet with the confidence of an old pro. And when I, more than once, caught sight of Luz smiling at something overheard in English, it became clear to me just how quickly, and thoroughly, she was catching on.

I loved the way everyone circled the wagons to take care of Luz. That seemed to be the way they did things on The Hill, I thought, as I observed women coming in and out of the open front door, tag-teaming each other as watchdogs for those kids who had run outside to play. A toddler falls down? The closest pair of arms picks him up and kisses his boo-boo. Someone's thirsty? Whoever hears the plea grabs the bottle. Everyone does what they can, what they know how to do, to help. It just seems to be who they are. They may not have the resources to keep kids in school, or the wherewithal to push them down a different path, or the courage to tell them to dare to be different, but if someone in the family needs a little help? There's a whole army of folks out there who will have their backs before they can even send out an SOS. They did what they could.

"Denis," I shouted above the din of the party, "I want to talk to you about something!"

"Uh-oh."

"Oh, just be quiet, and hear me out!" I yelled. "I have an idea!"

"Double uh-oh." He held up his pack of cigarettes and pointed to the door. I followed close behind.

"Okay," I continued, "tell me. What is it that I do best?"

Denis held his lighter in midair. "Is this a trick question?"

"Seriously, what am I really, really good at?"

He shrugged his shoulders. "Doing hair?"

"Exactly! And what is it that upsets me the most?"

"Um, when I watch TV and don't listen to what you say?"

"Besides that."

"When I go to Josi's store in my pajamas?"

"Those aren't pajamas. They're underwear! No, I mean what is it that I see around here that makes me crazy, that makes me want to do something but I never know what?"

"I don't know, the sewage in the street? Too much spandex?"

"It's the girls! You know, like the flower girls, and the others on the streets. And not just them, it's a lot of these girls, too." I pointed back inside the house. "These girls need to know that they can be somebody, anybody, if they try hard enough. And then there are the others—the girls who have no family, or families that don't care—the kids in orphanages and homes. You know how many of those there are around here. There are fund-raisers just about every night of the week."

"So you're going to do everybody's hair?"

"Don't be silly. Of course not."

"You're going to give everyone a job at Tippy Toes?"

"I'm practically doing that already." In fact, Martha's mother's living room did look a little like a Tippy Toes company picnic that afternoon. It made me feel good that the salon was providing work for so many of my extended family. In my own way, I sort of had their backs. It's what I could bring to the table. But I knew that I had the capability to do more, and with that came a *responsibility* to do more. And I had to do it in the way that *I* knew best.

"You're not going to start a beauty school, are you?" Poor Denis had been habitually subjected to my tales of woe over the anguish of having to leave behind all I had built in Kabul, and had been a witness to my vows to never do anything like it again.

"Lord no," I assured him. "But you're close!" I took a deep breath. "I am going to figure out a way to send some of the girls down here to beauty school." Denis raised his bushy white eyebrows. "No, really. It makes so much sense. If these girls knew a trade, they'd always have a way to support themselves, and their children when they have them. And everybody, everywhere, needs a hairdresser, right?" Denis nodded. "And even if they don't stick with hairdressing, at least they'll gain the confidence that comes with actually accomplishing something; at least they'll know they have the capability to do more than sell flowers, or worse."

Hearing my idea spoken out loud was a little scary, but my mind was already swimming with things I had to do to get the ball rolling. Poor Denis, I thought. He probably thought he was getting some chilled-out retiree to kick back with for his golden years, and here I was running a crazy business and starting a whole new project on top of it. But to his credit, and to my delight, his only response was to take my hand in his and say, "Go for it."

"Pi-ña-ta! Pi-ña-ta! Pi-ña-ta!" The house behind us was suddenly filled with squeals of excitement, with kids leaping over each other for the chance to be first in line to whack the red and blue Spider-Man piñata (which looked about as much like Spider-Man as I did) strung up in effigy from a rope across the ceiling. Of course, the birthday boy went first, and after a few determined swings, the cardboard burst open, sending everyone scrambling on their bellies in a free-for-all. I'd seen full-grown adults, my Tippy Toes girls, in fact, practically kill each other over piñata spillage during a fiesta. They dived into the frenzy in their stilettos, pushed each other out of the way, and actually sat on their claimed treasure to keep anyone else from getting it. All this over a few cheap sweets.

"Those must be really good candies," I said to Martha as she beamed at her son with pride.

"It is for good luck, Debbie." She tucked one into my pocket and peered out the door. I followed her gaze to the darkening sky. "You should go now. It will be night soon."

WHEN RENEE FIRST SHOWED UP AT TIPPY Toes, she looked like a little drowned pup. Her baby-fine blond hair seemed to have melted in the heat and humidity, and it was sticking to her scalp like skinny wet linguine. Of course, she was a walk-in who had asked only for a mani-pedi, so what could I say? Well, let's just say that whatever I said, by the time she left I had her booked for a full eight-hour session of hair extensions, and armed with explicit instructions on where and how to buy the hair herself, online, as the tax we'd have to pay on imported hair down here would double her cost, and she was heading back to the States for a while. I gave her a warning: beware of the scams. There are so many hair cowboys ripping people off out there these days it's ridiculous. Human hair has become so valuable that salons are being robbed for their hair, with the cash left behind in the register. Ukraine, I told Renee. Make sure the hair is Ukrainian. I provided her with my connection in Kiev and wished her luck.

When she returned a couple of months later, she proudly plopped her bag of hair down in front of me like a cat presenting a dead mouse at his master's feet. I nearly gasped. Renee had obviously asked for the lightest blond hair in all of Ukraine. She got it. Hooker bleached-blond hair, so overprocessed that it was going to be a hairdresser's nightmare. Daniela shot me a look, and I shot one back. Then we politely excused ourselves and headed to the back room to perform a miracle.

I grabbed one ponytail and Daniela grabbed the other, and we frantically began to mix. We needed to darken half the hair so the colors would blend. "Keep trying," I whispered to Daniela as I headed back to talk to Renee about style and length.

"Debbie!" came a panicky voice from the back room. "Debbie! Come!"

Behind the door, Daniela held up two olive green ponytails. "Verde, Debbie," she said with a frown. "Green."

Renee waited patiently, unaware of the behind-the-scenes maneuvers that were being done to turn her very expensive hair not-green. After all, we still had eight long hours of togetherness ahead, and there was no way I was about to get started on the wrong foot. It took every bit of color in my cupboards and every bit of hairdresser knowledge in my head to save that hair that day.

Once Daniela and I actually got started on Renee, it was like three old friends swapping tales at a high school reunion. When you spend eight hours together, committed to a tedious job that can't be left half done, you'd better pray you'll find plenty to talk about—never a problem for me. Luckily my two partners in crime were up to the task.

Renee told us she was married to a successful Texas car dealer. But her privileged life came with a large dose of pain—she had lost her son under tragic circumstances six years earlier. A tear came to Daniela's eye as she picked up the gist of Renee's story. In an attempt to change the channel from sad to happy, I shared some video I had on my phone of Daniela's little girl dancing with Derek at his birthday party, and told Renee a little about life on The Hill. Later I shared my story of Kabul, and all I had left behind. Eventually the conversation came around to my idea about sending girls to beauty school. Renee seemed fascinated.

"Why, Deb," she said in her sweet Texas drawl, "how on earth did you ever come up with that idea?"

I pointed to the copy of my *Kabul Beauty School* book that stood on display by the register. "Not such a wild idea. It just took me a while to find that part of me again."

"Well, I think it's awesome."

"You know," I said, "I just believe in my profession. And in a country like this, where an education is so tough to get, where birth control is so not the norm, at least from what I'm seeing, and where prostitution is legal, knowing how to do nails or hair can be a skill that gives girls a future they'd never have. It's really pretty simple."

"It sounds really exciting, Deb."

"And you know what I decided to call the whole thing? Project Mariposa. As in butterfly."

"Nice," said Renee with a little nod.

After another hour of exchanging chitchat about everything and anything, out of the clear blue sky Renee asked me a question.

"How much does it cost?"

"What, your extensions? Didn't I give you the price before—"

"No, how much does it cost to send a girl to beauty school?"

"Oh. Well, from what I've learned, it can come to anywhere from three to five thousand dollars before they're done, depending on what's included: equipment, uniform, tuition . . . you know."

Renee paused for a second. "Put me down for three."

"Three what?" I asked.

"Three students."

"But that could be fifteen thousand dollars!" I saw myself frozen in the mirror with my mouth hanging open like an empty coin purse, a strand of Renee's Ukrainian hair dangling from my motionless hand.

Renee just nodded. "You know, Debbie, I've been coming to my house down here for three years now. I love this place, and I've been trying to figure out a way to give something back. This, I can do. I can get the money. If there is one thing I know I'm good at, it's getting my friends to say yes." She smiled a sweet smile that left me no doubt about that. "It's time for me to rally the troops."

It was time for me to find more girls! And it was time for me to put my money (or rather Renee and her friends' money) where my mouth was. I had been planning on starting up slowly, and small, just to see how things went before I began hitting up my own friends and clients for donations. So far I only had one girl, Rosa, enrolled. I had heard about her from a few of the expat gang who had gotten involved with La Casa Nueva Vida, the home for girls. She was only fifteen years old, and had seen more trouble in her life than most of us do in an entire lifetime. Things got so bad at home that the social services therapist recommended she be removed from the situation. She was getting lots of support at the Casa, and she seemed determined and responsible enough to take beauty school seriously. But I was paying her tuition a week at a time, just in case.

I didn't want to rush into a decision about who

to choose as Renee's girls. This was a lot of money we were talking about, and I wanted to find girls who would be sure to stick with the program, who would do us proud. I already had one in mind. Lupe had been in an orphanage since she was seven years old. Now she was seventeen. I had heard from several clients who volunteered there that this girl would tell anyone who would listen that she wanted to become a hairdresser. Perfect! But I didn't want her starting alone. Mexican women, I knew from watching my Tippy Toes staff, worked better in teams. They hated doing things on their own. Everything was always in pairs. I'd send Selena to the beauty supply store for polish, and when I'd turn around Daniela would be gone, too. I needed to find a partner for Lupe. For weeks I kept my eyes and ears open, and asked everyone I knew for suggestions. I felt a lot of pressure to make the right choice.

One morning, as I entered Tippy Toes I saw Martha and Teresa deep in conversation. Teresa was clucking her tongue and shaking her head, clearly concerned by something, or someone. "What?" I asked Martha. "Is something wrong?"

"It's Gaby. Our niece. You know, Luz's little sister."

"What's the matter with her now?" I'd heard some rumblings about Gaby before.

"We are worried, Debbie. She is sick, she does

not leave the house. She won't eat. She does nothing all day. Her mother is very upset."

"Is she sick-sick? Has she been to the doctor?"

"Yes, but it's not like that, Debbie. She is unhappy; she is shy. She doesn't go to school anymore. We don't know why she is so sad."

I pictured tall, beautiful Gaby lying around day after day, with nothing to get out of bed for, no reason to venture out of her house. It broke my heart that she was joining the ranks of so many other kids on The Hill, dropping out just a few years after they'd gone through the mandatory six grades, and then what? How could they possibly figure out a future for themselves? Then it occurred to me. Here I'd been searching high and low for my next beauty school candidate, and there had been one right under my nose all along. I had no idea if Gaby had any interest in hairdressing or not, but I knew it was just the ticket for her low self-esteem and lack of confidence. I told Martha my idea and sent her off to talk to her niece.

I filled in Renee on my plans. We were on our way to the orphanage to meet with Lupe and the nuns.

"Don't worry, Deb," she said when I expressed my worry that Gaby might already be too deep into her depression to latch on to a dream, and my frustration at not being able to communicate directly with her. "I've got a team of prayer warriors who will start praying for Gaby this very day. We'll get her off that hill and into school in no time."

"Well, I haven't heard a word from her yet. I'm going to leave the door open for one more week, and that's it. We've got to get things moving!"

The orphanage gate was halfway open when we arrived. They must be expecting us, I thought. The shaded courtyard was filled with picnic tables, climbing bars, swings, a slide, and in the middle a huge statue of a saint, or maybe a priest. Inside, boys were playing video games, older girls were comforting littler ones, and a bevy of nuns who looked like they had been inside those walls for a hundred years kept a watchful eye. "Lupe?" we asked of everyone we passed. Finally we were pointed to a picnic table out back, where a pretty young girl with long dark hair and perfect makeup sat quietly next to a tiny nun in a crisp blue dress and a gray pixie cut. The nun's eyes were glued to a laptop. She barely looked up as I made our introductions.

"What is this beauty school?" she snarled. "What kind of school is this with a surfboard in the front?" She turned the screen around to face us. I had to bite my lip to keep from laughing. The nun's research had led her to my Trip Advisor page for Tippy Toes, which shows an image of the Margaritaville Adirondack chairs and surfboard we have out front for "atmosphere."

It did sort of look more like a bar than anything else.

"No," I quickly assured her. "That's not the school." I pulled a brochure from my purse. "This is it. Instituto de Belleza. This is the school I'm thinking of for Lupe."

Now all we needed was Gaby. I had promised the nun that Lupe would be attending school with another girl. At first Martha had told me that Gaby had said no to the idea, she was too afraid. Working at Tippy Toes might be okay, being among family and all, but going to a place filled with strangers, that was just too scary. Now I was even more worried, not so much about the project, but about Gaby. She was too young to give up. Because it's acceptable down here for children to stay in their parents' homes for life, too many of them don't feel any pressure to make anything of themselves. A lot of the girls just figure if anything's going to get them out of the house, it's going to be a man. There is no need to become independent. Even Martha, who was always a hard worker, didn't move out until Noah came along. Maybe Gaby didn't want to be a hairdresser, but I knew that just doing this would be a life-changing experience for her, no matter what. I dug in my heels and sent Luz to talk some sense into her sister. Luz was thriving at Tippy Toes. She never missed a day of work, and was never late. And by now she even had earned enough money, and gained enough confidence, to go to tattoo school at night. Judging from what I saw in Luz, I knew that if we could get Gaby to commit, she would take beauty school seriously. Her mother, Alicia, would make sure of that, as would just about everyone else on The Hill.

The next Monday Renee and I enrolled the girls at Instituto de Belleza. Gaby, with two days left to make up her mind, had finally said yes. I was more than relieved. The two girls sat silently in the back of the Mini as we wound our way through the crowded downtown streets. Though I had asked my friend Lisa to come along to translate, she bowed out at the last minute with a stomach bug, so I was going to have to rely on Google Translate to make this happen. And it almost didn't. The guy who sashayed up to the door of the school greeted us with an attitude befitting a Hollywood diva. He rolled his eyes when he saw it was me again. We had met before, when I dropped by to check out the school and get the tuition rates. The first time I was there, someone had taken me into the office and rattled off the list of rates, then immediately slashed everything on the list and gave me a new set of prices. It felt like a time-share presentation. I was confused, so they waved the diva guy over, assuring me that he spoke English. I offered my best smile and said, "Usted habla inglés?"

"No," he said with the wag of a finger. "No English." Then he turned and left the room.

This time he led us to a tiny plastic table. Doubting he'd have the patience to wait while I typed my questions into my phone, I instead called Lisa and asked her to translate via speakerphone. He then started pointing at pictures in a binder as he explained the curriculum. Or at least that's what I gathered he was doing, because about two minutes in, Lisa's voice came booming through the phone. "Deb! This guy's speaking so fast I have no idea what he's saying. It doesn't even sound like Spanish to me." We moved on to the price list. I wrote down what I had been quoted and handed it to him.

"No," he said. "Es más." It's more.

"But that's what the other guy told me!"

"Es lo que dijo el otro hombre," Lisa translated.

"Lo despidieron," he replied almost before she had the words out.

"He's been fired, Deb."

"Ask him if I can speak to the manager. Maybe if I tell him we're nonprofit he'll cut us a break. Tell him we're going to be sending lots of students here."

Lisa asked. "He is the manager, Deb."

"Then ask if we can speak to the owner." It was only later that I learned from Martha that in Mexico you never, ever ask to speak to an owner of a business, as they will suspect you might be a kidnapper out for ransom.

So we got off on the wrong foot. But after all the schools I had checked out, this still seemed like the best one, so I sent Martha to iron out the details. She came back mad as a hornet, insisting we change schools.

"What happened?" I asked.

"The Argentinian," she answered, her lips curling in disgust.

But that day, nothing mattered but what happened when the Argentinian diva told Lupe and Gaby that they could start tomorrow. At first Gaby's look was one of sheer terror. But then something shifted. She stood up a little taller, her shoulders relaxed, and I could almost see a sense of purpose and pride filling up her insides bit by bit. It was as if she had gone in an instant from a scared little girl to the person in charge. And for the first time since I met her, Lupe smiled, revealing a mouthful of beautiful white teeth that I swear would glow in the dark. Renee and I struggled to fight back our tears.

Now it was time to go shop for uniforms and shoes. The pants were easy: black and sturdy enough to withstand multiple washings. Then it was upstairs for the shoes, sensible shoes that would help a person survive standing on her feet all day. I knew all about that, and Renee, a former nurse, knew all about that as well. But the girls balked at the sneakers and walking shoes we pointed them toward.

"Zapatos de la abuela," I overheard Lupe whisper into Gaby's ear. Grandma shoes. I took a stiletto from Lupe's hand and placed it back on the rack.

We tried another store. Renee shook her head at the red patent ballet slippers Gaby was eyeing. "No arch support, no school," she said, shaking her head. The girls looked outraged by the whole ordeal, as if insisting on comfortable shoes were a form of abuse. How I wished I knew how to say *get with the program* in Spanish. I was a little embarrassed by the girls' behavior, as I had so wanted them to make a good impression on Renee. I tried using the eye I used to give my own kids when they misbehaved in a public place, but Lupe just wouldn't quit with the heels and platforms and wedges. Gaby must have known from hearing about me that this was a battle she wasn't going to win, and luckily she took charge in the nick of time, before I totally lost it. A few choice words into Lupe's ear and we were good to go, with two brand-spanking-new pairs of sneakers under our arms.

Back at Tippy Toes, it was time for a pep talk. "Tell them that they need to wear their uniforms every single day," I instructed Martha before sending the girls off. "Including the shoes. And under no circumstances can they ever be late." I remembered my no-tolerance policy in Kabul. *It was a suicide bomb,* they'd claim. *It was a rocket attack!* You live in Afghanistan, I'd tell them. These things happen. If you live in New York, you plan on traffic. You just leave earlier. I was not going to change my rules for Mazatlán.

And then came Jessie. Down here there's always some story about someone's brother's sister's cousin's sister's mother's son's stepchild who did something or needed something or saw something, so when Martha started telling me about how she was sort of related to a girl named Jessie in some convoluted way that I doubt included bloodlines, I was barely listening. But when she came to the part where she asked me to send Jessie to beauty school, my ears perked up. Martha is not the bleeding-heart type, so I knew this girl's story had to be serious. And it was. Jessie was fourteen when her mother died. She and her brother were shipped off by their stepfather, to go live with their father in Mazatlán. He had no interest in raising his children, so off they went to stay with their other brother and his wife, Celina, a couple barely out of their own childhood. Jessie was forced to help the little group survive by selling pots and pans door-to-door. Between that and caring for her little brother, there was no time for school. Besides, when she had been sent north to Mazatlán all her school records had been left behind. Nobody had bothered to retrieve them. Now Celina was pregnant, and things were about to become even more desperate.

So down to Instituto de Belleza Martha and I marched, a solemn Jessie lagging slightly behind, squinting in the midafternoon sun. But once inside, she continued to squint, her eyes tiny slits piercing her broad, smooth face.

"I don't think she can see, Debbie." Martha frowned.

I pointed to a diagram of fingernails posted behind the desk. "Ask her what that says."

Jessie just shrugged at the question.

"Oh my Lord," I said out loud. "You have got to be kidding."

On our way to the optician Martha got the rest of Jessie's story. She used to wear glasses, but around the time her mother died her eyes worsened, and her glasses broke. There was no one around to get her another pair, so for three years she had been walking around nearly blind. The eye doctor told us she could barely see two feet in front of her.

When Jessie came by Tippy Toes a week later with her Coke-bottle lenses perched on her nose, I wanted to melt.

"Cómo están?" I asked. How are they?

"She says she gets a headache," Martha told me.

"Well, remind her that the doctor said it will take time to get used to the glasses."

Jessie remained silent.

"Tell her it will be okay, Martha. The headaches will go away, school starts on Saturday, it's all good." I wanted so badly to see this girl's smile.

As Jessie slowly turned to leave the salon, I was suddenly caught off guard by a memory so painfully overwhelming I had to sit. Seven years earlier I had shown up for a visit to the Kabul Welayat, a women's prison in Afghanistan, loaded with a big box of Paul Mitchell gift bags stuffed with hair ribbons and nail polish and all sorts of girly stuff donated by church groups and schools back in Michigan. One look at the place and the women inside sent me reeling into a spiral of shame. Here these women had been locked inside this hellhole because they'd been raped, because they'd been beaten by their husbands, because they'd dared to run away with a man they loved, and I was all excited to be bringing them friggin' goodie bags? What on earth had I been thinking? It was the same with Jessie, I thought. She needed so much more than a stupid pair of glasses and a beauty school diploma to hang on her wall. She needed someone to care for her, to love her, to tell her she was someone special. She needed a mom. And here I was thinking I was doing enough for her?

I felt the tears start to roll down my cheeks. And it wasn't just her, I thought. It was all the girls. There was no way I'd be able to give them all everything they needed. A part of me wished I'd never heard their stories, wished I'd just stayed on the outside barely looking in, maybe writing a check here and there or plucking a card off an angel tree. It's so much easier not to know, because once you do, you have no choice. You have to act. You have to figure out something to do about it. It's like with that damn iguana—the minute you open your eyes and really *see* something, there is no turning back.

I heaved a huge sigh and wiped my cheeks with the back of my hand. Keep your eye on the ball, Deb, I told myself. You're doing what you're supposed to be doing. Keep your blubbering to yourself. Stay focused. Keep the girls on course, and let them know you are there for them. And for God's sake, learn to speak Spanish already, would you?

THE SEASONS HAD CHANGED BY THE TIME I got back to Pátzcuaro. Of course, you'd never know it in Mazatlán, where it was still so hot that you could fry a tortilla just by dropping it on the sidewalk. But dropping a tortilla would mean you'd have to prepare for a lot of company, or so my girls told me. I took off on a Wednesday, as starting *anything* on a Tuesday, including a journey, they also told me, will bring bad luck. Why take chances? It would still give me plenty of time to spend with Cynthia before everything started.

Cynthia had talked me into coming for El Día de los Muertos—the Day of the Dead. While in Mazatlán the Day of the Dead is celebrated with a parade, and by chasing a donkey cart down the street in pursuit of free beers (at least as far as I could tell), in Pátzcuaro it's the real deal, and a huge draw for the thousands of people who flock there every November 1. I was curious and excited, but also a little trepidatious. Death had always creeped me out, going way back to that childhood fear of my parents dying and leaving me all alone. Their way of dealing with that was to do everything in their power to shield me from the experience of death, including bringing another, identical Chihuahua into the house when Spot died. To be fair, they did try to broach the subject of their own mortality after I was well into my twenties, but every time they'd start to talk about wills and "arrangements," I'd cover my ears and drown out their words with a shrill *la-la-la*. In fact, I'd never had much experience with death, except for my father's, and I wasn't even around for that. He had been wheelchair-bound and suffering from Alzheimer's for years before I left for Kabul, and since I was originally going there for only one month I figured nothing would change. Besides, my dad had always played the *I could be dead tomorrow* card, for all sorts of purposes, and by then I had learned to blow it off. When I heard my mom's voice on the phone from Michigan, I could tell things weren't going well. But she knew I couldn't get home until the end of the month, so she never came out and said just how bad things were. When I checked in during a layover in New York, stuck in a storm, nobody told me he had already passed while I was in flight. Back in Holland, they took me straight from the airport to the funeral home, where Mom wanted me to see Dad before he was cremated. It pained me that we never got to say good-bye to each other. Though it had been nearly ten years by now, I still hadn't really dealt with the grief, as I'd never been able to get past the guilt of being in Kabul, and not by his side.

But in Pátzcuaro, during Day of the Dead, it wasn't about grief. In fact, despite all the images of skulls and skeletons and coffins and bones slapped onto everything from T-shirts to bread, it was life that was being celebrated—the lives of those who were no longer living. And Cynthia had promised a transforming experience. *Energy changes,* she told me. *Things happen.*

IT FEELS SO GOOD TO BE ABLE TO PULL ON A sweater, I thought as I headed out from my room into the cool courtyard of Casa Encantada to meet Cynthia for a day of shopping. I found her in the open dining area, surrounded by B&B guests eager for sightseeing and restaurant suggestions. The town was packed with tourists from all over Mexico, and all around the world, judging from the jumble of languages I'd heard swirling around since I'd arrived.

"Ready?" asked Cynthia after she handed a map to a young couple with three kids. I held up one finger in the air and gulped down my coffee as fast as I could. Our first stop was to be Santa Clara del Cobre, an old copper mining town known for its handmade crafts, which these days were completely made from recycled wire and cable.

A light drizzle began to fall as we started to make our way through the mountains, their peaks barely visible through the mist. Though the air was thick with moisture, somehow it felt more like a cozy blanket than the murky mess it really was, judging from the muddy fields and increasingly slick roads. I watched through the window as the scrubby roadside pulsed from color to black-and-white to color again as the sun struggled to break free from the clouds. Even the cattle seemed to have been lulled into a state of blind contentment, as was clear by the look on one surprised cow's face as she found herself skidding across two lanes of cars on her knees, scrambling frantically to her feet as she safely reached the other side.

We kept our pace to a crawl as we neared the entrance of Santa Clara, much to the delight of the wily children who had strategically positioned themselves on both sides of the speed bumps, thrusting their hollowed-out gourds toward our windows in hopes of scoring some holiday candy or loose change. Once our pockets were empty, we continued down the main street past the low whitewashed buildings, with their tiled roofs and uniform black and red lettering, each façade painted with a broad, horizontal red stripe across its base to camouflage the dirt. If I didn't know any better, I would have sworn we'd just completed a huge circle ending back at Pátzcuaro, where all the buildings were identical to these. But with the glare bouncing off the copper gazebo in the middle of the town square, and the copper pots, pans, plates, shot glasses, clocks, jewelry, vases, beds, tables, chairs, light switches, counters, sinks, and even bathtubs lining the streets, there was no mistaking where we were.

Cynthia led me into her favorite shop, where I was stopped dead in my tracks, right inside the doorway, by a mound of bright yellow flowers cradling an ornate copper cross. Directly above, on a shelf lined with even more flowers, sat a photo of a rakish-looking guy in jeans, a hand in one pocket. And above that, on yet another flower-lined shelf, was his straw hat, its brim curled upward in a sporty arc.

"Oh my," I said out loud, suddenly sad for this family for their recent loss.

"Es nuestro padre," said a woman who had slid in beside me. I looked up, surprised to see her smile.

Cynthia's laugh tinkled across the room. "It's okay, Deb. This guy probably died years ago. You're going to see lots of altars and shrines everywhere this week. Beautiful, eh?"

The workmanship displayed on the shelves of the little shop was stunning. My favorites were the etched copper plates, each depicting a different image related to the Day of the Dead, in a sort of bold, minimalistic style. The woman told us they were designed by her daughter, the most recent member of the family to apprentice in the craft. She then took us to their workshop out back, which, if it weren't for the still-warm embers in the open fire pit, I would have sworn was a stage set, with its primitive tools and tree-stump benches. I loved imagining this family, like mine, passing down the tricks of their trade from generation to generation, but in a parallel universe on the other side of the world.

I BEGAN TO NOTICE SIGNS OF THE APPROACHING holiday all around the lake as we headed back to Pátzcuaro with three of those magnificent copper plates and four copper pedicure tubs tucked safely away in the trunk. Pickup trucks, some practically buried under piles of orange marigolds and purple cockscomb, and others crammed with passengers standing shoulder to shoulder like penned-in livestock in the back, sped past us on their way to who knew where. Near a crossroad leading into one village, we stopped to watch a group of men constructing a huge wooden arch, which Cynthia explained would later be completely covered by flowers and erected over the intersection as a guide for the spirits of loved ones heading back home for their yearly visit, sort of like when you put balloons outside your house to let everyone know where the party is.

That afternoon was when my blood really got

pumping. The annual crafts market had been set up in the Plaza Grande. As I strolled those aisles, serenaded by the music of a soft rain falling on the tarps overhead, the experience seemed for me like what spending a long winter's afternoon in the Louvre must be for some people. But even better, because the artists were right there beside you—the indigenous women with gray braids and long, tiered skirts proudly displaying their elaborately embroidered linens and blouses, and the sturdy, ruddy men with their carved masks and rich, glossy pottery. These people had come from all over Mexico with their creations, with the best of the best vying in a formal competition up in the basilica. One Indian woman handed me a card that described the embroiderers of her town as story-tellers. *We tell our stories with needle and thread.* And indeed, when I looked closely at their work, I saw amazingly complex tales of love and marriage, of the harvest, of death. It wasn't long before I was forced to stop and buy one of those giant plastic totes to carry around all my new treasures. There were dishes and hats and purses and scarves, toys and mittens and sweaters and candelabras. And, of course, Catrinas. Rows and rows of Catrinas that, despite their gaping jaws and empty eye sockets, were alive with color and bursting with a whimsy that made the whole gravity of death seem like such a silly notion.

I was in heaven, wandering from booth to booth,

admiring the artisans' work, fingering their wares, bargaining for deals. A friend once told me that my true calling was marketplace ministry. When I first got to Kabul, I'd defy the security restrictions and sneak out by myself to wander around Chicken Street, where the vendors and I got to know each other by name. "Miss Debbie!" they'd call out, inviting me in for some tea and conversation. In fact, I'd made friends with vendors from Addis Ababa to Nepal. Just name a town or mountain village, and I'll tell you about the shops and the people who own them, how many children they have and what their wives' names are. Knowing whose hands made what has always made every purchase seem just that much more special to me.

More recently, on a road trip near Oaxaca, I spent a whole afternoon trying to locate the woman who had embroidered a fringed scarf I found in the market. I wanted more, and I wanted to meet the person behind these beautiful creations. We wound up in a teeny town in the pouring rain. Nothing looked open, but when I showed the scarf to the one man on the sidewalk, he motioned for me to follow, leaving me in front of an eight-by-ten countertop in a shop. I could see a woman seated inside, and next to her, on another plastic chair, was a young, pimply kid with the telltale crisp white shirt and skinny black tie of a Mormon missionary. What I didn't see were any scarves that came close to resembling the one I held in my hand.

"Do you want me to help you?" the boy offered as I stood in the doorway trying to figure out how to make this happen.

"Do you speak Spanish?" I asked hopefully. Before I knew it, despite his language skills, which were barely better than mine, the woman apparently told the boy to watch the store, and was out the door, hopefully to return with more scarves.

"These people are so nice," the boy said, gesturing for me to sit. "We've baptized quite a lot of them." Then he eagerly began his spiel on me.

"Thanks, but I'm good," I interrupted. "I'm not really that into being converted right now." He slumped his shoulders, lowering his gaze to the ground. "Though I do enjoy watching *Big Love*," I added.

IT WASN'T UNTIL AFTER THE LAST OF CYNTHIA'S guests had settled in for the night that we got a chance to relax. She grabbed a bottle of wine and some chips from the kitchen and the two of us plopped ourselves down on the terrace outside her room.

"So are you feeling it, Deb?" she asked as Señorita and Max sailed onto her lap.

I lifted my feet onto the empty chair facing me

and moaned. "Right now I'm feeling something, but I doubt it's what you're asking about."

Cynthia laughed. "You *are* a champion shopper, eh?" She took a sip of her wine. "Did you know that shopping can be an addiction?"

"Whoa, back off there, missy. Don't be messing with my shopping."

"No, seriously, Deb. It can be a coping strategy for people affected by trauma, just like eating disorders, or drug abuse. It's what some people call dissociative behavior, a way of avoiding whatever's going on."

"Thanks a lot, pal. I thought you said I was getting better. Now you tell me I'm suffering from shopping sickness?"

"I'm just saying, Deb. But seriously, shopping can provide a shot of dopamine for some people, which makes them feel happy and satisfied, for however long it lasts. That's how it becomes an addiction."

I didn't want to admit it out loud to Cynthia, but I could remember the rush I used to get from staying up all night shopping online in California, and the withdrawal I went through after moving to Mexico, where the customs hassles I'd have to face and the duty I'd have to pay on anything I ordered forced me to go cold turkey. I had always suspected my weight problems were somehow connected to bigger issues, but shopping? Really?

Cynthia wasn't through with me yet. "And yes,

I do think you are definitely on the road to healing, but I don't want you to think it's going to be like getting over a cold, or beating cancer. It's not going to be like you have it one minute, and then poof, it's gone."

"Damn." I unzipped my boots and kicked them off under the table. "You know, I still don't quite get it. Unless I'm blocking something, for the life of me I just can't pinpoint whatever it was or whoever it was that did its number on me."

"But it's not always like that. In your case, it could very well be a chain of escalating events; it could be a series of abusive situations throughout your life. And I suspect it probably started when you were a kid."

"But I've told you, my parents weren't abusive!" I protested. I was all too familiar by now with stories of rough childhoods. Mine was idyllic by comparison.

"Don't be offended, Deb. That's not what I said. All I'm saying is that there are all different kinds of abuse. Some of us grow up with parents who are so caught up in their own drama that they don't attune to us emotionally, and then we don't learn to attune to ourselves."

Cynthia and I had discussed the dynamics between me, my mom, and my dad, and how my mom had used me in a game of two against one. "But I obviously survived my childhood, and that obviously was a long, long time ago."

"Yes it was, you old lady. But childhood is when we develop our beliefs about how we fit in, what we deserve, how we interact with others."

"Lots of people grow up in less-than-perfect households, right? So why have I been the one walking around like a ticking bomb?"

"Because people don't all break the same. In a way, trauma is just part of being human. Most of us have had at least one experience where something was a threat to our security or well-being, but most people manage to cope. Some even use it to their benefit. I heard someone say once that it's like dropping two glass bottles at the same time. One might crumble and one might break into giant sharp pieces. The same thing that crushes one person might make another stronger."

"But my parents? Even though they might not have gotten along so well, they were always supportive of my decisions, good or bad."

"Good people can do harmful things, Deb. Without even realizing it. And like I said, if they are a part of the picture, they're no doubt just a part of it. But I do believe your heightened arousal level probably started when you were a kid, because you don't seem to have much of a sense of missing your lower gears."

"I don't know. Maybe I'm just a high-energy person or something."

Cynthia ignored my theory. "But whatever the root of our trauma, we tend to re-create the sensation by sending ourselves into familiar situations. Look at your own life. You went from one lion's den to the next, into relationships where you were a victim, where sometimes somebody was intimidating and controlling, where there was emotional abuse. And look at where you've put yourself, geographically. Just being at Ground Zero right after 9/11 had to be traumatic. And then Afghanistan? You weren't just surrounded by danger, it was sitting in your living room having a smoke! It's like you went from the frying pan into the fire into a roaring blaze. We're talking cumulative trauma."

"My friend Karen from Michigan likes to say that in Afghanistan I was like a frog dropped into a pot of cold water put on to boil. The frog just sits there as the water heats up slowly, but it won't jump out of the pot. It doesn't even know it's being boiled to death."

"But you did jump out. Escaping from Afghanistan was your launching point toward the healing process."

"Yeah, but that wasn't my choice. It was more like a giant hand came and grabbed me by the collar, and yanked me out."

Cynthia shook her head. "It doesn't matter, girl. Even though that brain of yours might not have known how to take charge, your body did, at least once you created enough safety around yourself to free up your natural impulses, to allow yourself to change, to start processing all that shit you'd been thrashing around in for all those years."

"But I wasn't looking to create safety. I was way more comfortable in a war zone than I was in the suburbs. Trust me."

"Still doesn't matter. Stop going there. As painful as it was, all that sitting out there in Napa is what led you down here. It's all part of the process."

"So Mexico is my safe haven."

"Well, in a way."

"All I know is that something about this place just feels right." I stood and leaned over the railing, my gaze resting on the back wall of the empty courtyard below. "You know, when I first arrived in Mexico I felt like I was taking in my first full breath of air. And now, with Tippy Toes and the girls in school, even though my days are crazy busy, I actually feel calmer than I've ever felt."

"It's called being happy, Debbie."

"Who knew?" I poured us each a touch more wine and sat back down in my chair.

"Seriously, Deb, it's a huge shift for you to be able to enjoy that feeling of happiness. People with trauma tend to develop these core beliefs that they're not worthy, to the point where they don't think they deserve to have positive feelings."

"And you know what, Cyn? When I come up here, to Pátzcuaro, everything feels even more right, if that makes any sense to you."

"Aha, so you *are* feeling it." Cynthia sat back and rocked Señorita in her arms. "You've found your place, Deb. Not just geographically, but energetically. There are certain places on the planet that feel more like a fit for certain people. There's a *physical* reason you feel differently here. Don't forget about the vortexes. It's an energetic match for you down here."

I had to laugh. "Right now I feel like an energetic match for a mausoleum. I'm exhausted." The truth was, I had barely slept the night before. I didn't know if it was the place or if it was Cynthia's unrelenting poking at my psyche, but Pátzcuaro seemed to bring out the most vivid dreams and graphic memories in me. Last night's dream was one I had had before. It was clear that it stemmed from Noah's growing desperation to get the baby her American passport to allow for a visit to Michigan before it was too late, before my mom's dementia progressed much further, or worse. But in my dream, Italya and my mom finally do get to meet for the first time. My mom's mind is still all there, and they take to each other as though they have known one another forever. Italya is just old enough to say a few words and hears everyone calling my mom by her first name, Loie. *Can you say Nana?* Noah asks the baby. *Loibella*, she answers, clear as a bell, reaching out for my mother's arms. *Loibella.* Beautiful Loie.

"I wish my parents could see all this." I sighed. Cynthia raised one eyebrow.

"I mean, my life. To get to know the baby. To see what a good father Noah is, to see how well Zach is doing. We all went through a lot together. They'd be so proud of my kids, and of me, too. Mom would get such a kick out of the idea of the girls in beauty school, but it's hard to know how much she's actually grasping these days. And my dad, he never even got to witness what I built in Kabul, let alone any of this stuff. He would have loved to have seen a happily-ever-after to the roller coaster we were all on for so long." I shuddered a little at the thought of what a wild ride it had been.

Cynthia must have noticed. "You know what, Deb? Tomorrow we're going to build an altar for your father. You're going to welcome him back, tell him about Mexico, and Italya, and the boys, Tippy Toes, your beauty school project, and Denis. All of it. It's time for the two of you to spend some time together."

"Really?" I asked, as I felt a tear springing from my eye. Though the shrines that had been popping up in doorways and courtyards all around Pátzcuaro were incredibly captivating, it had never occurred to me to build one myself. But now the thought of it kind of made me tingle all over.

"Why not?" Really, I thought. Why not? The

thought of it felt somehow right, to show some respect for Dad, even if it was a little late for that. And who knew? Maybe it wasn't too late. I'd learned by now not to discount any of life's possibilities, especially down here. "I'll go with you to pick up everything we need." And with that, Cynthia stood and embraced me in one of her legendary bone-cracking hugs, and headed to her room with Max and Señorita close behind.

ARMINDA WAS ALREADY WAITING IN THE courtyard when I opened my door the next morning. Cynthia had hired her to lead a group of us on a preliminary tour of the cemeteries the day before the Day, to see firsthand what goes into the preparation for the big night. Being a Purépecha, a direct descendant of the indigenous people of the area, she was well versed in all of the Day of the Dead traditions.

"Isn't it sort of like the Mexican Halloween?" asked a stout man in Bermuda shorts and knee socks.

Arminda slowly shook her head. "Even though the Day of the Dead comes one day after Halloween, it was not always on that day. It was the Spanish who moved it to Todos los Santos— All Saints Day—because before, we celebrated in August, during the, how do you say, harvest time, when we were offering corn and squash and beans. Also wild duck from the lake, with molé. We had no chickens then."

My stomach growled as I tiptoed behind

Arminda to grab a breakfast cookie from the kitchen counter.

"It is very important to receive the spirits with enthusiasm. They are very hungry after their long journey. And thirsty. They are coming from far away. I don't know from where, but it is very far."

The small crowd nodded in unison, as if they had already experienced that journey themselves.

"Somebody asked me, is this sad for everybody? Personally, when my mom died I was very sad. But now I am very happy." Arminda took a deep breath. "I am very happy, because I am going to check with her, and stay with her, and it is only once a year we can do this. So I am very happy." She paused and smiled a little wistfully. "What you will see most today is the cleaning of the graves. This has been happening all week. They will pull the weeds, and make the dirt fresh. After, the family will decorate. You will see lots of cans, which will be filled with candles. It is the light which will guide the spirits to the cemetery or to the home where their family is waiting. It is believed that if they don't have a candle they have to light their finger to find their way, and they will be very sad because their loved ones have forgotten them. You can bring candles for graves who have no family there. It is important to have candles so the dead can find you. My mother told us, please, when I die, bring me a candle. I don't want to burn my finger looking for my place."

A polite laughter echoed through the courtyard. Cynthia hugged Arminda and began herding the group to the vans waiting on the street.

"A parade!" squealed one of the guests standing close to the gate. Outside, the cobblestone streets were jammed with schoolchildren, walking slowly and silently toward Plaza Grande as they scanned our faces for admiring looks. There were little girls in wide-brimmed, plumed hats, parasols, and fancy gowns, and boys in black suits, bow ties, and top hats, all with painted white faces and the blackened eyes of a skeletal corpse. There were veiled Catrina brides carrying flowers, and others who looked like they were celebrating a macabre First Communion, or like they could have been tiny grieving widows. Mustachioed little skeletons twirled their canes in their hands, stopping only to strike a serious pose for the awestruck tourists lining the sidewalk. A parade of dead children, I thought. But then again, I guess it wasn't any weirder than the zombies and mummies and Freddy Kruegers that were roaming around the streets up north this very day. But these kids were all so quiet! Eerily quiet. It was hard to imagine kids in the States being so well behaved and respectful. These little guys apparently knew better than to mess with the dead.

ARMINDA CONTINUED HER LESSON ON THE traditions of the day when we reached our first destination. I trailed behind the rest of the enthusiastic group, a little wary since, until now, setting foot in a cemetery was an experience I'd managed to avoid. Although I'm not sure what I had expected, whatever it was certainly wasn't this. Behind us, entire families were pouring through the gates with shovels and buckets and small machetes, their arms full of marigolds and baby's breath and tall white candles. I could see men hacking away at long pieces of sugarcane, which Arminda had explained would be used to build the arches adorning each grave. There was so much activity it was hard to imagine that this was supposed to be the ultimate place of rest.

We stood in a light mist, surrounded by mounds of freshly turned soil. Arminda quickly explained that these were not new graves, simply newly "renovated," in a way. They had been spruced up in preparation for the festivities. Cameras began to click as she continued with some advice. "Tomorrow night when you come, be, how do you say, respectful. If you see people who look sad, it is better to leave it alone. That means that person died this year, so they are still sad. Next year they will have a big celebration. You can take pictures, but no flash. Do not disturb people. But if someone offers you something, say 'muchas gracias.' Do not say 'no thank you.' They are making you a gift from the deceased. And now, please walk around and look. By tomorrow night, it will be transformed."

As I navigated the narrow rows between the graves, trying my damnedest not to step on the dead, I marveled at the works in progress. There were tiered mounds of wet dirt, looking almost like little adobe pyramids, and others that were just shallow piles of fresh soil bearing simple crosses. Others were more elaborate elevated marble or concrete monuments. Some were half covered with petals, while others supported ornate marigold lattices or sculptures that had been already erected. It was already a beautiful sight. I couldn't imagine it getting much better than this.

IT'S HARD TO EXPLAIN WHAT HAPPENED THE next day. Everything started out normal enough. Sticking to her promise to help with Dad's shrine, Cynthia led me to the flower market that had popped up next to the basilica, where dozens of trucks overflowed with fresh marigolds and cockscomb and baby's breath. The men who had climbed to the tops of the piles couldn't toss their bundles down fast enough to the waiting customers below. We passed through the long row of tables sagging under the weight of more blooms than I had ever seen in one place at one time, Cynthia filling my outstretched arms until I was forced to cry uncle. I felt like Miss America cradling the massive bouquet against my chest. I hoped Dad would appreciate the effort, and I also hoped that my allergies would be kind enough to grant me a day off.

The ton of flowers, added to those spare pounds I was still carrying around, made keeping up with Cynthia a chore. She was like a mountain goat on those hills. I struggled to catch my breath as we maneuvered our way through the crowded sidewalks. On the street across from the plaza, we managed to jostle ourselves up to the rickety tables covered with elaborately decorated sugar skulls, some with bright green eyelashes or neon pink teeth and sequin eyes, all swarming with bees that had hit a holiday jackpot. It was hard to make a choice. There were sugar skeletons sitting upright on top of their coffins, wearing sombreros and waving bottles of tequila, candy skeleton couples sitting on park benches made of Popsicle sticks, tiny sugar infants tucked into their little sugar coffins. It amazed me that something so incredibly sad could seem so cute and playful.

The afternoon was spent building the altar. First I cut the stems from all the flowers, as I had seen others do the day before in the cemetery. Then I began to arrange everything on the table Cynthia had put out for me in the courtyard. A glass of water in case Dad got thirsty, and cup of coffee, because he never really was too fond of water. In fact, I couldn't really remember him without a cup of coffee, either in his hand or on the table next to his favorite chair. A few pesos and a few dollars, because I figured he could probably use some cash while he was here, and who knew, he might want to pop up to D.C. to see Zach, or over to Michigan to drop in on Mom while he was out and about. Then came the five ducks made out of sugar, which I placed gently among the flowers. When I was a kid, my parents bought a house in the woods. A house that, for some reason, came with five ducks. Those ducks adored my dad. When my dad went to the mailbox, five ducks went with him. When Dad mowed the lawn, five ducks followed behind. He loved it. He'd put on his cowboy hat and boots, call the ducks, and march around the driveway like he was the commander of a duck platoon.

Next I added a bottle of Bohemia, a Dos Equis, and a Victoria. Why shouldn't Dad sample all the local beers while he had the chance, right? I couldn't not include a piece of cake, for the man who loved his sweets, for the man who once dipped into a bowl of potpourri thinking it must be some sort of fancy candy. And of course, the traditional Pan de Muerto, a sugary loaf criss-crossed with what looked like chicken bones sculpted from the dough. Oh, and a bowl of fruit, in the unlikely event that he'd decided to turn healthy in the afterlife. The final touch was a picture I had printed out in Cynthia's office. In it, a towheaded Zach, with a grin stretching ear to ear, is seated on the lap of a very large Santa in those big glasses that can only mean the 1980s. My dad. My dad the way I liked to remember him best.

"How's it going, Dad?" I whispered as I lit the candle, its flame dancing a crazy hula in the wind darting through the courtyard. "Long time no talk. Hell, we probably never really have talked, right? Why is that?"

I pulled up a patio chair and sat. By now I knew the answer to my own question. I cleared my throat and began to speak a little louder. "So, Dad, first of all I want you to know that things are going great for me." I pulled out my iPhone and scrolled through the photos. "See? This is Italya. Your great-granddaughter. She's a feisty little one. Just like me, right?" I propped the phone up next to Dad's photo. *And like you, too.* The smile remained frozen across the face beneath the red Santa hat, making me smile as well.

"I swear, Dad, if you could be here now, I think you'd be really proud. And honestly? I'm beginning to think I'm more like you than either of us probably ever realized. And you know what else? I'm proud of that." The words coming out of my mouth in the privacy of the empty courtyard took me by surprise. I had spent my entire life trying to not be like my dad.

"I wish I had understood a lot of things earlier. I realize now just how tough it must have been for you. Mom didn't leave much room for you in our little triangle, did she? No wonder you were grouchy." The flame suddenly became eerily still. I glanced over my shoulder and pulled my chair in a little closer. "Between you and me, Dad," I whispered, "I'm thinking maybe she wasn't so perfect after all. I'm just saying."

I rearranged the little sugar ducks in a row facing my dad's photo. "You know, when push came to shove, you were always there for me. And don't think I don't realize that. 'Cause I do. And you know what else? Without you I would never have had the balls to do half the stuff I've done. Sure, Mom always said I could be whatever I wanted to be, but you were the one who actually showed me that anything was possible, who went out and did anything and everything possible, or at least tried. And there's no way I'd be who I am without you."

I plucked a Dos Equis from the center of the shrine. I don't even like beer, but somehow if felt like the right thing to do. A sigh escaped from so deep inside that my entire torso deflated like a leaky balloon. I lifted the bottle into the air.

"Cheers, Dad. Wish you were here." The candle flickered wildly. "Oh, sorry. I guess you are."

I stood up and paused for a moment, slowly sipping at my beer, hoping with all my heart that there was some truth to the magic of this night. "Catch up with you later, Dad. I love you." I watched as the smoke from the candle disappeared into the darkening sky above.

"THE VEIL IS THIN TONIGHT," CYNTHIA reminded me on our way out the door that evening, all bundled up against the damp autumn air. "Just be conscious of it. Look around you. Let yourself feel the magic, eh?"

The first thing I felt was an overwhelming sense of claustrophobia. Traffic jams, police whistles, people pushing. The food carts and the dancers twirling on a stage set up in the parking lot made it feel more like a street fair than an ancient ritual. And the spot that Arminda had pointed to the day before, insisting that we "remember this place"? I had expected something really cool to appear there, not the port-o-potties that were already beginning to reek.

But the minute I walked through the towering iron gates the crowd seemed to melt away around me. I closed my eyes and took a deep breath. An almost sickly sweet odor, a blend of marigolds and smoke, filled my nostrils. I could taste it in the back of my throat. The heat generated by the thousands of candles illuminating the sloped earth was enough to make me loosen my scarf. And then there were the bells, ringing out their invitation to the departed souls. *Come, come, come,* they seemed to call.

I opened my eyes to a sea of orange. Cynthia

grabbed my hand and advised me to stay close. A little dizzy, I struggled to find my balance as we began to follow the nearly invisible pathways between the graves, our pace slow and sporadic, controlled by an almost involuntary unwillingness to pass even one of them by. Each had a story to tell. Some provided just hints at who lay below, with their simple crosses inscribed with *Descance en Paz* or *Recuerdo de su Familia*, along with the years marking the spans of their lives, ranging from tragically short to remarkably long. Other graves had been turned into elaborate exhibits, flamboyant tributes to the deceased, 3-D résumés of their jobs, hobbies, talents, and vices. These folks sure must have loved their cigarettes and tequila, and I'd never seen so many bottles of Coke in one place in my entire life.

One of the most spectacular sights was a life-size bicycle made completely of flowers, with a real helmet resting on its seat and a photo of the deceased, competing in a race, hanging from the crossbar. One grave sported a huge marigold guitar, and another featured a magnificent floral donkey ridden by a child-size skeleton figure. I looked up to see a photo of a young boy dressed in his white Communion suit. But seeing the huge circle of family gathered around in the mist, sharing food and drink and conversation, nodding kindly at trespassers like me, who stood, openmouthed, admiring their work, I just couldn't feel sad. Because the whole damn thing was just so sweet.

In this cemetery, nobody seemed to have been forgotten. Arminda had told us that sometimes, when the dead become abandoned by families moving up north, their graves are adopted by others who step in to fill their shoes. Even the sparsest plots were covered by a blanket of orange petals that made death look oddly cozy and inviting. But I couldn't help but be saddened by the sight of the tiniest mounds of dirt nestled between the larger plots. One in particular really got to me. Beside it, an elderly Purépecha woman sat alone, motionless in a low crouch, wrapped in a blanket, her deeply lined face expressionless and unseeing. Another, a large, soft mound butted up against another much smaller one, immediately drew a picture for me of a mother who had died in childbirth. Then there were the altars that spoke of some tragic accident or other catastrophic event, like the one with its floral arch topped with an angel. Hanging from the lattice were framed photos of four small children, along with little toys and dolls and baby shoes. Four little kids. What kind of horror must that family have gone through? I could not imagine. Yet I realized that however unbearable and alienating their loss might have felt, tonight they were not alone. They were a piece of a living, breathing entity that was bigger than just them, hundreds of people all sharing an experience, acknowledging and accepting death not as the opposite of life, but rather as a vital part of it.

It remained hard not to stop at every gravesite, feeling so keenly aware of the lives below. *The veil is thin.* I was curious, and also felt sort of duty-bound to find out who they all were. All I could be sure of was that, whoever they were, they were all people who once had hopes and dreams and successes and failures and joy and disappointment and who were, on this night, surrounded by others who had loved them, and who loved them still, no matter what.

Cynthia and I continued to weave our way through the sodden maze, no longer able to avoid treading on the dead, the place was so packed that night with the living. But nobody seemed to mind. More than one family welcomed us into their little space, offering tiny cups of mescal or posole with a smile. "Muchas gracias," I replied, just as Arminda had instructed. We soon found ourselves following the sound of a discordant choir of deep voices coming from the highest part of the cemetery. Under a wide gazebo, at least a dozen men stood together, somberly singing a slow, sad song about their lost fathers, their beautiful wives, their precious children. It was a touchingly fitting sound track for the scene below, now a hazy blur through the thickening smoke.

After the last chorus I turned to go, but Cynthia

was no longer by my side. But for once, it was okay. I knew she wouldn't leave without me, and besides, I had prepared for this possibility by snapping a photo of our van and its surroundings before we left the parking area.

I continued exploring on my own, carefully picking my way through the patchwork of plots, trying my best not to disturb the calm of the night. But I must have missed a stone or something because all of a sudden I found myself stumbling forward into the darkness. "Fuego!" gasped someone behind me as I fell gently into a pair of beefy arms, my scarf crackling and sizzling from the touch of a toppled candle. I quickly swatted at the fabric until the little flame disappeared, and straightened myself up to thank my savior. And that's when I saw it. Delia's grave.

Now, I didn't know Delia from Adam, but by the looks of her altar I wished I had. Her name was spelled out in big glittery letters across the foot of the grave. At the head, a long triple-tiered banquet table hosted a feast for a dozen tiny skeletons, sitting there all duded up in front of itty-bitty plates of clay food. On their left, a six-piece papier-mâché mariachi band strummed and tooted silently into the night. It looked like *some* party. And in the center, on a cross sculpted from sand and topped with silver sequins, a naked skeleton basked under a little spotlight, as if she were enjoying a glorious day by the sea.

"Tu mamá?" I asked the young man who had reached out to catch me, my voice cracking a little.

He nodded proudly, turning to the boy next to him. "Nuestra madre."

Brothers. Suddenly a swirling wind kicked up around me, causing the dozens of candles adorning Delia's grave to flicker wildly in the dark. "I hear you, Delia," I said with a little laugh. "You weren't by any chance a hairdresser, were you?" Delia's sons held up their beers toward me in the gesture of a toast, and I toasted them back with my empty fist.

The veil is thin.

I stood with Delia's sons, the three of us smiling down at the silent, miniature celebration happening below.

And then something happened. All of a sudden I was filled with a sense of lightness, a feeling of clarity I couldn't recall ever experiencing before. If I could have seen what I was feeling it would have looked like this—hundreds of tiny pieces of myself whirling around, connecting to each other bit by bit with a soft thwack, like Humpty Dumpty in reverse. It was the oddest sensation, but wow, was it amazing. The only way I can describe it is that it felt as though there was no such thing as time: my past and present and future all melded into one. And for one brief moment I felt, for the first time in my life, like the skin on my body was the most elegant, luxurious, custom-made outfit in the world, and that it fit me like a glove.

I swore to myself that I'd remember that feeling, forever, and headed down the hill to find my way home.

20

"WHEEEE!!!" ITALYA SQUEALS AS I SWING HER by the arms, her toes skimming across the surface of the warm blue water. It's Sunday on Stone Island. Family day. Behind us the whole gang, including my vacationing son Zach, is gathered around a shaded table, watching and laughing as I try my darnedest to keep my fussy two-year-old girl from losing interest, from wriggling out of my grip and running back into her daddy's lap. Noah needs a break. Tippy Toes has been honored with a "Best of Mazatlán" award from a popular local magazine for the second year in a row. We are busy. Very busy. Hell, *I* need a break. Especially because Tippy Toes is no longer just Tippy Toes. We are now officially Tippy Toes and Marrakesh Spa & Boutique. That's right. Manis, pedis, massages, facials, body scrubbing, hair, *and* shopping! Now I have an excuse, no, a *reason,* to shop my way across the entire country, finding all sorts of those kinds of handmade treasures that get my heart thumping. How cool is that? Talk about transforming evil into good.

Well, maybe not evil, but at least I've found a way to make my addiction a fruitful one.

Italya slithers away and I follow her across the warm sand toward the table. "Looking good, Deb," says Barb.

"Really? Thanks." I twist my wet T-shirt to wring out the salty water. I'm not so convinced. I may be in better shape than I was, but I'm still not a hundred percent comfortable baring my belly in front of a crowd.

"Cuidado!" Martha puts down her Coke and shields the bundle in her lap as Italya tries to climb aboard. Yes, we have a new baby in the family, a boy this time. Kai Milan popped out with the chubbiest cheeks I had ever seen. "He cried in English!" insisted the gorgeous young doctor who helped bring him into the world. I didn't care what language he cried in. We all were just happy for another little munchkin to cuddle as we open up in the mornings, another doll to pamper with kisses and hugs at the end of the day, another cutie to spoil with toys and treats anytime we feel like it, for no reason whatsoever.

I look around the table at my friends and family, remembering that day that doesn't really seem all that long ago, when we first met. Only Sharon and Glen, and Analisa, are missing, too busy to take a day off for the beach. All has been quiet on the streets of Mazatlán, and the tourists are back. Casa de Leyendas and Macaws (especially on Margarita Wednesdays!) are packed. In fact, all of Centro seems to be booming, with new galleries and boutiques and restaurants that are starting to make it feel like a little SoHo. The neighborhood's biggest issues these days seem to be limited to things like broken sewers. But we've learned how to deal with that. One call to the local TV station and abracadabra, a pipe is repaired or a road repaved, overnight. Sergio has still not stopped teasing me about my ranting and raving on the six o'clock news.

A cheer goes up from the table as Luz and Alex come whizzing by the shoreline on top of a banana boat, Derek squeezed between them, all three holding on for dear life. "Cuidado!" Teresa and Martha shout out, this time in unison. Me, I'm happy to see those kids letting loose. Alex has been working hard at Tippy Toes doing everything, even the mani-pedis Sergio and Teresa had objected to, at first. *That would make him more gay,* they had protested. Go figure. But we do have plenty of customers now asking specifically for the boy with the pink hair. And he's planning on going back to finish school this year. A chef, or a lawyer, he answered when I asked him about his future. I will keep my fingers and toes crossed. Oh, and his other plan? A float for Tippy Toes in Mazatlán's next Gay Pride parade. We are all looking forward to it.

Luz now has her own tattoo gun, and is keeping

herself in ink by doing tats in her spare time. She's still learning, but I have no doubt she'll soon be a star in her field. At home, her sister Gaby is doing better, she tells me, and is loving beauty school. I've seen evidence myself in the different style of braid Italya's wearing every single time she comes down from The Hill.

"Más rápido!" I yell to the kids as they make another pass near shore. Yes, my Spanish is finally improving. It started, as everyone told me it would, with my ears. If I just kept my mouth shut long enough to listen, I found I could pick up a few things. My tongue still feels thick and long when I try to speak, and my delivery sounds more like beauty shop Spanglish than proper Spanish, and there are times when a word pops out in Dari by mistake, but at least I'm getting somewhere.

"You still here?" I squeeze my chair into a spot next to Denis, who lets out a laugh so loud I have to cover my ear. "I didn't mean it that way!" I had thought Denis was planning to go home early, to get ready for a poker game. But yes, he is still here. And I mean that, this time, in the bigger sense. In fact, I think my relationship with Denis has almost set the record as my longest. I know it's my best. Even if he sometimes drives me crazy with his uncanny ability to sit and do nothing, which, to a chronic multitasker, is torture to watch. That, and his poker face. Unless Denis is laughing, you can't tell if he's mad, glad, or sad. I keep telling him I'm going to make him wear a mood ring just to help me out a little.

And one of my dreams has come true. Noah is planning a trip to Michigan, with Italya. He finally succeeded in getting her passport and visa, and they are going together to see my mom. I so wish I could be there to see their faces when they meet. But somebody has to hold down the fort at Tippy Toes. Besides, I need to be here to make sure my girls get to school.

There are now seven students involved with Project Mariposa. And we've actually started to supplement their education with a little mentoring, right upstairs from Tippy Toes. The whole thing just came out of the blue, and I went with it. I was introduced to Rick when he tagged along with his friend, a furniture maker who had come by my house with a bid. "It's you!" he screamed. "It's her!" Turns out he was a hairdresser from Denver, and a big fan of my first book, who had recently retired in Mazatlán. He had no interest in working behind the chair anymore, but was looking for volunteer teaching opportunities to keep himself active in the industry. *And* he was fluent in Spanish. How could I say no? Now he parks himself upstairs with the students every Monday, sharing the tricks of the trade that can come only from a seasoned pro. I have to admit it is starting to feel a bit like Kabul up there, but in the good way.

Our first Project Mariposa girl is about nine months away from graduation. When Rosa recently dropped by Tippy Toes to say hello, I made her a promise: the day she shows up with a high school diploma, a beauty school diploma, and *no* pregnant belly (I made this last demand with a scowl at the teenage boyfriend who had tagged along with her), that will be the day I give her a job at Tippy Toes. Guaranteed. Her face lit up as if she had won the lottery.

Oh, and now we have one boy in the program! It was sort of my mistake, but one I'm glad to have made. Here's how it happened. You see, no matter how much Spanish I pick up, I will never understand María, who cleans my house. We've had several miscommunications, ending in things like a washer full of chicken feathers. She had heard about Project Mariposa through Martha, and mentioned her own child, who apparently liked to do hair. I knew María's life was pretty much hand to mouth, and even though she wasn't the world's best housekeeper, she was still a good, honest, warmhearted woman. So I told her to bring her daughter to meet me the following Saturday at the school. Imagine my surprise when a sweet teenage boy showed up in a bright pink-striped shirt, matching pink shoelaces, a pair of crisp white pants, and blond-tipped bangs.

So I welcomed him to class and did what I do on most Saturdays: I park myself on the sidewalk in front of the building on Juárez Street, just to make sure my girls—and now my boy—get there, get there on time, and get there in uniform. One by one, they come flying around the corner, head mannequins tucked under their arms. I tap my watch and shuffle them inside, where they'll spend the next four hours learning to cut and style, buff and polish, clean and steam. Someday these kids will have a real job, and a real pay-check, and Mazatlán will have a never-ending supply of top-of-the-line beauticians! Maybe someday some of them will be ready to do hair beside me. Then I'll be able to kick back any damn time I please. Maybe.

But for the moment I'll have to settle for kicking back on Sundays, which, honestly, feels pretty good to me right now. A warm breeze. A table loaded with platters of fresh shrimp, baskets of crispy chips, and bowls of chunky guacamole. An ocean that seems to go on forever, teeming with kids and moms and dads playing in the waves as if they didn't have a care in the world. My growing family around me, and friends who have made that family circle about more than just flesh and blood.

I wonder about something. If there were someone like me sitting at our table right now, the me of a few years ago, the me who was trying so hard to figure out the who and what and why of this place on that day at this beach, I wonder what I'd answer when she'd ask why I came to Mexico. I think I'd have only one thing to say. *It's a long story.*

ACKNOWLEDGMENTS

I AM ALWAYS AND FOREVER THE STORY-TELLER, and am so proud to work with great people who guide me through my endless notes and help me make sense of what is going on in my head—not always an easy task.

Margarita Wednesdays would not have been possible without wonderful, talented people, the first of whom I am so thankful to have worked with being Ellen Kaye. She is one of the most talented writers and one of the most gracious people I have ever met. I often wonder if she really knew what she was getting herself into when she took on the job of working with me, but man oh man, did we ever have fun—that is, if "fun" means getting lost in the mountains of Mexico and drinking tequila at midnight in smoky cemeteries. Ellen, I promise next time we do a road trip, I will admit to you when I am lost and will never listen to the GPS lady again. Ellen, you were at my side throughout the entire process. If I had to say what the best thing that came out of this book is, I would say my friendship with you.

This book would not have happened without wonderful publishers like Gallery at Simon & Schuster, and talented editors like Karen Kosztolnyik and her excellent team. Sometimes when you have a vision for something not everyone catches it. When I explained the vision for this book to Karen, Louise Burke, and the Gallery team, I instantly saw in their eyes that they got it. I knew the book would be in safe hands. Thank you, Karen, for guiding this very personal book with tender loving care.

Marly Rusoff, you are amazing and always so supportive of all my craziness and the books they become. I love your creative side, and love how you are not afraid to take risks. You and Michael Radulescu (Mihai), your wonderful, sweet, funny husband, have always guided me through every step of this journey. I love how you and your husband work as such a great literary team. My life has changed because of you. You have made possible so many things, for me and for others (the butterfly effect!). Michael, I know you always have my back, and I love that. Quality people and agents like you only come around once in a lifetime. I am the most blessed story-teller in the world.

Safety Mom, better known as Karen Kinne, you are my BFF. You have been, and always will be, my muse. I am not sure why this happens, but I am thankful for it. I can't even count the hours we spent together, you helping me purge the stories, sort them out, and remember all the funny things that happened. Thank you so much for always being only a phone call away.

Chris Gara, I will always be grateful to you. You saw me as a writer, even when I didn't see it in myself. I thank you from the bottom of my heart.

Mireille Coney is one of those people who can see through to your soul. When I told her I wanted to write another book and asked if she could help me with some ideas, it was as if she went into that deep place and pulled pieces out of me that I didn't even know were there. Mireille—you, Dan, and your beautiful children are a bright spot in my life.

My dear eldest son, Noah Lentz, thank you for taking this journey with me. I am sure that years ago, when we were running out the door into the muddy streets of Kabul, you never thought in your wildest dreams that you would be running a salon in Mexico with a beautiful Mexican wife and three beautiful children. I am so proud of you, Noah. Zach, I can hear you thinking that you're glad it was your brother's turn to be in a book and not you. You did that wild ride in Kabul already. Zach, you have always offered me the love and support I adore.

Martha, thank you for loving my son Noah, and for giving me beautiful grandbabies. There is nothing better in a mother's life than to see her children happy. You have given me the best reasons in the world to love Mexico forever.

Martha's family (you know who you are), thank you for coming to all my silly gringo parties just to be polite, and thank you for being a wonderful family to Noah and my sweet grandbabies.

Denis Asahara (aka Mr. Miyagi) makes me crazy, but in a good way. I am sure if you asked him, he would have plenty of stories of how I drive him nuts. Thank you, Denis, for supporting me with the book, Tippy Toes, the grandkids, the girls at the beauty school, and all the millions of projects I seem to take on. I know this was not your retirement plan, but hey, look how much fun you are having! You are such a great man, and you have the best laugh in the entire world. You are my happy ending.

Sharon Sorri, you are the sister I never had. We fight like sisters and cry like sisters. You and Glen are true family to me, and I cannot even imagine Mexico without you. I love how I can drop into your home (Macaws) and know that when frustrations mount I have family I can turn to. You make me laugh and you make me crazy. Glen and Sharon, your vision has changed the landscape of Mazatlán and my life forever.

Cynthia DeRozea, thank you for being a trusted friend, and for helping me sort through my PTSD. Thank you for opening my eyes and for opening your home to me. When you introduced me to the Day of the Dead, you forever changed my view of life and its possibilities.

Bodie Kellogg, you were the first person who made sure I never sat alone in a restaurant. Thank you for all the wonderful conversations, and for introducing me to such awesome people.

Tippy Toes crew, you are the best. You've had to wear Halloween costumes, act as Santa's helpers, be filmed on a reality TV show. I know we have cultural differences, and you've helped me through many of them. You have graciously learned English because, frankly, my Spanish sucks. Thank you for making Tippy Toes such a special place.

A huge thank-you to the people who live in, and love, Mazatlán. You've taught me so much about this beautiful city and its wonderful people. I've made so many friendships in this special town, a place that attracts so many—not only for its ocean beaches and beautiful weather, but for its ability to provide a welcoming home for quirky people, me included.

A huge shout-out to all the customers and friends of Tippy Toes. If it were not for this wild group in Mazatlán, Tippy Toes would not have happened. You got your toes painted and your body scrubbed and waxed (even when you didn't want to), and were kind to my staff. Thank you for making Tippy Toes a wonderful, fun place to be.

Polly, you are still a scaredy cat, but you have embraced Mexico and the music. Thank you for keeping the mice out of my house. We've come a long way, haven't we?

Bob the dog, you were a good dog, and you made for a great story. RIP.

My neighbors, thanks for sharing the stories of Carnaval Street.You are right, we live on the best street in Mazatlán.

Mazatlán, the Pearl of the Pacific. Mazatlán, you are a magical city, one that has weathered many storms and won. Thank you for opening your shores to me, and for giving me a new life and my wonderful home by the sea.

Lisa's Classic Margarita
(This makes one margarita, usually several are needed)

INGREDIENTS
  Ice cubes
  A shot of your favorite tequila
  The juice of 2 freshly squeezed limes
  A shot of simple syrup (recipe below), more or less depending on sweetness desired
  1 teaspoon orange liqueur, such as Grand Marnier
  1 tablespoon lime-salt-sugar (recipe below)

Fill a cocktail shaker with ice. Add tequila, lime juice, liqueur, and simple syrup. Cover and shake until mixed and chilled, about 30 seconds (can also be mixed up in a pitcher). Place lime-salt-sugar on a plate. Run a lime quarter around the rim of a chilled margarita glass, then press the rim of the glass into the lime-salt-sugar mixture to rim the edge. Strain margarita into the glass.

SIMPLE SYRUP
  1 cup sugar
  1 cup water

In a small saucepan, heat sugar and water over

low heat, stirring until the sugar dissolves. Keep in a sealed container in the fridge for up to 2 weeks.

LIME-SALT-SUGAR
    Zest from two limes
    3 tablespoons sea salt
    3 tablespoons sugar

Mix all ingredients in a bowl; follow instructions above. Serve.

Lisa's Salsa Tatemada (Roasted Salsa)

INGREDIENTS
    4 medium whole tomatoes
    2 large white onions, peeled and cut in half
    2 whole jalapeños (more if you like it hot)
    ½ cup water

Put all of the above on a grill or barbecue, or in a hot pan with olive oil, and turn until they are well roasted and blackened on the outside.

Place the blackened tomatoes in your blender along with ½ cup of water.

Blend until liquid (add a little more water if necessary).

Add the rest of the grilled vegetables, along with the following, to the blender:

4 large cloves of garlic, peeled
Juice of 2 limes
A large handful of cilantro
1 teaspoon of salt
½ teaspoon of pepper
Pinch of cumin
Optional: a few drops of liquid smoke

Blend all ingredients, but not a lot. I like to keep it a little chunky. Eat with chips, in tacos, or over meats and fish.

Serves 4 with tortilla chips.

Center Point Large Print

600 Brooks Road / PO Box 1
Thorndike ME 04986-0001 USA

(207) 568-3717

US & Canada:
1 800 929-9108
www.centerpointlargeprint.com